SPIRAL GUIDES

Travel with Someone You Trust®

Contents

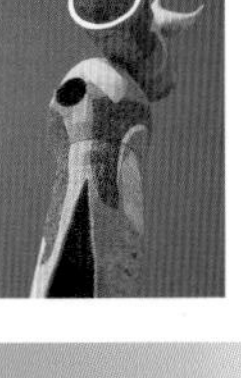

Written by Andrew Benson
Magazine by Teresa Fisher
Where to...Eat and Drink and Where to...Stay by Clarissa Hyman
Copy edited by Rebecca Snelling and Tony Kelly
Verified by Mona King
Indexed by Marie Lorimer

American editor Laura Breen-Galante

Edited, designed and produced by AA Publishing

This edition first published in the United States 2006

Published in the United States by AAA Publishing,
1000 AAA Drive, Heathrow, Florida 32746
Published in the United Kingdom by AA Publishing

ISBN-13: 978-1-59508-107-0
ISBN-10: 1-59508-107-0

Cover design and binding style by permission of AA Publishing

Color separation by Keenes, Andover
Printed and bound in China by Leo Paper Products

10 9 8 7 6 5 4 3 2 1

A02354

the magazine

Catalan

Catalans, and especially Barcelonans, will repeatedly tell you that Catalonia and its capital city are not Spanish. Over the centuries, the border regions of both Spain and France have clung fiercely to their unique culture, despite various attempts to eradicate it.

Wilfred "The Hairy" (*c*860–98)
Count Guifré "el Pilós", founder of the Catalan nation, met an early death in battle against the Saracens. It is said that, in recognition of his heroism, the Emperor dipped his fingers into Wilfred's wounds then ran them down his golden shield, so creating the four red stripes on yellow of today's Catalan flag – the *Quatre Barres* (Four Bars) – the oldest national flag in Europe. What nobody seems to know, though, is why or in what way he was so hairy!

Jaume I (1213–76)
Jaume I (right) was one of the most successful Catalan kings. Not only did he establish the *Corts* (Catalonia's first parliament) and the *Generalitat* (a governing committee of the *Corts*) (➤ 58), he also encouraged economic development and established Barcelona as a great Mediterranean power, by retaking the Balearic Islands from the Moors. His reign was a time of great prosperity, and impressive new buildings sprung up – including the cathedral, Santa Maria del Mar and the Drassanes shipyards – which radically changed the appearance of the city.

Capital

A Spanish-Catalan state existed as early as 878, when Wilfred "The Hairy" (► panel, page 6) succeeded in uniting several northeastern counties, creating the basis for a future Catalan nation. He named himself the first Count of Barcelona, founding a dynastic line that was to rule a powerful nation for several centuries before it was eventually absorbed into an expanding Spain in the 15th century.

The Spanish-Catalans were suppressed by Castilian rule until 1635, when Spain and France were at war, and Catalans on both sides of the border revolted and declared themselves an independent republic. The uprising was soon quashed. Barcelona surrendered to the Spanish army in 1652 and Spain lost control of the border districts of France. The Treaty of the Pyrenees was eventually signed in 1659, thus splitting the historical lands of Catalonia.

> "I would rather be Count of Barcelona than King of the Romans."
>
> *Charles V Holy Roman Emperor, 1519*

The Renaixença

During the 18th century, Catalonia began to re-emerge, thanks to a steady growth in agriculture, the export of wine, and increased shipping. Indeed, following the Napoleonic Wars, the region experienced such an industrial boom that Barcelona became the fastest-expanding city in Spain. This pre-empted the Catalan *Renaixença* (Renaissance) of the mid-19th century. Despite being previously banned in public life, the Catalan language had never died out and, as Catalan literature began to flourish once more, the language was revived in bourgeois circles. Hand-in-hand with the cultural "renaissance" came the Modernista movement (the Catalan response to art nouveau) which, together with the creation of the Eixample district (► 15–19), totally changed the face of Barcelona.

Facts & Figures
The autonomous region of Catalonia covers an area comprising 6.3 per cent of Spain and has a population of more than 6 million (11 per cent of the Spanish population), with 70 per cent of those living in Greater Barcelona. It is Spain's leading economic region, producing 20 per cent of the country's GNP. Nearly 40 per cent of all visitors to Spain go to Catalonia.

Spanish Civil War

The outbreak of the Spanish Civil War in 1936 marked the start of one of Spain's darkest periods, and, under the dictatorship of General Franco, Catalan national identity was totally repressed. Catalan language was banned once more in schools, churches and public life. The region was deliberately deprived of investment and new industry, resulting in strikes and riots in Barcelona. But despite the decades of cultural, commercial and political repression that ensued, Catalonia managed to cling onto its identity: the Catalan Church retained its independence; artists and writers continued to work; and Barcelona emerged as a major publishing centre. Not until Franco's death in 1975 and the new Spanish constitution of 1977 did Catalonia regain a measure of self-government. Eventually, in 1979, Catalonia became an Autonomous Community within Spain, with its own semi-autonomous government controlling education, health, industry, trade, social services, culture, tourism and agriculture.

The Catalan Capital

A strong Catalan identity has emerged in the aftermath of Franco's rule. The province is the wealthiest part of Spain and for a long time held the balance of power in the Madrid parliament. To its people, Barcelona is not so much Spain's second city as the capital of Catalonia, fervently European in both climate and culture. No other European city has reinvented itself as splendidly as Barcelona. A massive facelift, prior to the 1992 Olympics, converted the grand, old city into a chic, cosmopolitan metropolis, and the momentum continues as Barcelona becomes once more a leading centre of fashion and design. Without a doubt, Barcelona today is the richest, fastest-growing, and most stylish city in Spain. It has an undeniable vibrancy, a sense of pride and elegance – the result of Catalan refound self-confidence. Catalans will try to convince you that Barcelona, not Madrid, is Spain's premier city… and they could well be right.

Below: The changing face of the city: Palau Sant Jordi, a masterly feat of modern architecture

Speaking *"català"*

The resurgence of *català* (the Catalan language) is perhaps the most obvious manifestation of Catalan identity, even though Barcelona still has two official languages, Catalan and Castilian Spanish. Catalan is currently the second fastest-growing language in the world. In Barcelona and in most of Catalonia, Catalan has more or less taken over as the everyday language. As a local in a Barri Gòtic bar explained: "The language is the main guarantee of our nationality as Catalan people."

Although another Romance language, Catalan displays many differences from Castilian, and its vocabulary has more in common with French and Italian. Grammatical rules differ considerably, as do various pronunciation rules: for instance, the unstressed "a" and "e" sounds are almost swallowed in Catalan but clear in Castilian Spanish, and the soft lisped Castilian "z" and "c" sounds don't apply in Catalan, so it's "Barcelona" not "Barthelona"! Any effort to speak either language will be appreciated, but don't get too upset if locals mistake your attempt at Catalan as mispronounced Spanish!

The Torres de Ávila night-club (right), built for the 1992 Olympics, was part of a face-lift that transformed the city

Key Catalan Sights

Palau Reial de Pedralbes (➤ 156–157), former residence of the Counts of Barcelona.
Palau de la Generalitat (➤ 58), home of the Government of Catalonia.
Parlament de Catalunya, in Parc de la Ciutadella (➤ 86–87).
Museu d'Història de Catalunya (➤ 89), a state-of-the-art museum illustrating the history of Catalonia from prehistoric times to the present day.
Museu Nacional d'Art de Catalunya (MNAC) (➤ 136–139), presenting a magnificent millennium of Catalan art from the Romanesque, Gothic and baroque to Modernist furniture and paintings, and 20th-century sculpture.
Palau de la Música Catalana (➤ 78–79), splendid home to Catalonia's choirs and orchestras, designed by Modernist architect Domènech i Montaner.

Fiesta Time

Barcelonans are addicted to fiestas, with more than 140 different festivals a year. The inspiration for many is religious, but rural traditions and historic events make their mark too. Here are some of the highlights:

January

New Year's Day (1 Jan) On the stroke of midnight, everyone eats 12 grapes for good luck in time with the chimes.

Reis Mags (5–6 Jan) The Three Kings arrive by boat, then tour the city, showering the crowd with sweets. Naughty children are given a lump of coal!

February

Carnestoltes A week of colourful pre-Lenten carnival celebrations, costumed processions and flamboyant firework displays ends on Ash Wednesday with the symbolic burial of a sardine.

March

Sant Medir de Gràcia (3 Mar) Showy procession of traditionally dressed horsemen from Gràcia who ride over Collserola to the Hermitage of Sant Medir (Saint of Broad Beans) for a bean-feast.

March/April

Setmana Santa Religious services, processions and celebrations for Easter week.

April

Sant Jordi (23 Apr) To celebrate the day of Sant Jordi (St George), Catalonia's patron saint, couples express their affection by exchanging gifts: a rose for the woman and a book for the man. The Ramblas become a huge outdoor bookshop, decorated with roses, and more than half of Catalonia's annual book sales take place on this day, which is also the anniversary of the deaths of Spanish novelist Miguel de Saavedra Cervantes and English playwright William Shakespeare.

May

Corpus Christi Parades of giants and big-heads (➤ panel, page 11). The fountain in the Catedral's cloister is the site of the traditional

Below: Joining in the fiesta

Costumed processions (below and right) and a traditional *castell* (far right) during La Mercè

Giants & Big-Heads
Dancing giants, dragons, *capgrossos* (big-heads) and demons play an important part in traditional Catalan folklore and fiestas. During La Mercè, there's even a *Ball de Gegants*, a dance of costumed, 5m (16-foot) giants and grinning papier-mâché big-heads stretching from Drassanes to Ciutadella, climaxing in the *Corre Foc* (fire-running), when devils and dragons scatter firecrackers throughout the old town.

Ou com Balla (dancing egg), when an empty egg is balanced on the jet of the fountain, symbolising water and birth.

June

Trobada Castellera (mid-June) A unique and wholeheartedly Catalan celebration of *castell* (human tower) building – young men stand on each other's shoulders in massive balancing acts up to nine people high.

September

Diada de Catalunya (11 Sep), Catalunya's National Day doesn't mark a victory, but the taking of the city by Felipe V in 1714. More a day of political manifestations than merrymaking.
La Mercè (17–24 Sep) In 1637, La Mercè (the Madonna) saved Barcelona from a plague of locusts, assuring her status as patron saint of the city. This is the biggest fiesta of the year – four days of dancing in the streets, boisterous parades of devils, dragons, giants and big-heads, dramatic *castellar* displays and musically choreographed fireworks.

December

Christmas festivities include a Christmas craft fair outside the Catedral (13–23 Dec) and a large crib in Plaça Sant Jaume.

La Cuina Catalana

American food critic Colman Andrews described Catalan cuisine as "the last great culinary secret in Europe". Rooted in the fresh local ingredients of the mountains, the plains and the sea, the food is delicious, varied and surprisingly subtle in flavour.

Catalan Specialities

Catalonia has one of the richest gastronomic traditions in Spain, drawing upon Moorish, French, Sicilian and Levantine influences. *La cuina catalana* relies heavily on garlic, tomatoes, olive oil, peppers and herbs which, when blended, form *samfaina*, a delicious sauce served with many dishes. Other popular sauces include *picada* (parsley, nuts, bread, garlic and saffron), *romesco* (ground almonds, tomatoes, spicy red peppers, garlic and oil) and *sofregit* (a simple sauce of tomato, onion and garlic).

For centuries pork has been the cornerstone of the Catalan diet, but lamb, chicken, duck, beef, snails and game also figure prominently, often prepared *a la brasa* (on an open charcoal grill) and served with lashings of *allioli* (a strong, garlicky mayonnaise). Look for *escudella*, a tasty all-in-one stew containing beef, pig's feet, poultry, lamb, sausage, potatoes, cabbage and haricot beans, and the spectacular range of local sausages and hams. Try *botifarra* (spicy black and white puddings) and *fuet* (long, thin sausages made from dried meat), both staples of Catalan country cuisine.

Meat is commonly combined with fruit, with such mouth-watering dishes as

Fish and shellfish figure strongly in Catalan cooking (above and right)

Fresh local ingredients are the key to Catalan cuisine

Feeling Peckish

If you like eating supper early, you'll dine alone in Barcelona. So, why not begin your evening instead with some tapas– small portions of delicacies such as mixed olives, *xoriç* (spicy sausage), *fabes a la catalana* (broad beans with ham), *pa amb tomàquet* (bread smeared with olive oil, garlic and ripe tomato), *truita* (omelette), squid, snails and whitebait? The choice is endless, the displays dazzling and the portions are sure to fortify you until the 10 pm fashionable dining hour.

At one time, tapas were served free with a drink, but now they are served by the portion. Don't expect a menu, just look at what the locals are eating then point at whatever you fancy. For a larger portion, ask for a *ració*.

Try the following:
La Bodegueta (► 107 and 142)
Café de la Ribera (► 93)
Euskal Etxea (► 92)
La Gran Bodega (► 123)
Quimet & Quimet (► 142)

Olives and *truita* are among the wide variety of tapas on offer

conill amb prunes (rabbit with prunes) and *pollastre amb peres* (chicken with pears). But, it is the unique *mar i muntanya* (sea and mountain) combinations that differentiate *la cuina catalana* from the cuisine of other Spanish regions: *mar i cel* ("sea and sky"), made with sausages, rabbit, shrimp and fish, and *sípia amb mandonguilles* (cuttlefish with meatballs) are especially tasty.

Near the coast, fish dishes reign supreme, from simple grilled *sardines* (sardines) to hearty *sarsuela* (seafood stew) and a wide variety of fish soups. Look also for *bacallà* (salt cod), *arròs negre* (rice blackened with squid ink), *arròs amb llamàntol* (rice with lobster) and *fideuà* (a local variant of paella using pasta instead of rice).

Seasonal accompaniments include white asparagus in summer, and wild mushrooms (especially *rovellons* or *lactarius fungi* from the Pyrenees) in the autumn and *calçots* in springtime, elongated spring onions, roasted until black over an open fire then dipped into a bowl of spicy *romesco* sauce. Be sure to try *escalivada*, among the region's most popular salads, made from roasted vegetables such as red peppers.

Crema catalana, **just one of many desserts on the menu**

CAVA CULTURE

Gradually people around the world are acquiring a taste for *cava* as they realise there's no need to pay a fortune for a decent bottle of fizz. The Barcelonans swear that their *cava* tastes better than French champagne, and it's made by the same method.

Production in Catalonia is centred on Sant Sadurní, just south of Barcelona, with Freixenet being the largest producer. Other popular labels include Codorniu, Juvé & Camps, Torello, Mestres and Parxet.

The locals drink *cava* mainly as an aperitif and as an accompaniment to the first dish. It's often drunk at home, and during Sunday family gatherings in particular, but you'll find bars that specialise in champagne and *cava*, known as *xampanyeries*, throughout the city. During the second week in October Sant Sadurní hosts a *cava* festival.

Best *Xampanyeries*

La Cava del Palau (Carrer de Verdaguer I Callis 10) – popular, large bar close by the Palau de la Música.

El Xampanyet (➤ 93)

Xampú Xampany (Gran Via 702) – stylish, modern *cava* bar open until 4 am on weekends.

Desserts

Catalan desserts are surprisingly varied. As well as the usual *flam* (crème caramel), *gelat* (ice cream), *crema catalana* (a sort of crème brûlée) and *macedònia* (fruit salad), try *postre de músic* (musician's dessert – a dish of nuts and fruit), *panellets* (marzipans), *torrons* (nougats) and *coques* (pastries sprinkled with sugar and pine nuts).

Superb regional cheeses include *formatge de Serrat* from Lérida, goat's-milk *mató*, and *recuit*, a ricotta-like cheese made with ewes' milk that is often served with honey.

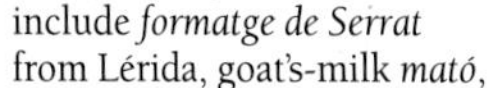

Wine

Bodegas Torres, produced in the Penedès region (➤ 166), is Catalonia's most successful and best-known wine. Connoisseurs should also hunt out the Marqués de Alella, Païmat Chardonnay, Perelada, René Barbier and Bach labels and the newly fashionable Prioratis, Ribera del Duero and Cigales. You shouldn't leave without having sampled a glass of *cava* (➤ panel, above right), the traditional sparkling wine of Spain.

Setting an Eixample

Few cities in the world can beat Barcelona for Modernist art and architecture. Its early 20th-century flowering coincided with the creation of a new district – the Eixample. Yet this radical new style met with mixed reactions. Some saw the daring creations of Gaudí and his peers as the perfect matching of money and ideals – a second Catalan "Golden Age" – while others declared it *l'època de mal gust* – the epoch of bad taste.

Pere Falqués i Urpí's elegant Modernist lampposts on the Passeig de Gràcia, the heart of the Eixample

TOP FIVE GAUDÍ SIGHTS

- La Sagrada Família (➤ 113)
- Parc Güell (➤ 110–112)
- Casa Milà (➤ 105–107)
- Palau Güell (➤ 60–62)
- Casa Batlló (➤ 104)

For over a century Barcelona has been a world leader in town-planning and modernity. Following centuries of repression exercised by Madrid, the city took the lead in Spanish industrial development, becoming a centre of art and design, nurturing such Modernists as Gaudí, Picasso and Miró. A period of considerable economic and demographic growth coincided with a wave of optimism, and from 1860 onwards an extension of the city beyond the medieval walls was built to reflect Catalonia's new-found prosperity – the Eixample.

The Eixample was the brain-child of engineer Ildefons Cerdà (➤ 24). A 9sq km ($3\frac{1}{2}$sq-mile) *barri* (district) of geometric uniformity, based on a grid pattern of 550 symmetrical square blocks (known as *illes*, meaning "islands"), each with their corners cut off, it is a visionary example of urban planning unique in Europe, with the aptly named Avinguda Diagonal cutting

WHAT IS MODERNISME?

Modernisme (defined as "a taste for what is modern") emerged at the turn of the 20th century with the aim of breaking away from the past through new art forms. Architecture throughout Europe had developed into an empty routine and a mish-mash of uninspired styles. Artists longed for a regeneration of art architecture based on curves rather than symmetry, and a new feeling for design was sweeping the continent, led by Belgian Victor Horta and Englishman William Morris. Flowers, foliage and oriental patterns were increasingly used for ornamentation, and each material (most notably iron, ceramics and stained glass) was exploited to the full.

These ideals gave rise to such movements as French art nouveau and German Jugendstil, each focusing on organic forms, sinuous lines and ornamentation. Modernisme was their Catalan equivalent – albeit a somewhat quirkier, longer-lasting version. And, largely thanks to Gaudí, Catalan Modernisme had the biggest impact, influencing all forms of European art, architecture, literature and theatre.

The stained-glass roof at the Palau de la Música Catalana, Lluís Domènech i Montaner's spectacular creation

through the rectilinear blocks at 45 degrees to add a touch of originality. Unfortunately though, the utopian features of Cerdà's plan – gardens in the middle of each block and buildings on only two sides – were not respected, and some today scorn the district for its monotony.

Just as Barcelona was building its new *barri*, Modernisme arrived in the city, bringing with it artistic geniuses who were to endow the district with architectural jewels to rival those of any city in Europe. The leading exponent of the movement in Barcelona was, without doubt, Antoni Gaudí, but he was by no means the only Modernist at work in the Eixample. Two other key players, local architects Lluís Domènech i Montaner and Josep Puig i Cadafalch, created such marvels as Palau de la Música Catalana (➤ 78–79), Casa Lléo Morera (➤ 102) and the Hospital de la Santa Creu i de Sant Pau

(➤ 120), which is set defiantly at 45 degrees to the street grid.

Domènech i Montaner is considered by many to be the father of Modernisme. He was the first to give art nouveau ideals "Catalan" expression, by drawing on the region's glorious past (in particular, its rich Romanesque and Gothic traditions) for inspiration in his designs. Unlike his pupil Puig i Cadafalch, or Gaudí, he frequently worked with entire artisan teams – architects, sculptors, glass- and metal-workers and ceramicists – to create his dazzlingly ornate yet always highly functional buildings, a contrast to the more idealistic, fanciful creations of Gaudí.

In the late 1990s, the Eixample received a face-lift, revealing the extent to which the city lavished decoration on itself during the latter years of the 19th century. Today, the Eixample is a *barri* for gazing not only at the masterpieces – such as La Sagrada Família (➤ 113–117), one of the great architectural wonders of the world, with its cloud-piercing, mosaic-clad spires – but also at the smaller details: the twisted wrought-ironwork of town house balconies and the ornate shop façades, right down to the doorknobs of hundreds of back-street buildings. Look closely as you walk around and you will be richly rewarded!

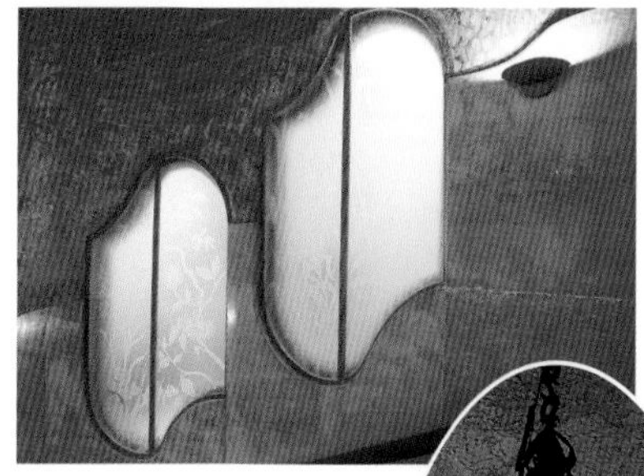

The Genius of Gaudí

No visit to Barcelona would be complete without paying homage to the eccentric genius of Antoni Gaudí i Cornet, one of Spain's most brilliant architects. Born in Reus in 1852, Gaudí studied at the Barcelona School of Architecture. Even his first work – the simple lampposts in Plaça Reial – revealed a distinctive architectural personality and a departure from the norm. A nonconformist, he conceived his buildings as "visions" and developed an idiosyncratic, organic style that reached a peak in the curvy, sinuous Casa Milà (➤ 105–107) and his neo-Gothic masterpiece, La Sagrada Família. No other architect had ever made such expressive use of stone and iron, and nobody else had ever gone to such painstaking lengths to embellish their buildings with ceramics, glass, wood and wrought iron. La Sagrada Família soon became his obsession. For the last years of his life (1908–26), he lived in a hut on the site and, having spent his entire finances on the project, he

Modernist architects based their designs on curved forms and drew much inspiration from nature

Gaudí's Casa Milà (above and right), supposedly built without a single straight line

"Gaudí must have been a jovial man. He has built a house in a main street in the form of waves with the inhabitants looking out of the windows like despairing swimmers."
Wolfgang Köppen, German author (*b*1906), writing about Gaudí's controversial apartment block, Casa Milà.

went begging from door to door through the streets of Barcelona so that work could continue. To this day it remains unfinished, and the original plans were lost in a fire.

A Love-Hate Relationship

As a mystic, recluse and celibate bachelor, during his lifetime Gaudí was considered a crank by many Catalans, and his designs were harshly criticised. Only after his death was his genius acknowledged. In 1926, aged 74, he was run over by a tram and died unrecognised in a hospital for the poor. When his identity was discovered, Barcelona gave him what was almost a state funeral. Since his death, all Gaudí's buildings have been listed as World Heritage Sites by UNESCO; he is rated among the most influential architects of all times; he is the first artist since Fra Angelico to be beatified by the Vatican; and his buildings have brought pleasure to millions. Perhaps it's more than mere coincidence that *gaudi* in Catalan means "delight"?

LESSER KNOWN GAUDÍ SIGHTS

- Pavellons de la Finca Güell (➤ 156).
- Casa Bellesguard (Carrer Bellesguard 16) – fantasy townhouse evoking a medieval past, built in 1900–02 (closed to the public).
- Casa Calvet (Carrer de Casp 48) – an apartment block from 1898 to 1900, with a conventional exterior but a more radical interior and the fine details typical of Gaudí.
- Casa Vicens (➤ 109) – an early work (1883 to 1888), with a grand round smoking-room and fine ironwork gates (closed to the public).
- Col.legi de les Teresianes (Carrer de Ganduxer 86–105) – the little-known but impressive school for nuns, constructed in 1890 (open by appointment only, tel: 93 212 3354).

FOOTBALL

Three or four disappointing FC Barcelona seasons plunged the city into a deep depression. Then salvation appeared in the form of Dutch manager Rijkaard and Brazilian superstar Ronaldinho. You see, Barcelona takes soccer very, very seriously.

The slogan of the city's top soccer club reads "More than a club", and it's true…FC Barcelona, or Barça for short, *is* much more than just Spain's top soccer club, the fifth most successful business in Spain, and the richest sports club in the world. It's one of Catalonia's flagship institutions, a symbol of identity for all Barcelonans.

The club – one of the oldest in Europe – was founded in 1899 by a Swiss, Hans Gamper. Ironically for such a patriotic club, many of the founder members were English or German, and the players still wear the blue and maroon (*blau grana*) colours of their founder's Swiss province.

THE BARÇA CLUB ANTHEM
"We are the reds and blues (*la gent blau grana*). It doesn't matter where We come from, North or South, On this we all agree, We're brothers under the flag, Red and blue in the wind. A cry of courage has made Our name known Throughout the world – Barça, Barça, Barça."

CRAZY

During the Franco era, it stood as a rallying point for Catalans, and this emotional identification remains today. It explains why Barça has the world's largest soccer-club membership – more than 108,000. For decades, Barça's matches against arch-rivals, Real Madrid, became the focus for the hatred of a centralised government. Such was the patriotic fervour whenever Barça beat Real Madrid, that from 1939 until the mid-1950s the club's board of directors was dominated by government vigilantes in an attempt to quash any patriotic stirrings.

At the height of Franco's dictatorship, match results were pre-ordained so that Madrid would win and the teams were made to share their best players. During the last years of oppression, the club came to symbolise freedom. Thousands of fans would assemble to wave the *blau grana* flag as a substitute for their own banned Catalan flag. Every goal scored was an assertion of the Catalan identity, and its players and supporters were an unofficial "army".

Today, support for Barça is undiminished as loyal Barcelonans of all ages crowd to Camp Nou stadium (► 157–158) for every match. Whenever they play Real Madrid, all of Spain is gripped by soccer mania, and when Barça wins, the streets erupt with excitement to the sound of car horns, fireworks and popping *cava* corks.

HOW TO GET TICKETS
Tickets for home league matches (played Saturday nights at 8:45 pm or Sunday afternoons) can be bought either at the stadium during the week or by credit card at the Servi-Caixa machines in La Caixa banks (► 42). Touting (scalping) is illegal.

Above: Barça fans at Camp Nou imitating the red and yellow of the Catalan flag

STREET SCULPTURE

Barcelona resembles a giant outdoor gallery, with more than 400 open-air monuments and sculptures. Some were erected during the Modernista craze of the early 20th century, but many were added in the 1980s as part of a programme to place modern sculptures in urban spaces to enhance them and to provide focal points in otherwise featureless suburban areas. In the 1990s, the slogan "Make Barcelona Beautiful", combined with the civic improvement plan for the 1992 Olympics, triggered yet more innovative projects as the latest trends in design found their way onto the city's streets and squares.

Moll de la Fusta

Several sculptures adorn the "Wooden Wharf" waterfront promenade, created prior to the 1992 Olympics, but the most impressive is undoubtedly Roy Lichtenstein's massive *Barcelona Head* (at the eastern end, just in front of the main post office), which uses Gaudí's technique of setting broken pieces of ceramic into cement to dramatic effect. Originally intended for Parc de Collserola so it could be viewed from a distance, it now surveys passers-by on the waterfront.

Parc del Clot

This park in the eastern suburbs was built on the site of an unused railway yard and ingeniously combines the walls and arches of the former railway buildings and an old chimney with a shady square and a playground. It is linked by a lengthy overhead walkway to a small grassy area of artificial hills and enigmatic sculptures, including the curious *Rites of Spring* by American sculptor Bryan Hunt.

Parc de la Creueta del Coll

Built in 1987 in an unused quarry by Olympic architects Martorell and Mackay and surrounded by dramatic cliff-faces, with a small sand-fringed boating lake and wooded pathways scattered with

Roy Lichtenstein's impressive *Barcelona Head*, on the Moll de la Fusta

modern sculptures, this park in the suburb of Vallcarca is always packed in summer. Look out for *Elogi de l'Aigua*, a hanging sculpture by Basque artist Eduardo Chillida, which is reflected in the water, and others by Ellsworth Kelly and Roy Lichtenstein.

On the Beach

Rebecca Horn's sculpture *Homage to Barceloneta* (Metro: Barceloneta) evokes memories of the *chiringuitos* (seafood kiosks) that were torn down to make way for the new waterfront development. Cast in bronze, it consists of a series of huts piled one on top of the other. At the far end of the beach (Metro: Ciutadella–Vila Olímpica), the glittering 50m (165-foot) copper *Fish* by American architect Frank Gehry has become the city's new maritime symbol.

Parc de l'Espanya Industrial

Barcelona's most controversial park, built between 1982 and 1985 on the site of an old textile factory in the Sants district (► 141), was designed by the Basque architect Luis Pena Ganchegui as a modern version of Roman baths. It is constructed on two levels, the lower part comprising a large lake and grassy area, with steep white steps up to the much-scorned upper esplanade, where there are ten "lighthouses", a series of water spouts and an immense metal play-sculpture entitled the *Dragon of St George* by Andrés Nagel, which contains children's slides. There are also sculptures by Antoni Caro, Pau Palazuelo and other contemporary Catalan artists.

Rebecca Horn's *Homage to Barceloneta*

The Parc de l'Espanya Industrial defies all traditional concepts of park design

MOVERS & SHAKERS

Christopher Columbus (1451–1506)

Many Mediterranean towns like to claim the Italian explorer Christopher Columbus (left) as their own, and the people of Barcelona are no exception. During the 19th century, the Catalan nation decided he was *their* discoverer, as he had returned to Barcelona following his triumphant first voyage to America in 1493 – hence the vast monument (➤ 52) erected in his honour for the 1888 Universal Exhibition outside the naval headquarters of Catalonia at the seaward end of the Ramblas. Ironically though, because of the lie of the coastline, the 8m (26-foot) statue of Columbus atop the mighty column points directly towards Italy, with his back turned on the New World!

Ildefons Cerdà (1815–76)

Nobody has had a greater influence on the appearance of Barcelona than Ildefons Cerdà i Sunyer (below left), the liberal-minded civil engineer and designer of the Eixample district. In his radical *Pla de Reforma i Eixample* (Plan for Renovation and Enlargement), Cerdà broke from traditional Spanish urban planning, proposing a unique and innovative grid design (➤ 15–19). Work began in 1859 and the elegant, new Eixample district immediately became *the* place to live for Barcelona's then-flourishing bourgeoisie.

Pablo Ruiz Picasso (1881–1973)

Málaga-born Picasso (below) spent his formative years between the ages of 14 and 23 in Barcelona, living with his parents in the Plaça de la Mercè and studying at the Llotja Art School. He is said to have considered himself more Catalan than Andalucian, and

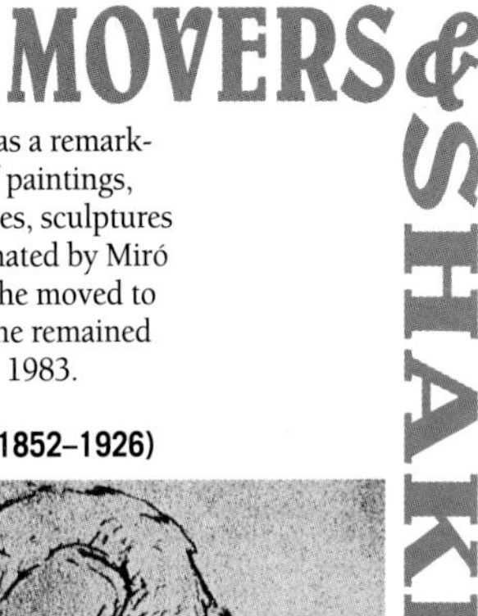

chose to stage his first public exhibition here – at the popular bar and restaurant Els Quatre Gats (➤ 70) in 1901. Even after his move to Paris in 1904, Picasso returned to Barcelona regularly, until the Civil War (the subject of his famous painting *Guernica*) put an end to his visits. Museu Picasso (➤ 82–85), in the Ribera district, contains one of the most important collections of his work in the world and is particularly rich in paintings from his Barcelona period.

Joan Miró (1893–1983)

One of Catalonia's greatest artists, Miró (below) was born in Barcelona and, apart from a brief spell in Paris, spent most of his life in the city developing his bold, childlike style of simple shapes, vigorous lines and vibrant primary colours. His works are regarded as one of the main links between surrealism and abstract art. One of his favourite early techniques was to spill paint onto a canvas and then move his brush around in it. The city is peppered with his sculptures, but the best place to see his work is the Fundació Joan Miró (➤ 134–135) on Montjuïc. This has a remarkable collection of paintings, graphics, tapestries, sculptures and ceramics donated by Miró himself. In 1956 he moved to Mallorca, where he remained until his death in 1983.

Antoni Gaudí (1852–1926)

Barcelona's most famous son (above) occupies a unique position in the history of modern architecture – a true genius of the Modernista movement, without predecessor or successor. To this day, his flamboyant style is unique (➤ 17–18).

Pau Casals (1876–1973)

The celebrated Catalan cellist (above), better known to the world as Pablo Casals, hailed from Barcelona. A veritable child prodigy, by the age of four he could play the violin, piano, flute and organ. Amazingly, his career began on a home-made instrument, constructed from a broom handle, a large gourd and some gut strings. As he progressed, his family bought a proper cello and he started to earn a living as a music student playing in the city cafés. His solo debut in Paris in 1899 launched him on a touring career that made him famous worldwide. Eventually, in 1920, he took up the baton and founded his own orchestra in Barcelona. His concerts were aimed particularly at the blue-collar class, and the orchestra performed regularly at the Palau de la Música Catalana (➤ 78–79).

José Carreras (*b*1946)

The world-famous Barcelonan tenor José Carreras (right) – known locally as Josep – loved singing from an early age. As a small boy he would sing to the customers in his mother's hairdressing shop, and by the age of 11 he was on the stage of Barcelona's great opera house, the Gran Teatre del Liceu (➤ 64). Carreras was singing more than 70 performances a year around the world's opera houses at the height of his career when, in 1987, he was diagnosed with acute leukaemia and given a one in ten chance of survival. He has since, miraculously, made a full recovery and resumed his career, concentrating more now on recitals than opera performances. Many of his concerts are held in aid of the José Carreras International Leukaemia Foundation, including the famous *Three Tenors* performances – flamboyant, box-office-busting concerts in which he is joined by the great Placido Domingo and Luciano Pavarotti.

Ferran Adrià (*b*1962)

Self-taught master chef Adrià, (above) born in the suburb of L'Hospitalet, has been dubbed the "Salvador Dalí of gastronomy" and voted one of the world's 100 leading creators by *Time* magazine. His story is one of dishcloths to riches: starting out washing pans and slaving in army kitchens, in the 1980s he converted remote El Bulli restaurant, near Roses, into his fiefdom. Inventor of "deconstructed cuisine" – most famously the tortilla-in-a-glass – he transforms whole meals from caipirinhas via paella to after-dinner coffee into scintillating sorbets, vacuum-packed sachets or foaming mousses. While his detractors dismiss his food as a lot of froth, his revolutionary influence is such that chefs now wield pressurised canisters at restaurants all around the world.

Antoni Tàpies (*b*1923)

Barcelona-born Tàpies (below right) is one of Catalonia's most important contemporary artists. His early works were influenced by Joan Miró. Many of his major works include every- day objects and symbols – newspaper, silver foil, cardboard, string and wire – and unusual materials, such as oil paint mixed with crushed marble. They can be seen periodically in exhibitions of his work at the Fundació Antoni Tàpies (➤ 118), founded by the artist to promote the study and understanding of modern art.

Snowflake the Gorilla (1964–2003)

Discovered as a baby in Equatorial Guinea, Snowflake (Copito de Nieve or Floquet de Neu) became the main attraction at Barcelona Zoo and the city's unofficial mascot. Possibly the only albino gorilla ever discovered, he was put to sleep after being diagnosed with incurable skin cancer at the grand age of 39 (nearly twice gorilla longevity in the wild); since then Barcelona has been in a state of mourning. He had sired 22 offspring with three different females but none was albino. Death has if anything enhanced his celebrity: his wrinkly face is on countless postcards, he starred in a novel and furry Snowflakes are best-selling souvenirs.

24 Hours of

Watch the Sun Rise
Take the Metro to Vallcarca and follow the signs for Gaudí's **Parc Güell** (► 110–112). It's a steep uphill trek but you'll be richly rewarded by the sensational views over the city to the sea beyond.

A Hearty Breakfast
Bar Salvador (Carrer de Canvis Nous 8) serves an authentic Catalan breakfast, with hearty chunks of rustic-style bread, smeared with olive oil, garlic and tomato, then served with a variety of toppings. For sheer volume, it's hard to beat the "international" breakfast buffet at **Hotel Le Meridien Barcelona** (► 37).

Go Shopping
Check out fashionable **Passeig de Gràcia**, **Rambla Catalunya** (which runs parallel), and the roads in between. Look out for Spanish designers **Adolfo Dominguez** and **Armand Basi**, Galician designer **Antonio Pernas** and local talent **Antoni Miró**.

Just Strolling
Stroll down the **Ramblas** (► 48–52), the vibrant heart and lungs of the city, and lap up the grand palaces, flower stalls, bird vendors, human "statues" and street entertainers along this charismatic, colourful avenue. Take in **La Boqueria**, Barcelona's largest market, and the **Café de l'Opera** (► 70) for a coffee *en route*.

It's Lunchtime
The atmospheric, old fishermen's quarter of **Barceloneta** (► 90) has always boasted the city's best choice of fish restaurants. Enjoy a mountainous platter of shellfish at **Agua** or **Can Ramonet** (► 91), **Can Ros** or **El Rey de la Gamba** (► 92) followed by a stroll along the beach.

See the Sights
"Must-sees" include the **Sagrada Família** (► 113–117) and the **Museu Picasso** (► 82–85), but don't forget the less obvious attractions – the **Manzana de la Discordia** ("The Apple of Discord",

➤ 102–104), so-named for its clashing architectural styles, or the vast stadium and museum of **Camp Nou** (➤ 157–158), the second most visited sight in the city.

Time for a Sundowner

Spit-and-sawdust **Celta** bar (Carrer de la Mercè 16) serves wine in traditional white

(➤ 91) is hard to beat. For a more traditional gastronomic experience that's easier on the wallet, enjoy dinner at **Senyor Parellada** (➤ 93), a hugely popular address in the same part of town.

Go Dancing

Barcelona easily lives up to its worldwide reputation for night-

Barcelona's Best

ceramic cups; stylish **Schilling** (➤ 70) in a converted gunsmith's shop, is currently an in early-evening meeting spot; or try ultra-chic **Goyescas** cocktail bar (in Hotel Arts, ➤ 36) with its dazzling sea views and its eye-poppingly arty tapas.

Best Dinner Venues

La Ribera's labyrinthine streets are where you will find many of the city's top restaurants. Offering delicious Catalan cuisine prepared with panache, an unbeatable cellar and impeccably discreet service, **Abac**

life. After the ultra-stylish lounge bar **White Pearl** (Carrer de Numància 179), move on to **Nick Havanna** (➤ 126), and then think about somewhere to dance. At **La Terrrazza** (➤ 144), a classic among the city's clubs, the action cranks up at 3 am, and expect to dance until dawn.

Grab a Late-Night Snack

Fidel (Carrer de Ferlandina 24) offers 500 varieties of sandwich. Open till around 3 am, it is a popular haunt for hungry clubbers!

Did you know?...

...that the metropolitan area of Barcelona covers 100sq km (62sq miles), with a population of more than 4 million – making it Spain's third largest city.

...that the city's official motto is Barcelona Es Teva (Barcelona Belongs to You).

...that visitors who drink from the fountain of Les Canaletes (➤ 49) are supposed to fall under the city's spell and are sure to return to Barcelona.

...that Barcelona is the leading cruiseship harbour in Europe and the Mediterranean, handling more than a million passengers every year.

...that Barcelona has more UNESCO World Heritage Sites than any other city in the world – five in all – including the first modern building to be selected.

...that Barcelonans are night owls. The city's flamboyant night-life is among the best in Europe, and the trendiest. Remember, tonight doesn't start until tomorrow!

...that Barcelona boasts more than 4km (2½ miles) of artificial beaches, stretching northwards from Barceloneta.

...that Gaudí's Casa Milà (➤ 105–107) is Spain's most original apartment block – seven rippling storeys, constructed, it is said, without a single straight line or right-angled corner.

...that Barcelona is the European city with the fastest growth in tourism.

Finding Your Feet

First Two Hours

Aeroport del Prat

Barcelona has just one national and international airport, located 12km (8 miles) south of the city centre, in the industrial suburb of **El Prat de Llobregat**. There are **three terminals**: Terminals A and B are for international and domestic flights, while Terminal C is reserved for the regular air-shuttle service to and from Madrid. Check your ticket to see which one concerns you.

Best Bets For Airport Transfers

By Taxi

A cab to the city centre will cost around €15 to 20 including an airport supplement. It is the most expensive option, but you'll be at your hotel door in 20–30 minutes, except in the worst rush-hour jams.

- Use only official taxis, easily recognisable by their **black-and-yellow paintwork**. Wait for these at the official stations outside each terminal.
- Taxi drivers should always use their meters, so there's no need to agree on a fare in advance. Each piece of luggage costs extra.

By Bus

The spacious, convenient **Aerobús** connects all three terminals to Plaça de Catalunya, stopping *en route* at Plaça d'Espanya, Gran Via de les Corts Catalanes (at the corner of Carrer del Comte d'Urgell) and Plaça de la Universitat.

- At the airport, **bus stops** are clearly marked from the Arrivals area.
- You buy **tickets** from the driver (who gives change). A discount pass for travel on the Aerobús, Metro and city buses is available (➤ 34).
- The **journey** takes about 30 minutes, and buses run every 15 minutes, between 6 am and midnight. At rush-hour the journey takes longer.
- On the **return to the airport**, the bus leaves from Plaça de Catalunya (opposite El Corte Inglés), stopping at Avinguda de Roma (at the corner of Carrer del Comte d'Urgell) and Sants-Estació (Sants station).

By Train

A regular train service runs from the airport station to Sants in about 20 minutes; the journey to Plaça de Catalunya and Arc de Triomf takes another five and ten minutes respectively. During rush-hour periods, the train can be a better option than the bus.

- A moving walkway across a bridge linking terminals A and B takes you to the **airport station**.
- You must buy your **ticket** before boarding. Tickets cost around €3, but you can use a **T-10 city transport card** (➤ 34) when outward bound.
- Trains **run daily** between 6 am and 10 pm.

Barcelona-Sants Train Station

Most **international and national trains** stop at Sants station. The station has its own tourist office, accommodation service, banks and convenient taxi ranks.

- Though the station is a fair distance from downtown Barcelona, **Line 3** (green) of the Metro (➤ 33) gets you to the Ramblas (Liceu station), central Plaça de Catalunya, and Passeig de Gràcia (where some mainline trains also stop) in a few minutes. Look for direction "Canyelles" on the signs.
- When using the Metro, **don't mistake** Plaça de Sants station for the Sants-Estació station, the one that connects with the train station.

Getting Around

The modern Metro system and air-conditioned buses provide good transport links in the city. Cable-cars and funicular railways (➤ 182) can also help you get around and are favourites with kids.

The Metro

The Metro is definitely the best way to travel where longer distances are involved. It is fast, frequent, quite modern, and most trains are air-conditioned – a relief during hot, sticky spells.

- Five lines make up the **Metro network**, which covers much of the city. The system is supplemented by the **Ferrocarrils de la Generalitat de Catalunya (FGC)**, two ultra-smart underground train services run by the Catalan government. The FGC line most likely to be of use is the one from Plaça de Catalunya up to Tibidabo (U7). Free maps are available from Metro stations.
- Both the **Metro** and **FGC** run from 5 am to 11 pm, starting and stopping slightly later on Sundays, and running till 2 am on Fridays, Saturdays and the day before a public holiday. Try to avoid **rush-hours**: roughly 7:30–9 am and 6–8 pm.
- You can expect a long walk at many interchanges, so do your best to avoid switching lines if you can.

How to Use the Metro

- **Lines** are identified by colours, while directions are denoted by the end-stations clearly marked on the Metro map.
- Individual **tickets** must be pushed through the slot in the turnstile (to your left at Metro stations) and retrieved – there are frequent ticket checks, but you don't need the ticket again to get out. When using **multiple tickets** (➤ 34) you'll see that a number is printed showing how many journeys you have left.
- Have enough **change ready** for ticket machines, in case the ticket offices are closed, often the case at night or on Sundays.

Buses

Like the Metro, buses are air-conditioned and comfortable. Useful routes take you where the Metro can't: up onto Montjuïc, for example, and to Parc Güell or Monestir de Pedralbes. Bus numbers have been given throughout, but free maps showing all routes are available from the Tourist Information Offices (➤ 34) and transport information offices in the major stations (Universitat, Diagonal, Sagrada Família, Sants-Estació and Catalunya).

- In general, Metro fares and times apply to the city buses, and single tickets can be bought from the driver, who gives change.
- Special **night buses** (*Nitbus*) run regularly from 11 pm to 5 am on selected routes.
- The **TombBus**, an ultra-comfortable, royal-blue single-decker, plies the Shopping Line, a route between Plaça de Catalunya and Plaça Pius XII, via Passeig de Gràcia and Avinguda Diagonal.
- The **Bus Turístic** also provides a hop-on, hop-off service. Open-topped double-deckers serve two interlinked circular routes (northern red and southern blue) that take in the city's main sights, such as La Sagrada Família and the football stadium, Camp Nou. **One-** or **two-day tickets** (discounts for children) can be bought at tourist offices or on the bus.

Discount Passes

Various types of transport passes provide differing access to the Metro, FGC and bus networks. Passes can be bought from ticket offices and automatic machines at all stations, from kiosks and lottery shops, and from Servi-Caixa machines (➤ 42). The ones most likely to be of interest are listed below.

- The **T-10** is valid for ten trips on all three networks and can be shared (pass it through the stamping machine once per passenger).
- **T-Dia** provides unlimited 24-hour travel for one person. **3 Dies** and **5 Dies** passes are available, which are valid for three and five days respectively.
- An **Aerobús+Bus+Metro** pass provides unlimited travel on Metro or buses, plus travel on the Aerobús (➤ 32) to and from the airport. You can buy three-day or five-day passes.
- The **Bus Turístic** fare (➤ 33) also entitles you to a booklet of discount vouchers for various attractions along the route.
- One-, two- and three-day **Barcelona Cards** (available at Tourist Information Offices) entitle you to unlimited Metro and bus travel and reductions at most museums, plus some restaurants and shops across the city.

Taxis

- Official taxis have distinctive **black-and-yellow** paintwork. The meter is set at around €2 and fare increments start after the first 2km (1 mile) or 2 minutes, whichever is sooner. Two fare bands operate: before 6 am and after 10 pm. On weekends and on public holidays, you will be charged 30 per cent more than at other times.
- A ***Lliure/Libre*** sign in the windscreen or a **green light** on the roof indicates that a taxi is looking for business, whether at a station or in the street.
- **Barnataxi** (tel: 93 357 77 55) and **Ràdio Taxi** (tel: 93 225 00 00) are two reliable phone-cab companies.

Driving

Driving in Barcelona can be tiresome, traffic systems complicated and parking downright frustrating. If you bring a car, the best advice is to leave it in the hotel garage. If you're determined to brave it, always wear a seatbelt and leave absolutely nothing in the car when it is parked.

Car Rental

The major companies have desks at the airport and city-centre offices, but local companies can work out a lot cheaper.

Avis (tel: 93 209 95 33)
Easy Link (tel: 93 453 41 88)
Laser (tel: 93 322 90 12)
Hertz (tel: 93 490 86 62)

Tourist Information Offices

Main Office 192 C5, Plaça de Catalunya (opposite El Corte Inglés), tel: 906 30 12 82, www.barcelonaturisme.com, open daily 9–9. Metro: Catalunya

Ajuntament (City Hall), 192 C3, Plaça de Sant Jaume, open Mon–Sat 10–8, Sun and holidays 10–2; closed 25 Dec, 1 Jan. Metro: Jaume I

Barcelona-Sants train station 198 C2, open daily 8–8, Jun–Sep; Mon–Fri 8–8, weekends and holidays 8–2, rest of year. Metro: Sants-Estació

Catalonia Tourist Office 200 B2, Palau Robert, Passeig de Gràcia 107, open Mon–Sat 10–7, Sun 10–2; closed holidays. Metro: Diagonal

Admission Charges

The cost of admission to places of interest mentioned in the text is indicated by three price categories.

inexpensive under €4 **moderate** €4–8 **expensive** over €8

Accommodation

Millions of people visit Barcelona each year, and there is a wide variety of accommodation to cater for all tastes and budgets. The 1992 Olympics transformed the hotel scene: old palaces were restored and turned into hotels, many new hotels were built and run-down establishments renovated. Most of the city's luxury hotels are very expensive, but since the city has become a year-round venue for trade fairs and conferences, more mid-range hotels have appeared. Quality budget accommodation and decent singles are still hard to find, but there are some good-value *hostals* (akin to an inexpensive hotel – not to be confused with a hostel) and apartment hotels suitable for longer stays.

Districts

The least expensive accommodation tends to be around the **Barri Gòtic**. This lively, atmospheric district is the heart of the old city, and many of Barcelona's first hotels were built along the Ramblas. Be warned, though, areas become seedier the closer you get to the port and you should take care when returning to your hotel late at night. Noise, particularly near the Ramblas and in the Barri Gòtic, may also be a problem.

The wide boulevards of the **Eixample** offer an extensive choice of hotels, particularly in the mid-range price bracket, although even these can be quite expensive. Be aware, though, that sometimes modern amenities take second place to Modernisme style. Beyond the Avinguda Diagonal is the neighbourhood of **Gràcia**, easily reached by public transport although farther away from the main attractions.

Reservations

Barcelona's booming popularity has meant increasing pressure on hotel rooms. **Advance booking** is strongly recommended, but if this is not possible, the hotel reservations office at the airport is open daily from 9 am to 9 pm and will book you a place to stay on arrival. Another hotel-finding agency, **Ultramar Express** (tel: 93 491 44 63), is located in the vestibule at Sants train station and is open 8 am–10 pm daily, but you need to give them a deposit against the bill. The **main tourist office** in Plaça de Catalunya (tel: 93 304 32 32, www.hotelsbcn.es, open 9–9) is very helpful but may also request a deposit. **Halcón Viajes** (Carrer Aribau 34, tel: 93 454 59 95), the giant Spanish travel agency, can book rooms, often combined with a car-rental deal, but they charge a commission.

Prices

Demand for rooms has pushed prices up in the last few years, and it is much harder to find the once-traditional cut-price weekend rates. There is also less distinction between high- and low-season prices, though you may still find some good deals, particularly if you shop around. Remember that all hotel bills are subject to 7 per cent **VAT** on top of the basic price. **Breakfasts** are additional, and there is usually a charge for secure hotel **car parking**.

Apartment Hotels

Small, self-contained flats with maid service are good for longer stays, although they will vary in cost depending on location and quality. **Apartaments Calàbria** (Carrer Calàbria 129, tel: 93 426 42 28) are good value but get booked well ahead. The mid-range **Aparthotel Senator** (Via Augusta 167, tel: 93 201 14 04; email: senator@city-hotels.es) has comfortable accommodation. Luxurious, high-tech apartments are available at the **Atenea Aparthotel** (Carrer Joan Güell 207-11, tel: 93 490 66 40; email: atenea@city-hotels.es).

B&B/Room Rentals

Barcelona Allotjament (Carrer Pelai 12, pral B, tel: 93 268 43 57; email: bcnacom@ibernet.com) charges a commission but can find a wide range of accommodation ranging from B&B with local families to whole apartments. It can also arrange special-interest courses. Other agencies include **B&B Norma Agency** (Carrer Ali Bei 11, tel: 93 232 37 66) and **Oh-Barcelona** (Carrer Fontanella 20 2D, tel: 93 304 07 69, www.oh-barcelona.com).

Youth Hostels

There are several official YHF youth hostels which offer pretty good rates, although charges are more if you don't have a membership card. Rooms in summer get snapped up quickly so **book ahead** if you can. Two of the best are **Alberg Pere Tarres** (Carrer Numància 149–151, tel: 93 410 23 09; email: alberg@peretarres.org), and **Alberg Mare de Déu de Montserrat** (Passeig de la Mare de Déu del Coll 41–51, tel: 93 210 51 51).

Accommodation Prices

Prices are for a double room (without tax)

€ under €60 **€€** €60–125 **€€€** €125–250 **€€€€** over €250

Hotel Actual €€€

The rooms at this resolutely modern hotel – the name means "up-to-date" – are sleek and easy on the eye, with internet access and well-stocked minibars. Though not large, they are not cramped, with efficient use of space, a small writing desk and inviting queen-size beds. For the location, the rates are unbeatable. Some rooms have wheelchair access.

200 B2 Carrer del Rosselló 238 93 552 05 50; www.hotelactual.com Diagonal

Hotel Arts €€€€

The towering, world-class Ritz-Carlton hotel, set in palm-filled gardens by the beach, boasts the only seafront pool in Barcelona, as well as fabulous interiors with specially commissioned artworks, a waterfall-lined lobby and fine views across the Mediterranean. Prices are equally sky-high; three of the upper floors are reserved for "The Club", those guests requiring an extra degree of privacy and privilege, and the top floors also have duplex apartments decorated by leading Catalan designer Jaume Tresserra. The hotel has its own fitness centre, hairdresser, restaurants and shops.

197 E2 Carrer de la Marina 19–21 93 221 10 00; email: info@harts.es Ciutadella

Hotel Axel €€€

Calling itself "heterofriendly", this extremely stylish hotel, in a converted Modernist corner-house, targets gay clients, attracted by the heart-of-Gayxample (► 125) location. A cocktail bar, a restaurant laying on weekly drag shows, a menswear boutique and fitness club with sauna and swimming pool are added attractions. The rooms are spacious and airy, with eye-catching details such as Kenzo fabrics and Alessi furniture. Some rooms boast mini-conservatories in the gorgeous Modernist stained-glass bow-windows. Guests have access to a library and business centre with internet access.

200 A1 Carrer d'Aribau 33 93 323 93 93; www.hotelaxel.com Passeig de Gràcia

Hotel Banys Orientals €€

All done out in cool greys and whites, the hotel is in stark contrast with the adjoining Senyor Parellada (► 93), but maintains the same impeccable quality. Each of the 43 rooms in this historic building is slightly different – some have four-poster beds – but all are extremely comfortable and stylish, with beautiful bathrooms.

193 E2 Carrer de l'Argenteria 37 93 268 84 60; www.hotelbanysorientals.com Jaume I

Hotel Condes de Barcelona €€€

This opulent hotel was designed as a private villa at the end of the 19th century, and it is still one of the city's most glamorous addresses. The curved lobby-bar with pentagonal skylight has an art deco look. The comfortable bedrooms have marble baths and also soundproof windows. A rooftop terrace and outdoor swimming pool are additional attractions. Rooms in the extension, however, are less characterful than in the original building.

200 B1 Passeig de Gràcia 75 93 467 47 80 Passeig de Gràcia

Hotel España €€

The public rooms of this popular hotel in El Raval are a showcase of Modernist design; the restaurant, in particular, has wonderful floral tiles and woodwork. The comfortable, spacious bedrooms have a more modern appearance, and many overlook a bright, interior patio.

192 A3 Carrer de Sant Pau 9–11 93 318 17 58; email: hotelspanya@tresnet.com Liceu

Hostal Jardí €€

You have to book well ahead to get a room here overlooking one of the old town's prettiest squares. These rooms also tend to be better furnished than interior ones. Those without a balcony, however, are cheaper. All rooms have telephone and bathroom.

192 C3 Plaça de Sant Josep Oriol I 93 301 59 00 Liceu

Hotel Jazz €€€

Part of a reliable local chain, the aptly named Hotel Jazz – it is cool, fashionable and relaxing – could not be more central, just off Plaça de Catalunya. Luckily the spacious, designer-decorated rooms are soundproofed, as this is not a quiet part of town. The views from the rooftop heated swimming pool and surrounding deck are simply fabulous.

192 B5 Carrer de Pelai 3 93 552 96 96; www.nnhotels.es Catalunya

Hostal Lausanne €

Despite the stylish staircase and attractive terrace, the rooms at this first-floor hostal are plainly furnished. A central location and friendly welcome, however, compensate for the lack of frills and make this a good budget choice. Some rooms have balconies overlooking the Portal de l'Angel.

192 C4 Avda del Portal de l'Angel 24 93 302 11 39 Catalunya

Hostal Layetana €

Although there are some good, inexpensive rooms to be had here, it may be worth paying a little more for a room with a shower, balcony and view. Noise may be a problem at night, but that's part of the fun of staying in this lively, ancient quarter near the Catedral. Some rooms have wheelchair access.

193 D3 Plaça de Ramon Berenguer el Gran 2 93 319 20 12 Jaume I

Hotel Le Meridien Barcelona €€€€

One of the first choices for visiting celebrities and pop stars, this luxury hotel is in a prime position right on the Ramblas. Built in classic Modernist style, it has double glazing which filters out most of the noise from the street below. Bedrooms, some no-smoking, are spacious with extra-large beds and luxuries such as heated bathroom floors. There is live music most nights in the chic lobby-bar, and Le Patio restaurant is recommended for its mix of fine continental and Catalan cuisine.

192 B4 La Rambla 111 93 318 62 00; www.meridienbarcelona.com Liceu

Hotel Mesón Castilla €€€

The combination of quiet, charming rooms in a central location at reasonable prices is hard to beat. This well-run, mid-range hotel has a wealth of art nouveau detailing and some of the comfortable rooms open onto large terraces. A generous breakfast buffet is served in the small dining room or on the patio. There are several rooms that are suitable for families (there are up to four beds in each).

192 A5 Carrer de Valldonzella 5 93 318 21 82; www.mesoncastilla.com Universitat

Hotel Neri €€€

If you want to stay in the historic centre, this is the place to go. A Gothic palace sumptuously converted into a boutique hotel, the Neri is tasteful, charming and utterly comfortable. While the cosy library is reserved exclusively for guests, the small restaurant is open to the public at lunch- and dinnertime, serving a limited but balanced menu. The luxurious rooms, some of them suites, are equipped with plasma-screen televisions and CD players. On the roof you can use a small sundeck and pool.

192 C3 Carrer de Sant Sever 5 93 304 06 55; www.hotelneri.com Liceu

Hostal-Residencia Oliva €

A delightfully antiquated lift takes you up to the fourth floor of this friendly, family-run *residencia* overlooking the Passeig de Gràcia. Most of the rooms are light and airy, and some have a balcony. Not all, however, have bathrooms. Great value given the location.

196 B5 Passeig de Gràcia 32 93 488 01 62 Catalunya/Passeig de Gràcia

Hotel Omm €€€€

On the outside it looks like a post-modernist pastiche of Gaudí's wavy and scaly Casa Milà (➤ 105–107), just around the corner. Inside the overriding feeling is of spaciousness and the very latest in design. Every part of the hotel, from the reception to the sundeck and swimming pool, grabs your attention with sleek lines and luxurious blends of wood, glass and textiles. Rooms are generously sized, with bathrooms that will make you want to have one just like them at home. The Moo Bar serves an outstanding selection of wines and haute cuisine in the coolest of settings, while Ommsession (➤ 126), down below, has fast become one of the city's hippest nightclubs.

200 B2 Carrer del Rosselló 265 93 445 40 00; www.hotelomm.es Diagonal

Hostal Palermo €

In an area packed with budget *hostals*, this is one of the best. The 34 refurbished rooms, with or without bath, are clean, bright and well kept. A friendly atmosphere soon makes you feel at home. Have breakfast at La Boqueria, the city's colourful central market, nearby.

192 B3 Carrer de la Boqueria 21 93 302 40 02 Liceu

Hotel Prestige Paseo de Gracia €€€

Facing the Manzana de la Discordia (➤ 102–104), this elegant hotel has 45 spacious rooms, some with large balconies. As prestigious as the name promises, the soothingly minimalist interior with fashionable details such as rectangular porcelain washbasins, is enhanced by top-quality linens, furnishings and fittings. The useful "Ask Me" service tracks down tickets to shows and provides information about unmissable events and cutting-edge shopping venues.

200 B1 Passeig de Gràcia 62 93 272 41 80; www.prestigepaseodegracia.com Passeig de Gràcia

Ritz Hotel €€€€

When the Ritz was founded in 1919, it was immediately dubbed "the grande dame" of Barcelona hotels. Following a period when it was called the Hotel Husa Palace, this most prestigious of hotels is once more named the Ritz. The interior is sumptuous, and the multilingual staff are discreetly omnipresent. The list of rich and famous patrons includes Salvador Dalí.

196 C5 Gran Via de les Corts Catalanes 668 93 318 52 00; email: ritz@ritzbcn.com Passeig de Gràcia

Food and Drink

It's hard to walk more than a few steps in Barcelona without coming across a good place to eat, from hole-in-the-wall cafés to exclusive restaurants. The enjoyment of good food and eating is considered one of life's priorities, and people in Barcelona are very demanding about the quality of food they eat.

Catalan cooking is at its finest in Barcelona, both traditional (➤ 12–14) and innovative, but you will also find many restaurants serving food from other regions of Spain. There's also a strong French presence, not surprising perhaps when you consider how close Barcelona is to the border, as well as a considerable number of foreign restaurants. There is some of the best seafood in the country, as well as an unusually high number of vegetarian eating places (see panel). Look out also for *tabernes catalanes* (Catalan inns) offering traditional home cooking.

When to Eat

It may take a few days to adjust to the rhythms of Catalan dining. Be prepared either to eat late or to sit in an empty restaurant.

- Most people eat **lunch** at around 2 pm, but many places serve food until about 4 pm.
- **Dinner** does not usually start until 9 pm and food can be served up till midnight. If you get peckish in the early evening, try some tapas (➤ 13).

Table Tips

- Good restaurants always get fully booked, especially on the weekend, so make a **reservation** to avoid disappointment. Many places are also closed on Sunday evenings as well as on the evening of a holiday, so those that are open tend to get very crowded. It's also worth checking annual holiday dates; many restaurants close for Easter and during August.

Best Seafood Restaurants
Botafumeiro (➤ 122)
Cal Pep (➤ 91)
Can Ramonet (➤ 91),
Can Ros (➤ 92)
El Rey de la Gamba (➤ 92)

Best Vegetarian Restaurants
Biocenter (➤ 68)
Comme Bio (➤ 92)
L'Hortet (➤ 69)
L'Illa de Gràcia (➤ 122)

- Those who eat neither fish nor meat will usually find plenty of vegetable, salad and egg dishes on most menus. In Barcelona, unlike many other cities in Spain, the number of vegetarian and vegan restaurants is growing. In ordinary restaurants, look for Catalan dishes such as *espinacs a la catalana* (spinach with raisins and pine nuts), *escalivada* (char-grilled vegetables) and, in early spring, *calçots* (➤ 13).
- There is no percentage rule on restaurant **tipping**; in most places, should you wish to leave a tip, €1–2 is more than acceptable. Many locals just leave a token sum, if that at all. **IVA** (VAT) at 7 per cent is generally included in the prices shown on the menu, but this is not always the case; it should say on the menu if you have to pay this.
- Don't be surprised to see napkins, toothpicks and olive stones just being dropped on the floor of old-fashioned tapas bars; however, this may not be acceptable in other places. Take your lead from the way locals behave.

- There are **different sets of prices** depending on whether you choose to stand at the bar to eat or sit at a table. Prices can be even more expensive if you decide to sit out on a terrace.

Cheap Eats

- Fill up at breakfast time on ***torrades*** (toasted rolls with butter and jam), ***truita*** (omelette), or ***xocolata amb xurros*** (delicious doughnuts with thick drinking chocolate).
- Throughout the day, you can get excellent ***bocadillos*** or ***entrepans*** (sandwiches), **tapas** (➤ 13) and pizza slices at bars and shops all over the city.
- ***Llesqueries*** specialise in open sandwiches of cheese, meat, ham, anchovies or vegetables on a base of ***pa amb tomàquet*** (toasted slices of country bread rubbed with garlic, the pulp of very ripe tomatoes, salt and olive oil). To sample this typical Catalan snack, try La Bodegueta (➤ 107).
- Try ***ensaimades*** (pastry spirals) and cakes from the city's excellent bakeries and pastry shops or indulge in some hot ***buñuelos***, doughnuts bought from a street-seller and eaten dusted with sugar.
- **Fast food** is as ubiquitous here as anywhere else and there are plenty of familiar burger chains around town. You'll also find an increasing number of falafel and kebab outlets, especially in the old town.
- The ***menú del dia***, the daily set menu, usually three or four courses and wine, always provides great value for money in Barcelona. The cheapest set menus are usually available at lunchtime only, but many decent restaurants have a good-value set menu in the evening.
- Several budget restaurants offer a ***plat combinat***, a combined plate of something like chicken and salad with bread and a drink included.

What to Drink

There is little difference on the whole between a bar and a café, although it's worth noting that *cellers* are really wine bars. Unlike many restaurants, most bars and cafés stay open throughout August.

- Most people drink wine with their meals and it is usually very inexpensive, especially house wine (served bottled or straight out of the barrel). Catalonia produces a variety of excellent wines (➤ 14). To sample the year's new wine, ask for *vi novell*.
- You'll find many ***xampanyeries*** in Barcelona (➤ 14). These specialise in champagne and *cava*, the traditional sparkling wine of Spain. You can sample a range of house *cavas* by the glass, either the sweetish *brut* or *brut nature*.
- ***Cerveseries*** serve mostly beers such as San Miguel, Estrella, Voll-Damm and draught *cerveza negra* – bitter, black, fizzy lager.
- ***Orxateries*** and ***granges*** serve *orxata*, an unusual but popular non-alcoholic, cold milky drink made from tiger nuts, *granissats* (refreshing iced fruit drinks), coffee, cakes, milkshakes and *suissos* (hot chocolate topped with whipped cream).

Best *Orxateries* and *Granges*

Dulcinea (➤ 70)
La Pallaresa (⊞ 192 B4, Carrer Petritxol 11), renowned for its *suissos*.
Orxateria-Gelateria Sirvent (⊞ 195 E3/E4, Ronda Sant Pau 3. Metro: Paral.lel) – one of the best places to try *orxata*.
El Tío Che (⊞ 197 off F3, Rambla del Poble Nou 44) – founded in 1912 and famous for malt-flavoured *granissat*.
La Valenciana (➤ 123)

Shopping

Shops in the city range from old-fashioned little businesses and trendy boutiques to glitzy shopping centres and large department stores selling just about anything you might want.

Where to Go

- The **Eixample** harbours the city's densest concentration of fashion emporia (➤ 124–125). The **more exclusive establishments**, and star designers, be they Catalan, Spanish or international, line the **Passeig de Gràcia** and other Eixample streets. **Antoni Miró** is one of the city's fashion gurus and you can find his beautiful shirts and dresses in his own outlets (➤ 124) and several other boutiques. Designers Adolfo Domínguez and Purificación García also boast prime-location shops along the Passeig de Gràcia.
- The northern reaches of the **Ramblas** or the pedestrian streets around the **Plaça de Catalunya**, are a good hunting ground for leather goods. Also in the vicinity are a myriad of fashion boutiques and crafts shops, as well as a massive branch of **El Corte Inglés**, the biggest store in town.
- **Avinguda Diagonal** is the third major commercial axis, seemingly sprouting a new shopping mall every week. Head out to its southernmost reaches (➤ 160) for leading international names and a branch of El Corte Inglés. **Diagonal Mar** is a brand new mall near Besòs Mar Metro station.
- If you're looking for **jewellery**, **glassware**, **textiles**, **prints** and **paintings**, the labyrinthine streets of La Ribera and, increasingly, El Raval, should come up trumps. Gràcia and the Barri Gòtic are also worth investigating. Try Roca (➤ 124) for jewellery and 1748 (➤ 94) for stylish pottery and glass.
- Try Camper's (➤ 71) for shoes and Calpa (➤ 72) for leather goods.
- Several of Barcelona's museums have shops attached. The best are at the Museu Tèxtil i de la Indumentària (➤ 86), Fundació Joan Miró (➤ 134–135), MACBA (➤ 63), CCCB (➤ 64), Fundació Antoni Tàpies (➤ 118), Museu d'Història de la Ciutat (➤ 64) and Casa Milà (➤ 105–107).
- If you want to put together a picnic to remember, the city's many colourful **food markets** are the best places to stock up. **Mercat de la Boqueria** (➤ 50–51) in particular shouldn't be missed.
- Several **specialist food shops** will tempt you with local specialities that travel well, including wine and olive oil, salt cod and hams, *torró* (Catalan nougat) and honey. Supermarkets are often a better-value alternative – try the Ramblas branch of **Champion** (113 La Rambla) or **El Corte Inglés**.

Opening Hours

- Bigger stores tend to stay open from 9 am to 9 pm. Smaller shops close during the siesta (usually 1–4:30 pm), close early on Saturdays, stay shut on Mondays and frequently pull down the shutters for the whole summer.
- *Fleques* and *pastisseries* (bakeries and cake shops) have always been allowed to open on Sundays, but otherwise **Sunday shopping** is still restricted. Larger shops, however, can open on a fixed number of Sundays throughout the year, and shopping malls are exempt from the restrictions.

Etiquette

- In most shops customer service is laid back, though you may be approached in exclusive boutiques. However, prodding fruit and vegetables is not appreciated.
- Old-fashioned stores and groceries have cashiers (*caixa*) whom you pay to get a ticket to be exchanged for your purchase. In small shops, people often ask who's last in line "*Qui es l'últim?*", answered by "*Soc jo*" (me).

Entertainment

Information

Pick up the weekly *Guia del Ocio* listings magazine at a kiosk or consult its website, www.guiadelociobcn.es. *La Vanguardia*, the best local paper, also has an informative arts and entertainments page. Two other websites worth visiting are www.red2000.com/spain/barcelon and www.city.net/countries/spain.

Clubs

- **Port Vell** and **Port Olímpic** (➤ 95–96), where clubs are free from time and noise restrictions, have become the focus of Barcelona's vibrant club culture and are *the* places to be seen after dark. There are, however, sophisticated clubs in the **Eixample** and **Gràcia** (➤ 125–126). The **Born** and **El Raval** are also lively at night. For a unique Barcelona clubbing experience, try La Terrrazza [sic] (➤ 144) or Torres de Avila (➤ 144).
- Most clubs **open** their doors at 10 or 11 pm, but you'll have the dance floor to yourself until at least 1 am, and in many places things don't really get going until around 3 or 4 am.
- Some of the fancier clubs in the Eixample and by the coast impose a **dress code**. Though scruffiness is definitely out, in the summer skimpiness is de rigueur. Many clubs allow ladies in free.

Opera and Music

- The **Gran Teatre del Liceu** (➤ 64) is one of the world's biggest and most celebrated opera houses and a night out there in its lavish velvet-and-gilt surroundings always smacks of a gala event. The **Palau de la Música Catalana** (➤ 78–79 and 95–96), another sumptuous auditorium, offers spectacular architecture as well as high-quality music, while the city's **L'Auditori** (➤ 96) hosts the world's leading musicians.
- **Jazz** and **rock**, **pop** and **salsa**, **flamenco** and **folk** are all on offer at a variety of haunts around the city.

Theatre, Dance and Cinema

Unless you speak Catalan or Spanish, your chances of finding drama to your liking are limited. However, ballet, dance and mime are all well represented. If you visit the city in late June or early August, try to catch one of the productions put on as part of the annual Festival del Grec (➤ 143–144).

Cinema is a different matter now that Spain's (and especially Barcelona's) cinema-goers prefer their films subtitled rather than dubbed, and a couple of great art-house **cinemas** regularly screen English-language films. Among the best are Meliès (➤ 126), Verdi (➤ 126) and Verdi Park (➤ 126).

Tickets

Two rival savings banks, La Caixa (de Pensions) and Caixa Catalunya, sell tickets for theatres and other entertainment venues, including the Teatre Nacional, Liceu and Festival del Grec. These services are called **Servi-Caixa** and **Tel-entrada**, respectively. You can order by phone or via the internet and pick up the tickets at the venue. **Servi-Caixa** also has special machines next to the Caixa's ATMs, which print the tickets out. **Tel-entrada** is operated out of most of Caixa Catalunya's branches and at a special desk at the Plaça de Catalunya tourist office (where theatre and certain other tickets are sold half-price, cash only, three hours before the performance).

Servi-Caixa (tel: 902 33 22 11; www.lacaixa.es/servicaixa)
Tel-entrada (tel: 902 10 12 12; www.cec.caixat.es)

Getting Your Bearings

There are few city streets in the world as well trodden as the Ramblas, one long thoroughfare divided into five distinct sections. As you saunter down the tree-lined avenue from Plaça de Catalunya, Barcelona's main square, towards the Mediterranean, you'll be drawn into the ceaseless flow of pedestrians.

On your left is the magnificent Barri Gòtic (Gothic Quarter), where the cathedral towers over one of the world's best-preserved sets of medieval palaces and churches. Beyond, at Port Vell (Old Port), the colourful harbourside, one of the major draws is a marvellous state-of-the-art aquarium, nestling among modern shops and multiscreen cinemas. Off the tail-end of the Ramblas, Antoni Gaudí's castle-like Palau Güell sits uneasily in the sleazy lower side of El Raval – a jumble of medieval streets, dingy alleyways and dead-ends. By contrast, El Raval's increasingly gentrified upper reaches are now dominated by the white hulk of the controversial Museu d'Art Contemporàni (MACBA), Barcelona's contemporary art museum set amid stylish restaurants and art galleries galore.

The Ramblas extend from Plaça de Catalunya to the Monument a Colom (left) overlooking the harbour

Previous page: The fountains of Rambla de Canaletes

The Ramblas and Either Side

★ Don't Miss

Passeig de Colom: tropical palms add a touch of the exotic to Barcelona's bustling waterfront

At Your Leisure

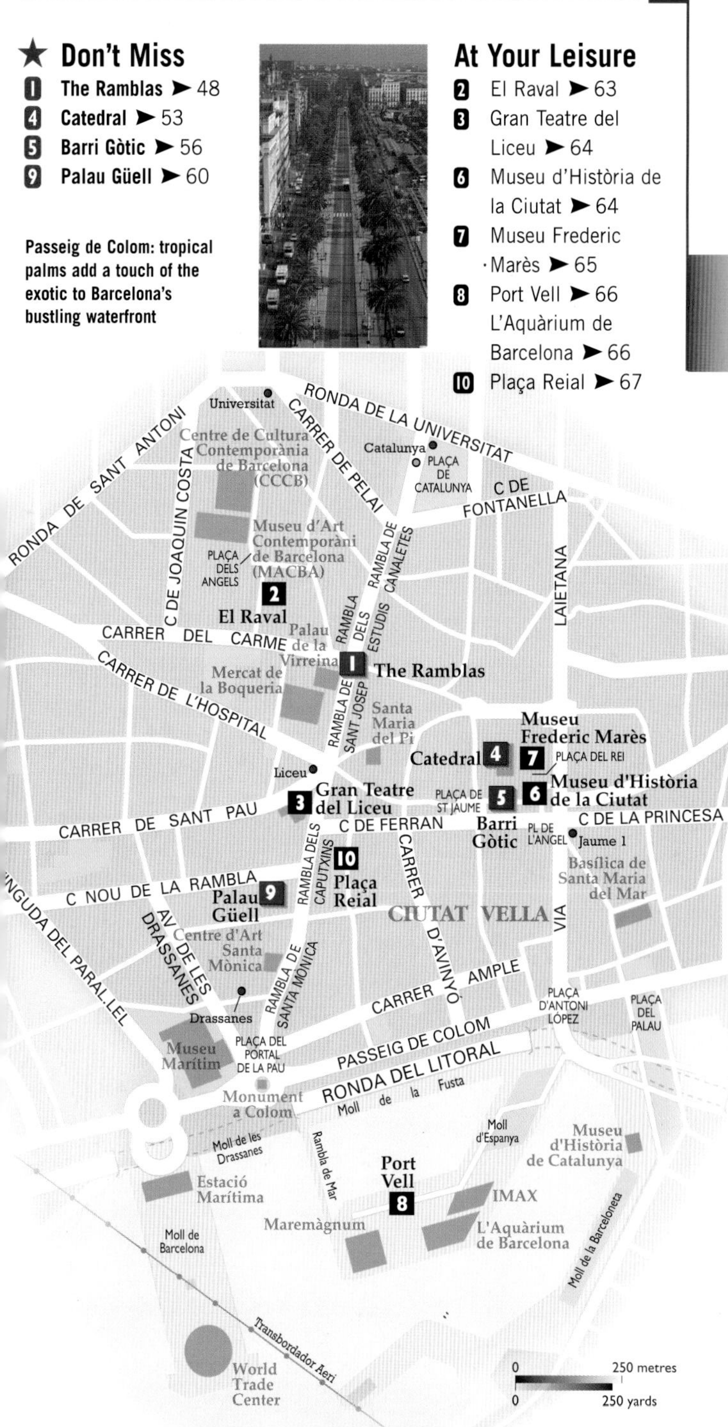

Wander down the Ramblas, then explore the Barri Gòtic dominated by the great cathedral, before reaching Port Vell, where the underwater marvels of the city's aquarium await you.

The Ramblas and Either Side in a Day

9:00 am

Make an early start, stopping for a coffee at Café Zurich on the Plaça de Catalunya (left), a locals' favourite meeting place. Then amble down the 1 **Ramblas** (➤ 48–52), which at this time of day is fairly quiet, as far as the 3 **Gran Teatre del Liceu** (➤ 64). You'll be exploring the avenue's nether reaches later in the day.

10:00 am

The morning is the prime time to visit the 4 **cathedral** (➤ 53–55) – best approached along delightful Carrer de Portaferrissa. After touring the cathedral and its cloisters, take the lift to the rooftops and survey the whole of the Barri Gòtic.

11:00 am

Start your exploration of the 5 **Barri Gòtic** (➤ 56–59) at Santa Maria del Pi, contemplating the church over a drink on one of the adjoining squares. Soak up more history on the Plaça de Sant Jaume before taking your pick of the museums around the Plaça del Rei (➤ 56).

1:30 pm

It's early for a midday meal in Barcelona, but at least you'll be sure of a table. Either opt for something like sausage and beans at La Cuineta, just behind the cathedral, or try the unpretentious Catalan cooking at the lively Els Quatre Gats (➤ 70).

3:00 pm

Make your way to the lower end of the Ramblas for a guided visit round the 9 **Palau Güell** (➤ 60–62) (below; closed for renovation until late 2006). Then treat yourself to a drink at the 10 **Plaça Reial** (➤ 67), where Gaudí designed the lampposts.

5:30 pm

Your next stop is 8 **Port Vell** (➤ 66–67), at the bottom of Via Laietana. Enjoy a stroll around the marina, then visit **L'Aquàrium de Barcelona** (above), where a slow-moving walkway takes you right into a fascinating underwater world of stingrays and sharks.

8:30 pm

Dinner at Silenus (➤ 70) in the trendy Raval district, and maybe a concert at the **CCCB** (➤ 64), would wind up a perfect day. Or else enjoy another drink before a sophisticated supper at Ca l'Isidre (➤ 68), the height of refinement and elegance. Alternatively, don your glad rags and attend an opera at the opulent Gran Teatre del Liceu (➤ 64).

The Ramblas

Once just a dried-up riverbed, the Ramblas are now flooded with people 24 hours a day. The avenue, flanked by flaky-trunked plane trees, acts as a long magnet, attracting crowds who flock to watch or add to its never-ending ferment. People chat, buy flowers, catch up on world news, have a drink, observe the ever-more inventive human statues, or simply join the flow of other people who wander up and down during the early-evening *paseo* (stroll) and on weekend afternoons. Not only the best-known street in Barcelona, the Ramblas are also a non-stop human spectacle, and you can have it all for free – unless you toss the street entertainers a coin or two.

The Ramblas
192 B2
Catalunya, Liceu, Drassanes, FGC Catalunya
14, 38, 59, 91, N9, N12

Palau de la Virreina
192 B4
93 316 10 00;
www.bcn.es/virreinaexposicions
Tue–Sat 11–8:30, Sun and public holidays 11–3
Liceu 14, 38, 59, 91
Exhibitions: inexpensive

Mercat de la Boqueria
192 B4
93 318 25 84
Mon–Sat 8 am–8:30 pm
Liceu 14, 38, 59, 91

Monument a Colom
192 A1
93 302 52 24
Daily 9–8:30, Jun–Sep; 10–6:30, rest of year Drassanes
14, 36, 38, 57, 59, 64, 91
Inexpensive

The Ramblas funnel you from Plaça de Catalunya, the city's main square, to the harbourside, where the Monument a Colom (➤ 52) stands like the full stop finishing off an enormous exclamation mark. The total distance is little over a kilometre, but there are so many diversions that you need to allow plenty of time. This has been a popular promenade since the 18th century, when the walls that once protected the Barri Gòtic were torn down and the first street lamps were put up. Although it has seen many changes since, the present character of the Ramblas owes most to the 19th century, when the opera house, market and cast-iron flower stalls were built.

Above: Modernist mosaic

Left: Street art by Joan Miró

Rambla de Canaletes

Although people often walk it as one continuous promenade, the street is divided into five fairly distinct sections. Starting at the top end, adjoining Plaça de Catalunya, is the Rambla de Canaletes, named after a black-and-bronze drinking fountain – if you quench your thirst here, so the legend goes, you're bound to return to Barcelona. For a small fee you can sit on one of the rickety seats and watch the world stroll by, or listen to the elderly men who gather here to talk about politics or soccer. Also along this stretch are enormous bunker-like news-kiosks, selling papers and magazines from all around the world, plus everything from postcards to hard-core videos.

Rambla dels Estudis

The character of the Ramblas changes several times as you continue down towards the port. After the first cross-roads, you enter the Rambla dels Estudis, also known as the Rambla dels Ocells (*ocell* is Catalan for bird). A dozen or so stands sell canaries, budgies and prize parrots, distressingly cooped up in cages, while pathetic goldfish and rabbits stare out from an assortment of cramped abodes.

Església de Betlem, at the corner of Carrer del Carme, is a splendid baroque church; its once glorious interior was destroyed during the Civil War. It dates from the late 17th century, before the Ramblas became Barcelona's main thoroughfare, which is why its severe façade and majestic doorway are actually on a side street. Busy Carrer de Portaferrissa, on your left, runs straight to the Catedral (➤ 53–55) and the Barri Gòtic (➤ 56–59).

What's in a Name?

The word *rambla* is now accepted in Spain as the word for a main city promenade, but it is actually derived from the Arabic *raml*, meaning "river-bed". It originally referred to the gullies running through most Catalan towns, which were dry for most of the year and only filled with water after heavy rains. It has even given rise to a tailor-made Catalan verb, *ramblejar*, meaning "to wander up and down the Ramblas".

Flower stalls line the Rambla de Sant Josep, dubbed the Rambla de les Flors

Patterns of parasols decorate the Casa Bruno Quadros, once an umbrella shop, on Rambla de Sant Josep

Rambla de Sant Josep

Next comes the Rambla de Sant Josep, nicknamed the Rambla de les Flors on account of its colourful flower stalls. Impressive displays of cut-flowers, pot plants, shrubs and even huge palms brighten up the street along this stretch. At No 99, on your right, is the late 18th-century **Palau de la Virreina**, built by the Viceroy of Peru for his wife Vicereine Maria Francesca. The story goes that she was due to marry his nephew, but when the Viceroy saw the bride-to-be dressed up for her wedding, he fell in love with her and declared that he would have married her himself if he had not been too old. She replied that she lived in a very old convent, which pleased her greatly; he took the hint and married her after all, leaving the nephew somewhat in the lurch. Later, the Viceroy made his fortune in Lima, kept a famous mistress, and built this palace to placate his wife when she found out (forgetting that she preferred older things). The palace is now used as an eclectic exhibition hall and a tourist information office where tickets are sold for artistic and cultural events.

A little way farther down on the right lies the **Mercat de la Boqueria**, Barcelona's central market. Although it's officially called the Mercat de Sant Josep, everyone knows it as La Boqueria (the butchery). The market, housed in an airy iron-and-glass structure, with token Modernist touches at the Ramblas entrance, is where the city's top chefs come to buy the freshest ingredients. It is a great place to pick up picnic ingredients such as cheeses, olives and tomatoes, or to wander around the mouthwatering displays of huge hams,

A cornucopia of fresh produce is on sale at the Mercat de la Boqueria, the city's central market

Catalan sausages, seafood, vegetables, herbs, mushrooms and dried fruits.

Across the street at No 82, **Casa Bruno Quadros** (1883–5), now a bank, occupies a former umbrella shop. The façade is decorated with ornate parasols, part of a theatrical, oriental design of dragons and lanterns. Criminals were hanged on this site in the Middle Ages.

Rambla dels Caputxins

Pla de l'Os, on the central walkway, marks the halfway point of the Ramblas and the start of the Rambla dels Caputxins. It also offers a rare opportunity to walk over a work of modern art: Joan Miró's colourful ***Mosaic*** (1976) is crying out to be trampled on. The next stretch of the street is always one of the liveliest, with street musicians and magicians competing for attention with human statues swathed in large quantities of gold paint. The **Gran Teatre del Liceu** (➤ 64), Barcelona's opera house, extends between Carrer de Sant Pau and Carrer Unió. To the right, a short distance along Carrer Nou de la Rambla, is **Palau Güell** (➤ 60–62) and, immediately opposite, **Plaça Reial** (➤ 67).

Street musicians ensure that a stroll down the Ramblas is a lively experience

Rambla de Santa Mònica

Performance artists give way to portrait painters as you reach the Rambla de Santa Mònica, the final stretch of the Ramblas at its seaward end. As you might expect in a port city, this area is decidedly seedy. Drug-dealers and transvestite prostitutes, though less visible than in the past, still ply their trade here after dark. Although some people find the atmosphere on this section of the Ramblas threatening, it is generally safe for streetwise visitors – just hang on to your valuables. This is also where you will find the **Centre d'Art Santa Mònica**, an avant-garde art gallery housed in a converted convent.

Monument a Colom

At the bottom of the Ramblas, in the middle of the busy Plaça del Portal de la Pau, stands the Monument a Colom, erected for the 1888 Universal Exhibition. From the top of the 60m (200-foot) column, a statue of Christopher Columbus (► 24) points out to sea, while at his feet is a viewing platform that offers a panorama of the city and its harbour. Pigeons appear to treat the statue with utter contempt, providing the great explorer with a permanent white wig. To enjoy the views up the Ramblas and along the harbourfront, you have to take the lift up. It's a shame about the inevitable X-loves-Y graffiti scratched onto the glass.

TAKING A BREAK

Food comes no fresher than at **Garduña** (Carrer Morera 17–19, tel: 93 302 43 23), a ramshackle restaurant within the famous food market La Boqueria. You can either eat downstairs at the crowded bar or more formally (and quietly) upstairs. There's great seafood such as grilled hake with herbs or *zarzuela* (fish stew). Although open in the evening, the atmosphere is best at lunchtime.

Visitors can enjoy a bird's-eye view of the city and Port Vell from the Monument a Colom

THE RAMBLAS: INSIDE INFO

Top tips The heaving crowds, the distraction of the entertainments and the large numbers of foreign visitors mean that **petty crime is a problem**, especially down at the rougher end of the Ramblas. Don't let the mostly harmless but very light-fingered pickpockets who congregate here spoil your stay. Keep your hands firmly on all belongings, especially valuables, at all times; don't let yourself be distracted, and watch out for suspicious behaviour.

One to miss However enticing the advertisements or the blonde bombshell dishing out flyers at the door, you're better off giving the **Museu de l'Eròtica** (Rambla de Sant Josep 96) a miss. Its displays are poorly presented and not even erotic!

Hidden gem Light years away in terms of atmosphere is the **Rambla de Catalunya** (► 196 B5), which slices through the Eixample above Plaça de Catalunya, at the top end of the Ramblas proper. Here the cafés are costlier and the shops unashamedly chic. This is the Rambla for you, though, if madding crowds drive you crazy – and it's ideal for a late afternoon stroll.

4

Catedral

Barcelona's great cathedral, at the spiritual and physical heart of the splendid Barri Gòtic, is a beautiful example of Catalan Gothic architecture. Its shady cloisters are a delight, and from the rooftops you can admire the impeccably preserved medieval buildings spread out below.

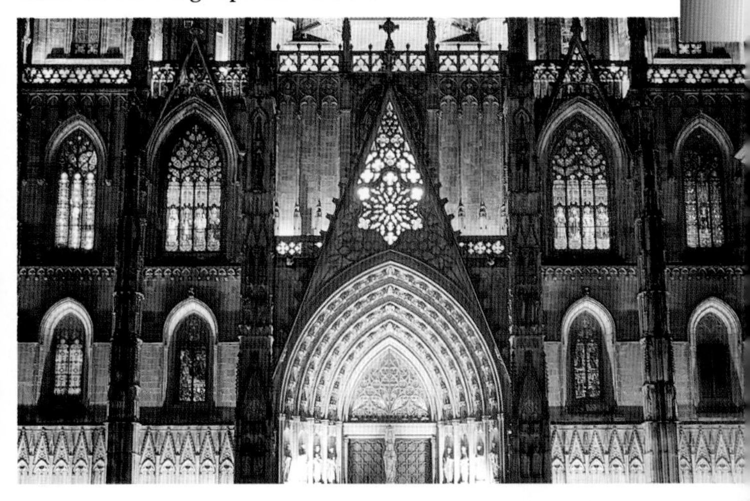

While the cathedral's façade is impressive at first glance, a closer look reveals that it is a late 19th-century neo-Gothic addition. Compared with more typically plain Catalan churches, such as the Basílica de Santa Maria del Mar (➤ 80–81) or Santa Maria del Pi (➤ 59), this façade, with its detailed stone carving and slender pinnacles, looks rather more northern European than southern. That said, at sunset, when the stone glows coppery brown, or at night, when the building is illuminated, it can be mesmerising. Until late 2005, however, the pollution-damaged exterior is under wraps for cleaning.

The cathedral's elaborate 19th-century façade

---

193 D3 | Plaça de la Seu | Mon–Fri 8–1:30, 4–7:30, Sat–Sun 8–1:30, 5–7:30; cloisters and choir open slightly later and close earlier | Jaume I, Liceu | 17, 19, 40, 45 | Cathedral: free. Choir and crypt: inexpensive

Museu de la Catedral
Daily 10–1 | Inexpensive

Colourful candles light up the cathedral's dark interior

The Interior

Inside, the building dates back to the 14th century. The huge space is divided into two broad aisles, nearly as wide as the cavernous central nave, that soar heavenwards.

Immediately to your right after you enter is the **baptistery**, where, as a plaque records, the six Native Americans brought back from the New World in 1493 by Christopher Columbus were christened. But your eye is quickly drawn to the central enclosed **choir** (separate entrance fee), where there are exquisitely carved 14th-century stalls. This is where the Chapter of the Order of the Golden Fleece, a kind of early European summit meeting, was convened by Emperor Charles V and attended by England's King Henry VIII and a host of European monarchs in 1519. Look at the royal coats of arms, including that of Henry VIII, painted on the backs of the stalls. The intricate wooden **pulpit** of 1403 and Italianate Renaissance **choir-screen** (1519–64) also stand out as masterpieces.

Your entrance fee to the choir entitles you to descend to the **crypt** where, among other relics, you'll find a gorgeous alabaster sarcophagus (1327) thought to contain the remains of Santa Eulàlia, Barcelona's patron saint (along with the Virgin of Mercy). The 4th-century martyr converted to Christianity at the age of 13 and was subjected to unspeakable tortures at the hands of Roman governor Dacian.

Soaring heights are a typical feature of Catalan Gothic architecture

The magnificent cloisters are the highlight of the cathedral for many visitors

The Cloisters

The cloisters, for many visitors, are the best part of the cathedral. Orange and medlar trees, glossy magnolias and shaggy palms held up by trapeze-wires blend in beautifully with the lush floral motifs of the Flamboyant Gothic iron and stonework, some dating back to the 14th century. In the middle of the garden, a mossy green **fountain**, sheltered by a stone tabernacle decorated with a carving of St George (Catalonia's patron saint) and the Dragon, tinkles into an emerald pond. Here you'll find a half-dozen gaggle of geese; there were originally 13, one for every year of St Eulàlia's life. Legend has it that they either hark back to Barcelona's Roman past (geese guarded the Capitol in ancient times), or that their pure white feathers symbolise the martyr's virginity.

Leading off the other side of the cloisters is the simple but beguiling Romanesque **Chapel of Santa Llúcia** (13th century), where many visitors come to pray. If you leave the cathedral on this side, you'll be facing the handsome **Casa de l'Ardiaca**, a renovated 15th-century palace now housing the city archives. Within the tiled courtyard stands a spindly palm, but the palace's special feature is on the outside wall: a Modernist letter-box carved with a tortoise and swallows.

The stone carving on the cathedral's outer walls rewards closer attention

From the Rooftops

Before leaving the cathedral, don't forget to take the lift to the rooftops for a bird's-eye view of the medieval district and a closer look at the beautiful late 19th-century bell-towers; the lift entrance is beyond the choir, to the left as you look at the main altar.

TAKING A BREAK

Pablo Picasso's first paid commission was to design the menu cover at **Els Quatre Gats** (➤ 70), once the meeting place of bohemian Barcelona. Now smartly restored, the café is an animated spot for coffee, snacks and good-value meals.

CATEDRAL: INSIDE INFO

Top tips Try to come on **a sunny day**, when the light filters through the stained-glass windows into the nave and through the lush canopy of palms and shrubbery into the cloisters.

• Every Sunday, from noon to 2 pm, you can watch the ***sardana***, Catalonia's national folk dance, on the cathedral square. The dancers are accompanied by an instrumental group (*cobla*), which includes tenor and soprano oboes, a *flabiol* (long flute) and a *tambori* (drum).

One to miss The **Museu de la Catedral**, in the 17th-century chapter house off the cloisters, charges extra for a glance at some rather dull religious paintings.

Hidden gem Look for the **stone carvings** around the door overlooking the Plaça de Sant Iu – these are the oldest feature of the exterior.

5

Barri Gòtic

A maze of dark, twisting medieval streets and sunny squares lined with venerable churches and lavish palaces huddles around the cathedral. The Barri Gòtic (Gothic Quarter), a part of the city once overlooked by visitors, was extensively restored in the 1920s and has now regained much of its former splendour. A couple of the city's finest museums flank the medieval Plaça del Rei, while the magnificent Ajuntament (City Hall) and Palau de la Generalitat (Government Palace) face each other across Plaça de Sant Jaume, the monumental, historic heart of old Barcelona.

Below: Plaça del Rei, the movie-set showpiece of the Barri Gòtic

Right: The Bridge of Sighs was part of Barcelona's 1920s Gothic revival

Plaça del Rei

Tucked away to the north of the cathedral is the Plaça del Rei, flanked by the stately buildings of the Palau Reial, the former royal palace. In medieval times, the square served as a market-place where hay and flour were sold; later locksmiths plied their trade here, making so much noise that the royal court moved out.

The mid-16th century **Mirador del Rei Martí** (King Martin's Watchtower), a curiously modern-looking building distinguished by five storeys of stone arches, and the svelte turret of the 14th-century **Capella de Santa Agata** (the royal chapel) tower over the square. They can be investigated as part of a visit to the Museu d'Història de la Ciutat (➤ 64–65). To your left as you look towards the Mirador is the stern **Palau del Loctinent**, built in 1549 as the official residence for the Viceroy of Catalonia.

Among the pigeons and street musicians, you'll see ***Topo*** (1985), an abstract sculpture by Basque artist Eduardo Chillida. The work's enigmatic B-shapes may (or then again may not) stand for Barcelona.

---

193 D3
Jaume I, Liceu · 17, 19, 40, 45, N8

The Ajuntament
93 402 70 00
Sat–Sun 10–1:30 · Free

Palau de la Generalitat
93 402 46 00
2nd and 4th Sun of every month except Aug, 10:30–1:30, and all day 23 Apr (St George's Day), 11 Sep (Catalan National Holiday), and 24 Sep (La Mercè) · Free

Plaça de Sant Jaume

Nearby **Plaça de Sant Jaume**, the historical and political heart of the old city, is spacious and imposing, where Plaça del Rei is intimate and secluded. The square was a crossroads even in Roman times and today busy Carrer de Ferran slices through it. Two ancient rivals, the Casa de la Ciutat (or **Ajuntament)** and the **Palau de la Generalitat** face each other across the flagstones. The former is home of the Left-wing city council, the latter the official headquarters of the firmly conservative Catalan government. Both buildings have been added to piecemeal over the centuries, with the extravagant neo-classical façades a 19th-century addition.

Both the Ajuntament and Palau de la Generalitat reward visitors. Outstanding work in the Ajuntament includes Josep Maria Sert's 1928 murals depicting great moments from Catalan history in the **Saló de les Cròniques** (Hall of the Chronicles); Sert later decorated New York's Rockefeller Center. In the Palau de la Generalitat, the frescoes of classical allegory by J. Torres-Garcia typify the Noucentisme movement. The Generalitat's highlight, though, is undoubtedly the Gothic inner courtyard, the raised **Pati de Tarongers** (Courtyard of the Oranges), with fine Renaissance columns and sweet-scented orange trees.

Below: Statues of saints remind you that this is Barcelona's spiritual heartland

Left: A spontaneous *sardana* on the Plaça de Sant Jaume in front of the Palau de la Generalitat

The Generalitat is joined to the **Casa dels Canonges**, a set of 14th-century cathedral canons' houses where the Catalan prime minister now has his official residence, by a bridge across Carrer del Bisbe. It may look Gothic from a distance but beware of appearances; the bridge, modelled on the Bridge of Sighs in Venice, was in fact built in the 1920s, when all things medieval were in vogue and this area of the city became known as the "Barri Gòtic".

Even the shop fronts are medieval in the Barri Gòtic

Santa Maria del Pi

The 14th- to 15th-century church of Santa Maria del Pi, a squat yet sumptuous Gothic masterpiece, lies just off the Ramblas. The interior is almost disconcertingly simple and empty, with a wide single nave without aisles. The gigantic rose window, however, is magnificent, filling the church with multicoloured light.

The church is surrounded by three delightful little squares (**Plaça del Pi**, where you'll find the church's main entrance, **Plaça Sant Josep Oriol** and **Placeta del Pi)**, and strolling between them gives you a chance to survey the church's sober exterior. At weekends and during the summer the squares are filled with artists and musicians. Choose one of the many café terraces from which to enjoy the spectacle of street life. Cheeses, sausages and other local produce are sold at makeshift stalls on the first Friday of the month.

The rose window of Santa Maria del Pi

TAKING A BREAK

Bar del Pi (Plaça Sant Josep Oriol 1, tel: 93 302 21 23) gets crowded, so pick a table outside in the lovely medieval square and be entertained by street performers. The tapas selection is limited but good.

BARRI GÒTIC: INSIDE INFO

Top tip If you want to immerse yourself further in Gothic architecture, follow the **Barri Gòtic** walk (➤ 170–172).

Hidden gems The **Museu Diocesà** (Diocesan Museum, ✚ 193 D3, Avinguda de la Catedral 4, tel: 93 315 22 13, open Tue–Sat 10–2, 5–8, Sun and holidays 11–2, moderate) is housed in a patchwork of Roman, Renaissance and later buildings, capped with some 20th-century elements. Occasionally, interesting exhibitions of mostly sacred art are staged here. Albeit chaotic, the permanent display offers some gems of Catalan religious sculpture and painting, including an altarpiece or two by Bernat Martorell – look for his Retable of St John the Baptist.
- The **Museu del Calçat** (Footwear Museum, ✚ 192 C3, Plaça de Sant Felip Neri 5, tel: 301 45 33, open Tue–Sun 11–2, inexpensive) is something of a curiosity. Many famous people, including cellist Pau Casals (➤ 26), have donated their shoes to the museum. One oddity is a shoe big enough for the Columbus statue.

9

Palau Güell

Chimney-pots decorated with glazed tiles crown the Palau Güell, Gaudí's glorious exercise in discreet opulence, while the intriguing interior (closed for renovation until the end of 2006) remains more or less as it was when it was completed in 1890.

When wealthy industrialist Eusebi Güell i Bacigalupi and his aristocratic wife decided to move into Carrer Nou de la Rambla to be near his parents' home on the Ramblas, Barcelona society drew gasps of amazement. Not only was everyone else moving out to fashionable addresses in the Eixample, the new residential district on the outskirts of the city, but the Güell's new home was on the edge of El Raval's red-light district, opposite Eden Concert, a notorious cabaret-cum-brothel (now a multi-storey car park). This insalubrious neighbourhood and the cramped plot of land would have posed almost insurmountable challenges for most architects, but Gaudí turned these restrictions to his advantage and produced a masterpiece.

Gaudí's genius at work: part medieval fortress, part mischievous fantasy

Not What it Seems

Don't be daunted by the austere façade; the cold limestone, portcullis-like grilles and fierce wrought-iron dragons were meant to ward off undesirables, of whom there were plenty. The Gothic, fortress-like windows, parabolic arches and doorways concealed behind metalwork – later to become decorative hallmarks of all Modernist architecture – served a dual purpose: they provided privacy and safety. Gaudí used many other architectural tricks. In the inner courtyard, while the tiles may look like stone they are actually made of Scots pine, which muffled the noise of horses' hoofs; and in the interior, false windows – in reality glass screens lit from behind – create an illusion of space. Other devices include the protruding bay windows and oriels, mezzanine minstrel galleries, hidden chapels and secret passages (including one linking the house to Güell's parents' home).

192 A2
Carrer Nou de la Rambla 3–5
93 317 39 74
Telephone for opening times during the restoration
Liceu 14, 18, 38, 59
Inexpensive

In the interior of the Palau Güell, Gaudí used many devices to create the illusion of space

A Guided Tour

The palace was donated to the city authorities in the early 20th century and is now open to the public. Visits are by guided tour only (given in Spanish, Catalan and English) at set times through the day. Despite being used as a detention centre during the Civil War and later by the Centre of Drama Studies, most of the palace's interior has survived intact and even some of Gaudí's original furniture remains.

The tour, lasting an hour, starts in the cellars, stables and kennels, which were reached by a ramp from the courtyard. Mushroom-shaped brick columns support the ceiling, creating a cave-like atmosphere. Back on ground level, you can admire the grand granite staircase with a red-and-yellow glass screen depicting the Catalan flag above it.

On the main floor are the reception hall, the dining-room and private apartments, all more or less as they were when the Güells lived here. The central feature of the house is a gallleried salon, rising up three storeys to a perforated dome which looks rather like the roof of a Turkish bath.

Throughout the palace, it is the attention to detail and the quality of the materials (supplied in large part from the stone-quarries, metalworks and glass and ceramics factories owned by the Güell family) that is so impressive. Beech and ebony, walnut and teak are just some of the dozens of different woods used for the ceilings and

Below: *Trencadí* (tile fragments) decorate the palace's chimneys

Left: The central tower of the Palau Güell is topped by a quirky weather-vane

windows, the lattice-work screens and furniture. Polished granite, alabaster and blood-red marble were used for the floors and the delicate columns.

Finally, you come to the **roof**, where there is a profusion of chimneys and turrets coated with *trencadí* (a mosaic of multicoloured ceramic-tile fragments). The views of El Raval and the harbour from here are wonderful.

Glove at First Sight?

Gaudí's patron and publicist, Eusebi Güell i Bacigalupi commissioned several projects that bear his name. It is said that Güell first came across Gaudí's work when he spied a glass cabinet for gloves that he was making for the 1878 Universal Exhibition in Paris.

TAKING A BREAK

Les Quinze Nits (Plaça Reial 6, tel: 93 318 95 76) offers a winning combination of low prices, modern Catalan food and elegant surroundings. There is no advance booking.

PALAU GÜELL: INSIDE INFO

Top tip The palace is **closed** for extensive renovation work until the end of 2006; when it reopens, the visits may differ from the description given here.

Hidden gem Notice the **iron bat weathervane** on top of the middle tower on the roof, an unusual decorative subject.

At Your Leisure

2 El Raval

Geographically, El Raval is a mirror-image of the Barri Gòtic, a warren of narrow streets and alleyways to the west of the Ramblas. For centuries this was an insalubrious part of the city, but the city authorities are now trying to shake off its seedy reputation with a programme of renovation and rebuilding.

In the lower, portside fringes of the neighbourhood (roughly beyond Carrer de l'Hospital), the seamier side of city life is more in evidence.

By contrast, in the upper reaches of the district, gentrification is well advanced. This is reflected in modern workshops and art galleries, hip bars, lively cafés and refined restaurants – all linked with the development of the MACBA and CCCB arts centres.

Museu d'Art Contemporàni de Barcelona (MACBA)

The brilliant white, glass-fronted museum dominates the Plaça dels Angels. After opening in 1995, American architect Richard Meier's startling building received mixed reactions: many local people felt that the ostentatious design was inappropriate in such a run-down area, and, furthermore, the exorbitant construction costs had left no money in the coffers to stock the gallery with worthwhile exhibits. However, continuing investment in the area has meant that the exhibition rooms are now filled with works by major artists such as Saura and Tàpies, Fontana and Dubuffet, Calder and Klee, while the regular temporary exhibitions of internationally acclaimed painters, sculptors, photographers, video artists and avant-garde performance artists are increasingly successful. For many, however, the clinical interior and wonderful views of the surrounding district from the upper floors linger in the memory longer than the exhibits.

192 A5 Plaça dels Angels 1 93 412 08 10; www.macba.es Mon, Wed–Fri 11–7:30 (also 7:30–8 Mon, Wed and Fri, 7:30–9 Thu, Jul–Sep), Sat 10–8, Sun 10–3. Guided visits Sat 6, Sun 11 Catalunya, Universitat, FGC Catalunya 9, 14, 16, 17, 22, 24, 38, 41, 55, 58, 59, 66, 91, 141 Moderate. Half-price Wed

MACBA, in El Raval, part of a programme of regeneration

Centre de Cultura Contemporània de Barcelona (CCCB)

Behind MACBA, across a rather stark playground area, is the Centre de Cultura Contemporània de Barcelona. Piñón and Viaplana, a duo of local architects known for their controversial designs, transformed an early 19th-century workhouse – the Casa de la Caritat – into this impressive arts centre. The high-quality exhibitions you can see inside range from architecture to design, fashion and photography. The tile-lined courtyard, where the cityscape and harbour are reflected in plate-glass panels, is used for theatre, dance and other performance arts.

192 A5 Carrer del Montalegre 5 93 306 41 00; www.cccb.org Tue–Sat 11–8, Sun and holidays 11–3, Jun–Sep; Tue, Thu, Fri 11–2, 4–8, Wed and Sat 11–8, Sun and holidays 11–7, rest of year Catalunya, Universitat, FGC Catalunya 9, 14, 16, 17, 22, 24, 38, 41, 55, 58, 59, 66, 91, 141 Moderate

3 Gran Teatre del Liceu

Tragedy struck Barcelona's prestigious opera house in 1994 when a spark from a welder's blowtorch set alight the stage-curtains, and the whole theatre went up in flames. Now, however, after a campaign led by local diva Montserrat Caballé, the Liceu has been restored to its former glory. The theatre, one of the world's largest, complete with modern extensions and the original understated façade (which survived the inferno), occupies a huge chunk of land along the Ramblas.

As you go inside, a marble staircase sweeps up to the Salon of Mirrors, lavishly decorated with mirrors, columns and chandeliers. The huge gilded auditorium, which can seat 2,334, was rebuilt to the design of the 19th-century original with improved acoustics and sightlines and a larger stage. Local designer Antoni Miró produced an incredibly lavish velvet curtain, and avant-garde Catalan artist Perejaume decorated the ceiling with landscapes made up of images of the red-velvet seats below. Behind the scenes, state-of-the-art machinery and electronics bring the theatre into the 21st century. Even if you don't make it to a performance – but do try, it's the experience of a lifetime – you can admire all these splendours on a guided tour.

The Gran Teatre del Liceu, devastated by a fire in the 1990s, has been painstakingly restored

192 B3 La Rambla 51–59 93 485 99 00; www.liceubarcelona.com Daily 11:30 am–1 pm; closed Aug. Guided visits 10 am Liceu 14, 38, 59, 91, N9, N12 Moderate

6 Museu d'Història de la Ciutat

The main body of the museum of the city's history is housed in a 15th-century mansion, the Casa Padellas, which was moved here stone by stone in the 1930s. During the work, the most extensive Roman city foundations in Europe were discovered and these are now beautifully laid out and lit.

A museum ticket also includes entry to three of the highlights of the Catalan royal palaces on the Plaça del Rei (► 56). The first is the divine royal chapel, **Capella de Santa Agata**, where the bare stone walls set off one of the most highly acclaimed works of Catalan Gothic art, the exquisitely painted 15th-century altarpiece by Jaume Huguet. From there you can climb the maze of passages and staircases to the top of **Mirador del Rei Martí** (King Martin's Watchtower) and peer down onto the square through the dark arches – you'll also be face to face with the grotesque gargoyles. The vistas of the cathedral and surroundings from the top are superb. You'll also be allowed into the staggering **Saló del Tinell**, a huge barrel-vaulted banqueting hall, where, it is claimed, Christopher Columbus was fêted by Ferdinand and Isabella when he got back from the Americas.

Temporary exhibitions of a historic nature are held here.

193 D3 Plaça del Rei/Carrer del Veguer 2 93 315 11 11 Tue–Sat 10–8, Sun and holidays 10–2, Jun–Sep; Tue–Sat 10–2, 4–8, Sun and holidays 10–2, rest of year Jaume I 17, 19, 40, 45 Moderate

7 Museu Frederic Marès

Frederic Marès i Deulovol (1893–1991) was a prolific sculptor and magpie-like collector who acquired all manner of curios during his long life. The museum houses his eclectic collection with row upon row of wooden Virgins and perfume bottles, labels and coins, fans and playing cards, photographs and crucifixes – you name it and there will be at least four-score-and-ten varieties of it. Jaume Huguet's moving Christ on his Way to Calvary (15th century) in the Gothic painting gallery is one of the museum's highlights.

Above: Huguet's *Christ on his Way to Calvary* in the Museu Frederic Marès
Left: Part of the treasure trove at the Museu d'Història de la Ciutat

The collection is fascinating, if only for the sheer number of exhibits, and will provide avid collectors with an excuse never to throw anything away again. Equally, it can be overwhelming, particularly as the artefacts lack any explanation. For some, the café-terrace in the beautiful courtyard may come as a welcome relief.

193 D3 Plaça Sant Iu 5–6 93 310 58 00; www.museumares.bcn.es Tue–Sat 10–7, Sun and holidays 10–3 Jaume I 17, 19, 40 and 45 Café d'Estiu Apr–Sep 10–10 Inexpensive. Free first Sun of the month and Wed afternoons

The wooden-planked Rambla de Mar connects the Ramblas to Port Vell

8 Port Vell

Prior to the 1992 Olympics, Barcelona made little of its shabby waterfront and harbour, but since then the Old Port has metamorphosed into a polished pleasure port, with the commercial harbour banished to the far-off Zona Franca.

You can admire luxury yachts and outsize catamarans as you saunter around the marina, along the Moll d'Espanya (Spanish Wharf), and over the wavy-banistered, wooden-planked swing-footbridge known as the Rambla de Mar – an extension of the Ramblas.

At the end of the Moll d'Espanya, the Maremàgnum, a shiny complex of aluminium and plate-glass designed by controversial local architects Piñón and Viaplana, houses shops, bars, eateries and a multiscreen cinema. Next door is the acclaimed L'Aquàrium de Barcelona and a state-of-the-art IMAX cinema. From the end of the jetty you can look across to the circular hulk of the World Trade Center. At the end of the port's other main pier, Moll de Barcelona, is the functional Estació Marítima, used by ferries plying to and from Mallorca, Ibiza, Menorca and Genoa. Finally, down by the old portside, you'll find hip nightspots where you can dance the night away (➤ 72).

For alternative ways of seeing the harbour, you can take the Transbordador cable cars that swing across from the Torre de Sant Sebastià at Barceloneta to Montjuïc (Mirador) via the Torre de Jaume I on the Moll de Barcelona, or board the little double-decker boats known as Golondrinas that run pleasure trips into the harbour and along the coast (➤ 182 for more information).

Visitors to the Aquàrium de Barcelona enjoy an up-close meeting with the sharks

L'Aquàrium de Barcelona

Children from 5 to 105 will adore this close encounter with the sea. Twenty-one mini-aquariums on the lower floor of the ultra-modern building re-create the environments of different marine habitats, from the Ebro Delta near Barcelona to the Red Sea, Australia's Great Barrier Reef and the coral reefs of Hawaii.

The aquarium's highlight is the 80m (260-foot) glass tunnel containing a moving walkway that plunges you into the silent universe of the Oceanario, where sharks and sting-rays slink past,

For Kids

- The honking **geese** in **the Catedral's cloisters** and **views** from the roof (► 53–5).
- The **touch-and-see installations** and **underwater tunnel** at **L'Aquàrium de Barcelona** (► 66–7).
- Rides on the **Golondrinas** or on the **cable-car** above the harbour (► 66).
- The **special kids' room** at the **MACBA** (► 63).

over or towards you. Many of the exhibits are interactive, with some brilliant child-oriented installations on the top floor. There are also good harbour views from the terrace.

196 B1 Moll d'Espanya 93 221 74 74; www.aquariumbcn.com Daily 9:30–9, Sep–Jun; 9:30 am–11 pm, Jul and Aug Drassanes, Barceloneta 14, 19, 36, 40, 57, 59, 64, 157, N6 Expensive. Free under 4s

10 Plaça Reial

Francesc Molina, architect of La Boqueria (► 50), the city's central market, designed this square in the 1840s. The tall palm trees, Gaudí's tree-like lampposts, and the much-copied *Three Graces* fountain, cast by the French ironworks Duresne in the 19th century, combine to give the square its tropical feel. Although the area became synonymous with drugs and drunkenness in the 1970s and 1980s, a permanent but fairly discreet police presence has turned things around, and the square's benches and café terraces (notably Glaciar at No 3) are now pleasant places to linger. A couple of good restaurants and unmissable night-spots occupy opposite corners of this lively space.

192 B2 Liceu 14, 38, 59, 91, N9, N12

Cooling off by the *Three Graces* fountain in the stylish Plaça Reial

Where to... Eat and Drink

Prices
Expect to pay per person for a meal, excluding drinks
€ under €15 €€ €15–35 €€€ over €35

Biocenter €
This is one of the largest and best-known vegetarian restaurants in Barcelona. Its walls are hung with paintings executed by the owner and his friends. There is a good special menu, a wide choice of seasonal vegetable casseroles and an extensive salad bar. A selection of interesting vegan dishes is also served, and there is a health food shop of the same name across the street.

192 B4 Carrer del Pintor Fortuny 25 93 301 45 83 Mon–Sat 9–5 Liceu

Cafè de l'Acadèmia €€
Although you can have breakfast or just a coffee here, the main attraction is the great-value special lunchtime menu, which packs the place with the city's civil servants. The appealing setting of beamed ceilings and bare stone- and brickwork make it ideal for a weekday dinner, too. Try the terrine with goat's cheese followed by lamb stuffed with pears and mushrooms. Salt cod is a house speciality served in a variety of ways; try it with chickpeas or a green pepper sauce.

193 D2 Carrer de Lledó 1 93 319 82 53 Mon–Fri 9–noon, 1:30–4, 8:45–11:30 Jaume I

Ca l'Isidre €€€
This small family-run restaurant in a quiet, obscure part of El Raval counts the King of Spain among its regulars. The discreet, subdued elegance of the interior suits the moneyed clientele who come to enjoy refined dishes such as artichoke hearts stuffed with wild mushrooms and duck liver. Booking is essential.

195 F3 Carrer de les Flors 12 93 441 11 39 Mon–Sat 1:30–4, 8:30–11:30; closed four weeks Jul/Aug Paral.lel

Can Culleretes €€
Can Culleretes in the Barri Gòtic has the distinction of being the oldest restaurant in Barcelona. Founded in 1786 as a pastry shop, it retains many of the original architectural features. The three rambling dining rooms are decorated with tiles and wrought-iron chandeliers, and the walls display signed celebrity photographs. The lengthy menu includes traditional Catalan dishes such as wild boar stew, *canelons* (pasta) and paella. Game is a speciality in season. Booking is recommended at weekends.

192 B3 Carrer d'en Quintana 5 93 317 30 22 Tue–Sat 1:30–4, 9–11, Sun 1:30–4 Liceu

Los Caracoles €€
This cavernous, split-level restaurant hidden away in a maze of narrow cobblestoned streets near Plaça Reial serves some of the best Catalan food in Barcelona. It may be touristy, but it's not a tourist trap. Join the list of celebs, from John Wayne to Salvador Dalí, who have sampled the snails in this colourful setting. The rest of the menu is equally earthy and aromatic – you can watch the cooks at work in the open kitchen framed with dried herbs, smoked hams and plaits of

garlic. The spit-roasted chicken on display in the street outside is particularly recommended.
192 B2 Carrer dels Escudellers 14 93 302 31 85 Daily 1–midnight Liceu

Cervantes €
Homely Catalan food such as *botifarra* (spicy sausages) and *escudella* (a tasty all-in-one stew containing beef, pig's feet, poultry, lamb, sausage, potatoes, cabbage and haricot beans) is cooked and served by three sisters to an appreciative mix of local city officials and art students. Note that credit cards are not accepted.
192 C2 Carrer de Cervantes 7 93 317 33 84 Mon–Fri 1:30–4:30; closed Aug Jaume I

El Convent €€
To the relief of many loyal customers, only the name changed when this lively old-style restaurant changed hands. It was taken over by former staff when the owners retired, and they have had the sense not to alter the tried-and-tested formula. The lengthy menu is based on freshly cooked Mediterranean dishes such as grilled fish. Salt cod in cream sauce is a speciality. Be warned, it can get very crowded at peak times.
192 B4 Carrer de Jerusalem 3 93 317 10 52 Daily 1–4, 8–midnight Liceu

És €€
Apart from its hip location near the MACBA (➤ 63), one of the main advantages of this bright and airy restaurant is that it is open from lunchtime until late at night every day of the year. The special lunchtime menu is a very good deal. The clean-cut designer interior, trendy waiters and waitresses, and mellow music fit with the arty surroundings.
192 A5 Carrer del Doctor Dou 14 93 301 00 68 Daily 1 pm–midnight Catalunya

Gaucho's €€
A meat-eater's heaven, this friendly Argentine restaurant serves a mean *parrillada mixta* (barbecue), plus other Buenos Aires' specialities such as beef- or corn-filled *empanadas* (pies) and *milanesas* (schnitzels), with bottles of punchy Malbec wine the perfect accompaniment. Dollops of *allioli* (garlic mayonnaise) add a Catalan touch to it all.
192 C2 Baixada de Sant Miquel 6 93 318 99 00 Daily 1 pm–midnight Liceu

L'Hortet €
Smoke-free, organic and resolutely vegetarian, this is a place to come for a fresh salad or a hefty serving of meat-free pasta. L'Hortet is on a street that seems to specialise in veggie eateries. The soups are recommended, too.
192 B4 Carrer del Pintor Fortuny 32 93 317 61 89 Mon–Wed 1–4, 8:30–11, Thu–Sun 8:30–11 Catalunya

Peimong €
Peruvian cooking makes a change from Catalan, so if you're in the mood to experiment with ceviche or duck stewed with peas, potatoes and white rice, this is the place to come. The décor is basic but that doesn't deter the crowds, so at weekends you need to make a reservation in advance.
192 C2 Carrer dels Templaris 6–10 93 318 28 73 Tue–Sun 1–4:30, 8–midnight Jaume I

Pla €€
This is an excellent place for a romantic meal in the Barri Gòtic. With candlelit tables for two and gentle background music, Pla is usually full every night. Dark walls, mock-medieval chandeliers and a sweeping archway lend this split-level restaurant its atmosphere. Interesting salads are dressed with apple and sherry, there is a moussaka made with white *botifarra* (spicy sausage), and carpaccios are conjured out of swordfish and pig's feet. Try the caramelised

tuna with salad, tomato marmalade and yucca chips.

193 D2 ✉ Carrer de Bellafila 5 ☎ 93 412 65 52 ⌚ Sun–Thu 9 pm–midnight, Fri and Sat 9 pm–1 am Ⓜ Jaume I

Pla del Àngels €€

Effectively the MACBA's canteen (➤ 63), this little place is very popular with artists and art-lovers alike. Attractively decorated with brightly painted walls and with some fun details, like menus printed on wine labels (in English as well as Spanish and Catalan), it specialises in a trio of impeccably seasoned carpaccios: duck, octopus and salmon. Dainty portions are great for weight-watching but the food is tasty, including the delicious tiramisu for dessert.

192 A5 ✉ Carrer de Ferlandina 23 ☎ 93 329 40 47 ⌚ Mon–Sat 1:30–4, Tue–Sat 9–midnight Ⓜ Universitat

Els Quatre Gats €€

The walls of "The Four Cats" were once hung with works by Picasso and other great artists of the day, and this legendary restaurant and meeting place has preserved its art nouveau look well. As you eat unpretentious market-fresh Catalan cooking in the large, lively inner dining-room, imagine this as the setting for poetry readings, piano recitals and impassioned cultural and political debates.

193 D4 ✉ Carrer de Montsió 3 ☎ 93 302 41 40 ⌚ Mon–Sat 1–4, 9–midnight Ⓜ Catalunya

Silenus €€

Proximity to the impressive MACBA (➤ 63) makes this airy, minimalist restaurant popular with artists and gallery owners, some of whom use the walls as extra exhibition space. The cooking is suitably stylish and offers a creative mix of modern Spanish and Catalan dishes. In the summer there are tables outside.

192 A5 ✉ Carrer dels Angels 8 ☎ 93 302 26 80 ⌚ Mon–Sat 1–4, Tue–Sat 9 pm–11:30 pm Ⓜ Catalunya

BARS AND CAFÉS

Café de l'Opera €€

Café de l'Opera remains one of the most popular and fashionable places in town. The coffees, drinks and snacks don't come cheap, but it's worth coming here at least once to enjoy the late 19th-century décor and savour the atmosphere. Splash out on a table on the Ramblas for the best people-watching spot in the city.

192 B3 ✉ La Rambla 74 ☎ 93 317 75 85 ⌚ Mon–Thu 8–2:15, Fri–Sun 8–3 Ⓜ Liceu

Dulcinea €

You can indulge in delicious cakes or milkshakes at Dulcinea, but it is the *suissos* (hot chocolate) that steals the show. This is the most famous place in the city to come for hot chocolate. The gorgeous, thick drink, topped by an avalanche of whipped cream, is served by super-fast white-coated waiters in traditional surroundings. *Melindros* (sugar-topped biscuits) are traditionally dunked into the chocolate.

192 B3/B4 ✉ Carrer de Petrixol 2 ☎ 93 302 68 24 ⌚ Daily 9–1, 5–9; closed late Jul to mid-Aug Ⓜ Catalunya/Liceu

Schilling €

This ultra-fashionable, gay-friendly bar is a stylish, spacious place to stop for a cup of tea or coffee and serves good *entrepans* (sandwiches). When you eventually get a seat (it's always full) you won't be hurried to leave.

192 B3/C3 ✉ Carrer de Ferran 23 ☎ 93 317 67 87 ⌚ Mon–Sat 10 am–2:30 am, Sun noon–2:30 am Ⓜ Liceu

Xocoa €

Chocoholics congregate at this and other branches of a reliable chain of cafés. Cocoa in many forms from beverages to brownies is served.

192 B3 ✉ Carrer de Petritxol 11 ☎ 93 301 11 97 ⌚ Daily 9–8 Ⓜ Liceu

Where to... Shop

The Ramblas are lined with all kinds of shops, ranging from classy *pâtisseries* to modest souvenir stalls. You'll also find the city's top food market, La Boqueria (➤ 50) here. Boutiques and specialist stores cluster in the Barri Gòtic and El Raval, while Portal de l'Angel and Plaça de Catalunya are home to the major department stores and boutiques.

DEPARTMENT STORE

El Corte Inglés (Plaça de Catalunya 14, tel: 93 306 38 00, Metro: Catalunya), Spain's ubiquitous chain, crams a tantalising variety of goods, from designer fashion to records, into this massive building that overflows into an annexe on nearby Avinguda del Portal de l'Angel.

LARGE STORES AND MALLS

On the Plaça de Catalunya, French megastore **Fnac** sells reasonably priced records and films; it's housed in the brand-new **El Triangle** complex, on Carrer de Pelai, where **Sephora** (tel: 93 306 39 00), the perfume temple, and one of **Camper's** (tel: 93 302 41 24) many footwear outlets jostle for space with Spain's famous mid-range clothes store **Zara** (tel: 93 301 09 78).

If malls are your thing, try **Gralla Hall** (Carrer de Portaferrissa 25, tel: 93 412 32 72, Metro: Liceu), a mecca for clubbers' attire. Glitzy **Maremàgnum** (Moll d'Espanya, tel: 93 225 81 00, Metro: Drassanes), down at Port Vell, is a fun place for window-shopping or snapping up a few last-minute souvenirs. Soccer fans invariably make a beeline for its **Botiga del Barça** in search of a blue-and-burgundy football shirt printed with their favourite player's name. A great place to stock up for a picnic or to grab some food or wine to take home is **Champion** supermarket (La Rambla 113); avoid busy shopping times such as early afternoon or evening.

GIFTS

If you're looking for unusual toys then either **Joguines Foye** (Carrer de Banys Nous 13, tel: 93 302 03 89, Metro: Liceu) or **Joguines Monforte** (Plaça de Sant Josep Oriol 3, tel: 93 318 22 85, Metro: Liceu) should come up with the goods. **Drap** (Carrer del Pi 14, tel: 93 318 14 87, Metro: Liceu) sells delightful dolls' houses, while **Travi** (Carrer d'Amargos 4, tel: 93 412 66 92, Metro: Urquinaona) is the perfect place to purchase a puppet.

For traditional candles, try **Cereria Subirà** (Baixada de la Llibreteria 7, tel: 93 315 26 06, Metro: Jaume I), or for something more innovative **Cereria Abella** (Carrer dels Boters 5, tel: 93 318 08 41, Metro: Jaume I); both will make candles to any shape you request, within reason.

Paperona (Plaça de Sant Josep Oriol 8, tel: 93 317 15 72, Metro: Liceu) sells Gaudíesque papier-mâché figures, while both **Raima** (Carrer de Comtal 27, tel: 93 317 49 66, Metro: Urquinaona) and **Papirum** (Baixada de la Llibreteria 2, tel: 93 310 52 42, Metro: Jaume I) offer ranges of beautiful stationery with a Barcelona theme, plus elegant photo albums.

FASHION AND ACCESSORIES

You can see espadrilles being handsewn at the proudly traditional **La Manual Alpargatera** (Carrer d'Avinyó 7, tel: 93 301 01 72, Metro: Liceu). Leather shoes are always good value at **Casas** (La Rambla 125, tel: 93 302 45 98, Metro: Catalunya and Avinguda del

Portal de l'Angel 40, tel: 93 317 90 40). **Sombrereria Obach** (Carrer Call 2, tel: 93 318 40 94, Metro: Liceu) has been selling bonnets and balaclavas for seven decades, while **Mil Barrets i Gorres** (Carrer de Fontanella 20, tel: 93 301 84 91, Metro: Catalunya) has provided hats for the rich and famous since 1850. **Preu Bo** (Carrer Comtal 22, tel: 93 318 03 31, Metro: Urquinaona) will amaze you with its designer bargains; **Zsu-Zsu** (Carrer d'Avinyó 50, tel: 93 412 49 65, Metro: Liceu) goes in for fashionable knitwear. Rather more classical is **Almacenes del Pilar** (Carrer de la Boqueria 43, tel: 93 317 79 84, Metro: Liceu), a shawl and mantilla specialist. Local household name **Calpa** (Carrer de Ferran 53, tel: 93 318 40 30, Metro: Liceu) is great for leather bags and cases.

FOOD AND DRINK

Escribà (La Rambla 83, tel: 93 301 60 27, Metro: Liceu) is one of the finest cake and chocolate makers in town and his Ramblas shop also happens to be a Modernist gem. The florentines are amazing – perfect with a cup of coffee on the tiny terrace. **Mel Viadiu** (Carrer de Comtal 20, tel: 93 317 04 23, Metro: Catalunya) specialises in honey and beeswax products, while the nearby **Casa del Bacalao** (Carrer de Comtal 8, tel: 93 301 65 39, Metro: Catalunya) somehow dresses lumps of salt cod to look like jewels. Many locals claim that **Planelles-Donat** (Portal de l'Angel 7 & 25, tel: 93 317 29 29, Metro: Catalunya) has the best *orxata*, *torrons* and ice cream in the city. Bon-bons and nougat at **Fargas** (Carrer dels Boters 2, tel: 93 317 94 35, Metro: Liceu) prove difficult to resist, as do the hams at **La Pineda** (Carrer del Pi 16, tel: 93 302 43 93, Metro: Liceu). **La Catedral dels Vins i Caves** (Plaça de Ramon Berenguer El Gran 1, tel: 93 319 07 27, Metro: Jaume I) is one of the city's best wine merchants, with a variety of vintages from Catalonia and the rest of Spain.

Where to... Be Entertained

CLASSICAL MUSIC

The **Gran Teatre del Liceu** (➤ 64) has been splendidly restored after the 1994 fire. Each season's programme includes classical ballet and modern dance, along with contemporary opera. Despite the massive 2,300-odd capacity, tickets are like gold-dust, but sometimes there are returns on the night.

Classical concerts are also held at the cathedral and the churches of Santa Maria del Pi, Sant Felip Neri and Santa Anna; keep an eye out for posters or ask at Tourist Information.

NIGHTLIFE

The mellow **Harlem Jazz Club** (Carrer de la Comtessa de Sobradiel 8, tel: 93 310 07 55, Metro: Jaume I) sometimes swaps jazz and blues for top-rate world-music concerts. **Jamboree** (Plaça Reial 17, tel: 93 301 75 64, Metro: Liceu) is always packed out, so arrive early for a good dose of jazz, blues or funk. **Los Tarantos**, right next door, is a great venue for flamenco, tango, salsa and other Latin rhythms. Join in the fun after 1 am when the two clubs open as one nightclub.

One of the classics of the lower Ramblas is **Moog** (Carrer Arc del Teatre 3, tel: 93 301 72 82, Metro: Drassanes), with varied music and a tiny dance floor. **La Paloma** (Carrer del Tigre 27, tel: 93 301 68 97, open Thu–Sun, Metro: Sant Antoni), is an institution: concerts by rock and pop stars vary the steady diet of ballroom sounds in this wonderfully retro all-ages-welcome place.

La Ribera to Port Olímpic

Getting Your Bearings

One of the oldest districts of Barcelona is undergoing a revival as one of the hottest places in the city. The street names of La Ribera – Argenteria (silverware), Sombrerers (hat-makers), Vidriera (glass-making) – may reflect its origins as a medieval centre of trade, but these days the streets are positively buzzing with tapas bars, wine bars, and stylish restaurants in Gothic palaces and Manhattan-style factory conversions.

La Ribera is reached from the Barri Gòtic by crossing busy Via Laietana, which cut a swathe through the medieval area of Barcelona in the early 20th century.

The northern half of the district, known as Sant Pere, contains the Modernist masterpiece Palau de la Música Catalana.

South of Carrer de la Princesa, you enter the Born, a warren of narrow streets which was an important mercantile trading district in the

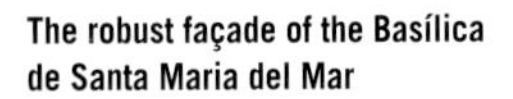

The robust façade of the Basílica de Santa Maria del Mar

Previous page: Frank Gehry's giant bronze sculpture in Barceloneta

★ Don't Miss

At Your Leisure

14th century. The rich merchants built their palaces along Carrer de Montcada, now a showcase of art galleries and museums, including one of Barcelona's biggest attractions, Museu Picasso. The lanes around Carrer de Montcada, known as "the artists' quarter", are full of workshops where craftspeople such as jewellers and potters carry on their trade much as they did in medieval times.

Passeig del Born, the main thoroughfare through the Born, once the scene of jousting tournaments, is now a lively promenade lined with jazz clubs and cocktail bars. This is where you will find the Basílica de Santa Maria del Mar, sometimes known as the fishermen's cathedral. This part of Barcelona has always had close links with the sea, and a pleasant waterfront walk leads from La Ribera around the fishing village of Barceloneta to the popular new beaches on either side of Port Olímpic.

A fairytale concert hall, a fabulous basilica and a fine collection of work by Picasso are the Ribera's highlights, while sandy beaches or a seaside promenade beckon after lunch.

La Ribera to Port Olímpic in a Day

10:00 am

Be at the **1 Palau de la Música Catalana** (left, ➤ 78–79) for the first guided tour of the day, which takes almost an hour. While you are here, maybe try to get tickets for an evening performance of Bach, Bartók or Bernstein.

11:00 am

Next wander down Via Laietana for a coffee break at the Mesón del Café (Carrer Llibreteria 16, just off Plaça del Angel), before making your way along Carrer de l'Argenteria to the **2 Basílica de Santa Maria del Mar** (➤ 80–81). The impressive interior (left) of this Gothic masterpiece is beautiful in the morning light.

12:00 noon

You should by now be prepared for one of the city's cultural highpoints, the 3 **Museu Picasso** (➤ 82–85), reached after a short walk up Carrer de Montcada. The museum's collection of ceramics, paintings and drawings is breathtaking.

1:30 pm

After admiring Picasso's works, visit either the nearby 4 **Museu Barbier-Mueller d'Art Precolombí** (➤ 86) or the 5 **Museu Tèxtil i de la Indumentària** (➤ 86) – or, if you're in the mood for a real museum marathon, both. Follow this with lunch at the Tèxtil Café (➤ 93), the delightful café-restaurant in the museum courtyard, or in one of the nearby tapas bars, such as El Xampanyet (above, ➤ 93) or Euskal Etxea (➤ 92).

4:30 pm

By now you may want to slow the pace. Head down Passeig Joan de Borbó and wander around the lively streets of nearby 8 **Barceloneta** (above, ➤ 89) for a real flavour of the seaside. In the summer this is exactly the right time to chill out on the beach – so look no further.

7:00 pm

Round off the day with sole or squid at Can Ramonet (➤ 91) or Les Set Portes (➤ 93), or attend a concert in the opulent surroundings of the Palau de la Música Catalana, if you picked up tickets in the morning. The choice is yours.

0

Palau de la Música Catalana

The Palau de la Música Catalana (Palace of Catalan Music) is a fantastic venue for choral, chamber and symphonic music, and attracts a galaxy of classical-music maestros. It is also a temple to Catalan tradition and history, testifying to the splendour of Barcelona's art nouveau movement.

The stupendous concert hall was built in 1908 as the headquarters of the Orfeó Català choral society by Lluís Domènech i Montaner, one of the leading exponents of Modernisme (► 16). The building is a masterpiece and was declared a World Heritage Site in 1997. Even if you don't make it to a concert (there are 300 each season), you can take a **guided tour** (in English, Catalan or Spanish) and learn why, how and when the concert hall was built.

Busts of famous composers adorn the façade

The Exterior

Before going inside, take a good look at the **façade**, complete with mosaic-coated columns, busts of Bach, Beethoven, Palestrina and Wagner, and across the upper storey, allegorical mosaics depicting a Catalan choir, with the jagged peaks of Montserrat in the background. On the corner of the building, a sugary sculpture symbolising Catalan popular song trickles down from a Moorish turret. Crowning it all is a mosque-like dome, decorated with the Catalan flag and St George shields.

The Interior

In the entrance hall and staircase, the prolific decoration continues. The theme of much of the work is floral; roses, lilies and fanciful blooms picked from Montaner's fertile imagination climb up pillars and trail across the ceilings and stained-glass windows. As always with Modernist design, there is a profusion but never an excess of detail.

The climax of the tour, however, is the magnificent **concert hall** on the upper floor. Ethereal stained-glass windows flank the great organ, and below it, behind the stage, are Muse-like figures with mosaic-tile bodies and terracotta statues for heads. On either side of the stage rise marble sculptures by local artists Didac Masana and Pau Gargallo, representing the cityfolk's taste in music: to the right, Richard Wagner's Valkyries ride over a stern bust of Beethoven, while to the left a tree of traditional song casts

---

193 E4 · Carrer de Sant Francesc de Paula 2 · 93 295 72 00 · Daily 10–3:30 (also 3:30–7, Jul and Aug); closed holidays · Urquinaona · 17, 19, 40, 45, N8 · Moderate

its leafy shade over 19th-century Catalan composer Anselm Clavé. The gorgeous blue-and-gold stained-glass **skylight** by Antoni Rigalt is encircled by 40 women's heads, representing a heavenly choir.

Now, imagine concerts by the likes of Richard Strauss, Pau Casals or Mstislav Rostropovich, all of whom have performed here, and the experience will be complete.

The lavish interior of the main auditorium shows architect Domènech i Montaner at his very best

TAKING A BREAK

For a special dinner try the **Mirador** (tel: 93 310 24 33), a classy restaurant located in the Palau's modern conservatory-style extension. The kitchen, presided over by French chef Jean-Luc Figueras (► 122), yields such delights as asparagus and cockerel-crest risotto along with more traditional Catalan offerings.

PALAU DE LA MÚSICA CATALANA: INSIDE INFO

Top tips **Tickets** for the hour-long tours (every 30 minutes) are sold at both Les Muses del Palau gift shop across Plaça de Lluís Millet, just off the Via Laietana, and at the ticket office located in the modern extension.

• The Palau's strongest musical tradition is **choral music**, so try to attend a concert by the Orfeó Català (► 95–96 for box office details). **World music concerts**, however, including Youssou N'Dour, Chinese classical music or Rom (gypsy) orchestras, are also popular.

Hidden gems Bring binoculars to scrutinise the fine details. The **columns** at the top of the side balconies inside the concert hall fan out along the tiled ceiling like peacock tails, and **ceramic roses** stud the ceiling.

2

Basílica de Santa Maria del Mar

Like all great stars, Santa Maria looks beautiful from every angle. Slim, tall and elegant, this is Barcelona's leading lady of churches, representing the high-point of Catalan architecture of the 14th century.

In medieval times, La Ribera was the centre of a thriving ship-building and fishing industry. As the Catalan empire grew, trade flourished, creating great wealth among a growing middle class. The wealthy citizens wanted to build a magnificent church, to keep in with God as well as Mammon. The resulting cathedral, built with funds collected to celebrate Catalonia's conquest of Sardinia, was completed within 55 years, which accounts for its astonishing architectural unity.

The **façade** is robust with decorative flourishes, typical of the Catalan Gothic style. Slender, pencil-like towers soar on either side of a plain curtain-wall, and it is easy to see why it has been likened to a mantelpiece with a pair of candlesticks. Before going inside, take a good look at the wood and bronze doors – the two little brass workmen carrying heavy loads on their backs are very finely crafted.

The Interior

Baroque and neo-classical additions and heavy decoration inside the basilica were destroyed by fire during the Civil War, leaving only the Gothic shell. But what a shell! The remarkably narrow **nave** accentuates the basilica's length and height, creating an effect of great elegance. Eight octagonal pillars punctuate the side aisles, off which side chapels radiate. Another eight pillars form an arcade behind the main altar.

From the altar, look back at the **rose window**, which depicts the Virgin's Coronation. It was manufactured in Toulouse and installed in 1458 after an earthquake shattered the original. Finally, leave by the strangely angled door on Carrer del Born; the carving of the Virgin Mary over the doorway is by Frederic Marès (➤ 65).

193 E2 · Plaça de Santa Maria · 93 310 23 90 · Daily 9–1:30, 4:30–8 · Jaume I · 17, 19, 40, 45 · Free

BASÍLICA DE SANTA MARIA DEL MAR: INSIDE INFO

Top tips **Concerts**, mostly classical, are held in the basilica from time to time, which bring the place to life. Ask at the basilica for details.

• The best time to **view the interior** is in the morning light.

Hidden gem **Fossar de les Moreres** (Mulberry Graveyard) is a small square along Carrer Santa Maria shaded by mulberry trees. A granite slab inscribed with lines of verse and an eternal flame commemorate Barcelona's invasion by the Spanish in 1714.

Fire destroyed the basilica's interior decoration, leaving only the Gothic shell

TAKING A BREAK

Choose one of the shady tables facing Santa Maria del Mar at **La Vinya del Senyor** (Plaça de Santa Maria 5, tel: 93 310 33 79). Look for the special selection of wines, *cavas* and sherry. Tapas are good, especially the Iberian ham, cheeses and slices of *coca*, rather like pizza.

3

Museu Picasso

Barcelona is where Picasso learned to paint, so it is appropriate that the city has one of the greatest repositories of his art. The collection, housed in not one but five handsome, medieval mansions on the elegant Carrer de Montcada, traces the artist's career through ceramics, paintings, drawings and lithographs; it has a particularly fine collection of early works.

The Museum Buildings

The three beautiful medieval palaces in which the museum is housed, Aguilar, Baró de Castellet and Meca, are well worth seeing in their own right. Opened in 1982, after years of painstaking renovation work which joined the three seamlessly together, they represent some of the world's finest domestic architecture from the 13th and 14th centuries. Built to fashionable styles influenced by Italian *palazzi*, each of these aristocratic homes was more beautiful and lavish than the previous one, testifying to the rivalry among the city's merchants. The museum was extended in the 1990s by converting two more fine medieval buildings, the Casa Mauri and Palau Finestres; the extra space is used to display the museum's top-notch temporary exhibitions, usually devoted to Picasso's contemporaries or particular aspects of his own work, such as linocuts or sculptures.

---

193 E3 · Carrer de Montcada 19–23 · 93 319 63 10; www.museupicasso.bcn.es · Tue–Sat and holidays 10–8, Sun 10–3 · Jaume I · 14, 17, 19, 39, 40, 45, 51, 59 · Café and excellent bookshop · Moderate

Picasso painted this portrait of his mother (left) when he was 14 years old

Far left and below: The collection is housed in medieval mansions on Carrer de Montcada

Picasso's family moved to Barcelona from Galicia in 1895, when Pablo was just 13 years old, after his father got a job teaching art at the city's School of Fine Arts. An amazingly early starter, Picasso began studying at the same school, La Llotja, in the autumn of the same year. After a year away in Madrid attending classes, he returned to Barcelona in 1898, by which time he had produced an incredible number of touching self-portraits, many of which are on display at the Museu Picasso.

Picasso never lost his affection for the city, despite decades of living in France. He effectively initiated the collection when he donated *The Harlequin* (1917). More generous donations followed, including a sizeable collection of his early paintings and a pledge to give Barcelona a copy of every print he produced until he died.

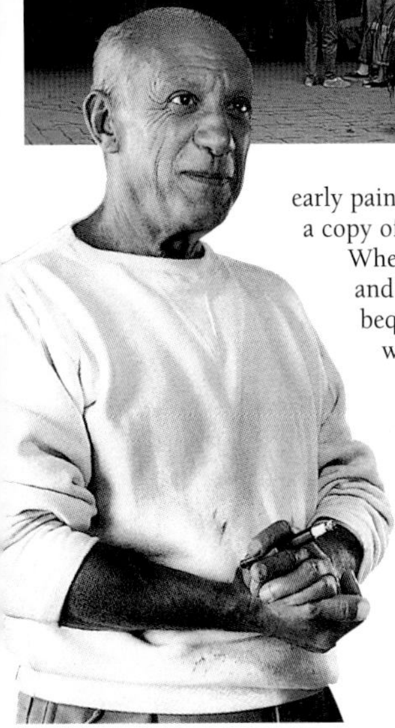

When Jaume Sabartés, Picasso's lifelong friend and personal secretary, died in 1968, he bequeathed his private collection of Picasso's works to the city authorities. Picasso paid tribute to him by matching his donation painting for painting.

The Permanent Collection

The circuit begins upstairs, and the works are arranged chronologically. In **Rooms 1** to **9** Picasso's earliest etchings and academic drawings, nudes and doodles, including some delightful miniature seascapes, are on display. Before Picasso reached the age of 20, he had produced a vast number of powerful studies, realistic landscapes and promising still lifes, and even one or two mocking self-portraits. At the far end of **Room 8** you'll see *Science and Charity* (1897), a huge, forceful work, portraying an old woman on her sick bed. Painted when Picasso was only 15, it is early proof of his immense talent.

In 1900 Picasso spent a few months in Paris, scouring its avant-garde galleries, cafés and cabarets. The experience greatly influenced the young painter, as is clearly visible in the colourful, Fauvist-influenced paintings such as *The Embrace* (1901) and *Margot* or the *Wait* (1901), both in **Room 10**.

A clutch of paintings in **Rooms 11** and **12** represents work from the Blue Period. Picasso, profoundly affected by the suicide of close friend Carles Casagemas, turned to a more limited palette dominated by cold blue tones. Look for *Dead Woman* (Barcelona, 1903).

In the **Sala Sabartés**, Picasso's irreverent *Portrait of Sabartés Wearing a 16th-century-style Ruff and Hat* (1939) is given prominence, along with a series of caricatures of his assistant. Some minor Cubist works from 1917 are shown in **Rooms 13** and **14**. Most of Picasso's work from the interwar years, however, went to collections in Paris, Madrid and New York.

In **Rooms 15** and **16,** you'll find the museum's real highlight, a set of Cubist reinterpretations of *Las Meninas,* a monumental 17th-century painting by Spanish master Diego Velázquez. Picasso broke the original composition up into its components, in a set of 44 canvases, reinterpreting the scene from different perspectives. The centre-piece is a mind-boggling monochrome reworking of the whole work in **Room 15**, painted in 1957. Nine versions of *The Pigeons*, inspired by the dovecote he installed at his Cannes studio in the 1950s, are displayed in **Room 17**.

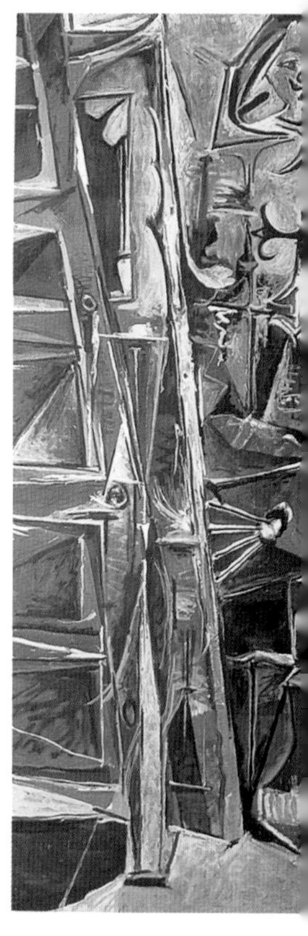

Picasso's Cubist reinterpretation of Velázquez's painting *Las Meninas*

The circuit is rounded off by an exquisite set of boldly painted ceramic plates and vases (**Rooms 18** and **19**), mostly fashioned in the 1950s and donated by Picasso's widow, Jacqueline, in 1982, just in time for the museum's opening. A portrait of Jacqueline (1957), plus a handful of the artist's final works, adorn the walls of these two rooms.

Gallery Highlights

- ***Portrait of the Artist's Mother*** (1896) Room 3
- ***Science and Charity*** (1897) Room 8
- ***Margot* or the *Wait*** (1901) Room 10
- ***Roofs of Barcelona*** (1902 and 1903) Room 11
- ***The Harlequin*** (1917) Room 12
- ***Las Meninas*** (1957) Rooms 15–16
- ***Ceramics*** Rooms 18–19

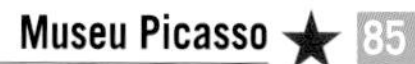

TAKING A BREAK

There is a good cafeteria in the museum. Close by the museum, **Txirimiri** (Carrer Princesa 11, tel: 93 310 18 05) serves up an appetising selection of Basque-style pintxos (tapas) and kaxuelitas (scrambled eggs with a variety of additions). Vegetarian dishes are available as are some delicious desserts.

MUSEU PICASSO: INSIDE INFO

Top tips Try to go on the **first Sunday of the month**, when admission is free.
• Always **get there early** (or time your visit during the afternoon siesta) as the museum is invariably busy.

Hidden gems Don't forget to look up at the marvellous **painted ceilings** in some of the rooms.
• A great place to catch your breath is the **19th-century neo-classical hall**, in the Palau del Baró de Castellet, next to the Sala Sabartés. It drips with sculpted cherubim, crystal chandeliers and gold-leaf decorations.

At Your Leisure

4 Museu Barbier-Mueller d'Art Precolombí

A compact museum, with a magnificent collection of pre-Colombian art, the Museu Barbier-Mueller occupies part of the medieval Palau Nadal, a masterpiece in itself.

The permanent exhibition, laid out in a series of connecting rooms, takes you from the origins of the oldest-known Mexican civilisations more than 3,000 years ago to an extremely rare 1,000-year-old set of figures and urns from Amazonia.

Every piece in the museum is of extraordinary quality, but the highlights include a very modern-looking female ceramic figure, in the Nayarit style, from northwest Mexico; a 1,000-year-old millstone from Nicaragua, unusually shaped like a stylised jaguar; and a fabulous fuchsite mask, with seashells for eyes and a tongue, made by Mayas more than 1,500 years ago.

193 E2 Carrer de Montcada 14 93 310 45 16; www.bcn.es/icub Tue–Sat 10–6, Sun 10–3 Jaume I 14, 17, 19, 39, 40, 45, 51 Inexpensive. Free on the first Sun of the month

5 Museu Tèxtil i de la Indumentària

The Museum of Textile and Clothing shares part of the Palau Nadal with the Museu Barbier-Mueller, next door, and the two can be visited on a joint ticket. It also occupies part of the 13th-century Palau dels Marquesos de Llió, worth seeing for its sumptuous painted ceilings alone. If you're really interested in fashion, you'll enjoy the museum, but be prepared for its rather dull layout. The exhibits start with some beautiful Hispano-Arabic textiles, and then take you through the history of clothes from baroque extravagance to the relatively sober styles of the 1960s. Cristóbal Balenciaga is one of the leading fashion houses to have made a donation to the collection.

193 E3 Carrer de Montcada 12 93 319 76 03 Tue–Sat 10–6, Sun 10–3 Jaume I 14, 17, 19, 39, 40, 45, 51 Café-restaurant in the courtyard and adjoining design shop Inexpensive. Free on the first Sun of the month

6 Parc de la Ciutadella

A leafy haven of tranquillity, the Parc de la Ciutadella is a great place to take a shaded walk, stop for a picnic, or go boating.

The park was the site of the Universal Exhibition of 1888, and several Modernist buildings constructed for the exhibition remain. The Arc de Triomf, an unusual Moorish-style arch on Passeig de Lluís Companys outside the park proper, formed the main entrance. Inside the park, look for the red-brick Castle of Three Dragons, a stupendous mock medieval fortress designed by the Modernist architect Lluís Domènech i Montaner as the exhibition café. It now houses a rather musty zoology

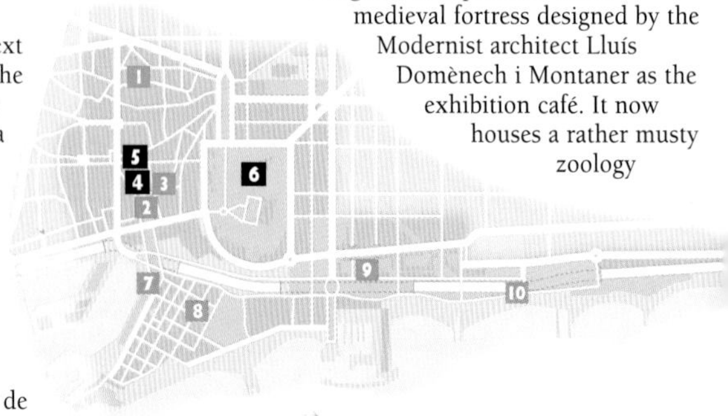

1 5 4 3 2 6 7 8 9 10

The Parlement de Catalunya in Parc de la Ciutadella

museum (one to miss). The L'Umbracle, a fanciful iron-and-glass vivarium, and the L'Hivernacle (➤ 93), or winter garden, also date from this time.

By the lake at the centre of the park, you'll find the **Cascada,** a monumental wedding-cake of a fountain complete with spouting griffins and sea-gods. The grotto at its centre was one of Gaudí's first projects.

197 D3 Daily 10–7, in summer; 10–5, in winter Arc de Triomf, Barceloneta 14, 39, 40, 41, 42, 51, 100, 141

The Spanish Citadel

The Parc de la Ciutadella occupies the site of the citadel built in the early 18th century by Felip V following the Spanish defeat of the Catalans. A symbol of Spanish oppression, it was eventually demolished and the park created.

For Kids

- The fantastic exhibits at the **Museu Barbier-Mueller d'Art Precolombí** (➤ 86).
- Row boats and a life-size elephant statue in the **Parc de la Ciutadella** (➤ 86–88).
- The interactive sections at the **Museu d'Història de Catalunya** (➤ 88–89).
- Frank Gehry's giant fish at the **Vila Olímpica** and the safe sandy beach beyond (➤ 89–90).

7 Museu d'Història de Catalunya

The Palau de Mar, a stunning ensemble of beautifully restored brick warehouses, dominates the northern, Barceloneta side of Port Vell. Inside, an extensive display takes you through the history of Catalonia from prehistoric times to the present day. The attractive exhibition is interactive and informative, with some excellent maps, photos and re-created interiors and environments.

Gaudí helped to design the monumental Cascada in the Parc de la Ciutadella

Highlights include a suit of armour that you can try on. Exhibits are labelled in Catalan only and non-Catalan speakers have to rely on the sketchy information given in the translated handbook issued with the ticket for much of the exhibition. The top-floor Mediateca, however, does have displays in English and, from June to September, the excellent guided tours on Wednesday evenings are given in English as well as Catalan.

196 C2 Plaça de Pau Vila 3 93 225 47 00; www.mhcat.net Thu–Sat, Tue 10–7, Wed 10–8, Sun and holidays 10–2:30; closed 25, 26 Dec and 1, 6 Jan. Guided tours Wed 10 pm–midnight, reservation only Barceloneta 14, 17, 39, 40, 45, 57, 64, 157 Café on fourth floor. Excellent bookshop and gift shop Inexpensive. Evening guided tours expensive. Free 1st Sun of month

8 Barceloneta

"Little Barcelona" is a honeycomb of lively, narrow streets lined with fishermen's houses and low-rise apartments, dotted with little squares and a park. Originally created in the mid-18th century by draining reclaimed land to house dockers and boatmen, it is now a great place to come for a taste of the Mediterranean. Its focal point is the delightful Plaça de la Barceloneta, with its 18th-century church and fountains, where people still come for drinking water. The park is a possible spot for an alfresco picnic lunch bought at the nearby market, whereas the old *chiringuitos*, or beach-hut restaurants, have mostly been replaced by permanent structures catering for a trendier crowd.

197 D1 Barceloneta, Ciutadella-Vila Olímpica 17, 45, 57, 59, 64

The Museu d'Història de Catalunya is housed in the Palau de Mar

9 Vila Olímpica

Barcelona's 1992 Olympiad bequeathed to the city an impressive complex of state-of-the-art apartment blocks and a smart marina (**Port Olímpic**), known collectively as the Vila Olímpica, a short and bracing stroll along the coast from Barceloneta.

Barceloneta's beach-hut restaurants (➤ 89) are an ideal place to kick-back and relax

A casino, shopping complex, seafood restaurants, assorted bars and raunchy nightclubs vie to draw in customers. Near the beach are Spain's two tallest towers. One is the impressive steel-framed Hotel Arts (➤ 36), while the other is Torre Mapfre, an office block. In their shadow, but holding its own in the popularity stakes, is the striking bronze sculpture of a giant whale-like fish by American architect Frank Gehry, renowned for designing the Guggenheim Museum in Bilbao.

197 F2 Ciutadella-Vila Olímpica 10, 36, 41, 45, 57, 59, 71, 92, 100, 157

10 Barcelona's Beaches

How many other big cities in the world – save for Rio and Sydney – can boast clean, sandy beaches (*platges*) on their doorstep? Barcelona enjoys 5km (3 miles) of them, stretching all the way from Barceloneta to Diagonal Mar, to the north. Behind them is a new promenade, the Passeig Marítim, lined with palm trees. Showers, bars, shops and restaurants along the beaches make the experience all the more pleasant. The water quality is monitored, and there are lifeguards and Red Cross stations aplenty, plus buoys to keep boats and jet-skis away from swimmers. All the beaches, easily accessible by public transport, have qualified for EU Blue Flag status to vouch for their safety and cleanliness.

The three beaches nearest the city, Platges Sant Sebastià, Barceloneta and Passeig Marítim, get very crowded on hot days, so it's worth going that bit farther to Nova Icària, Bogatell, Mar Bella or Nova Mar Bella. At the latter two beaches you can rent water-sports equipment such as sailing boats, windsurf boards and surfboards.

197 off F2 Barceloneta, Ciutadella-Vila Olímpica, Bogatell, Llacuna, Poble Nou, Selva de Mar 10, 36, 41, 45, 57, 59, 71, 92, 100, 157

Where to... Eat and Drink

Prices
Expect to pay per person for a three-course meal, excluding drinks
€ under €15 €€ €15–35 €€€ over €35

Abac €€€
In this sleek dining room, with onyx panels diffusing the light overhead, you can taste scintillating cuisine. Chef Xavier Pellicer concocts fabulous food; the likes of roast pigeon and figs or red mullet and wild mushrooms. Charming service, a breathtaking selection of Catalan and Spanish wines, and unusual desserts such as strawberries in vinaigrette all make this memorable dining.

193 F2 Carrer del Rec 79–89 93 319 66 00 Tue–Sat 1:30–3:30, Mon–Sat 8:30–10:30 Barceloneta

Agua €€
It's sometimes easy to forget that Barcelona is right beside the sea. When you long for beachfront eating head for Agua, next to the Hotel Arts (➤ 36) and near the Vila Olímpica (➤ 89). The menu offers a good range of Catalan and Spanish dishes such as salt cod with sun-dried tomatoes, and wild rice with green vegetables and ginger, although pastas, hamburgers and salads are also available. House specialities are prepared in a coal-fired oven. The interior of the Renaissance house has been beautifully modernised and a glass ceiling maximises the light. In summer, book in advance.

197 E1 Passeig Marítim de la Barceloneta 30 93 225 12 72 Mon–Sat 1:30–5, 8:30–midnight (also midnight–1 am Fri–Sat); Sun 1:30–5 Barceloneta

Cal Pep €€
Be prepared to wait at this hugely popular, small seafood restaurant run in idiosyncratic style by Pep himself. Grab a stool at the packed bar if you can and, unless you speak Catalan, simply point to any of the tapas that look good, or wait to be seated in the tiny, brick-lined restaurant. Don't miss dishes such as *pebrots del padró* (fried green peppers), chickpeas with spinach and Catalan sausage, and crayfish with chilli sauce.

193 E2 Plaça de les Olles 8 93 310 79 61 Tue–Sat 1–4:30, 8–midnight, Mon 8–midnight; closed Easter, Aug, public holidays Jaume I

Can Ramonet €€€
A new terrace has added to the attractions of this family-run restaurant, said to be the oldest in the port area. Set in a renovated square in the heart of Barceloneta, the restaurant has a front bar with stand-up tables and a few seated tables where you can enjoy seafood tapas, beer and some regional wines. This provides a crowded but less expensive option than dining in one of the two rooms at the rear, lined with wooden tables. The seafood is exceptionally good, and it's worth paying the price for spanking-fresh hake, monkfish and shellfish spectacularly displayed at the entrance. Specialities include lobster with clams, cod with *romesco* and marinated anchovies. Vegetarians can opt for braised artichokes or *tortilla* with spinach and beans.

193 F1 Carrer de la Maquinista 17 93 319 30 64 Daily noon–midnight Barceloneta

Can Ros €

As well as a lengthy list of tapas, there's a good choice of classic dishes such as paella and *arròs negre* (rice cooked with squid ink) at this popular Barceloneta seafood restaurant. You can nibble on a mixed platter of *peixets* (deep-fried whitebait), prawns and mussels while you wait for the main course. Prices are remarkably competitive, given the quality of the food.

196 C1 Carrer de l'Almirall Aixada 7 93 221 50 49 Thu– Tue 1–5, 8–midnight, Wed 1–5 Barceloneta

Comme Bio €

A large vegetarian restaurant, health-food shop selling organic fruit and vegetables, and craft gallery all rolled into one, Comme Bio offers plenty of choice. Everything is well prepared and reasonably priced.

193 D2 Via Laietana 28 93 319 89 68 Daily 9 am–midnight Jaume I

Euskal Etxea €€

Pintxos are the Basque version of tapas – reputedly the best in Spain. You need to get here early for the best selection, but even then you'll probably still have to stand. There is, however, a restaurant with a Basque menu at the back – but part of the fun is fighting at the bar for the laden plates of tuna chunks, crab claws and much, much more.

193 E2 Placeta de Montcada 1–3 93 310 21 85 Bar: Tue–Sat 8:30 am–11:30 pm, Sun 12:45–3:30. Restaurant: Tue–Sat 1–3:30, 9–11:30 Jaume I

Passadís d'en Pep €€€

Although this restaurant is virtually invisible from the street and fiendishly difficult to find (you have to go down a long unmarked passageway by the Caixa office), it's worth making the effort. The seafood here is fantastic. There's no menu, just whatever is fresh that day, but a mouthwatering buffet and *cava* are included in the price of the beautifully cooked Spanish/Catalan dishes. Advance booking is essential.

193 E1 Plaça del Palau 2 93 310 10 21 Mon–Sat 1:30–3:30, 9–11:30; closed three weeks in Aug Barceloneta

Restaurante Carpanta €€€

If you stick to one dish, perhaps a paella or *arròs negre*, the price is relatively inexpensive, but the bill soon starts to climb when you order a full meal. The wonderful setting, however, in a candlelit Gothic house around the back of Santa Maria del Mar, justifies the price and makes this the perfect place for a special, intimate dinner. Table reservations need to be made well in advance.

193 E2 Carrer dels Sombrerers 13 93 319 99 99 Mon–Sat 1:30–3:30, 9–11:30 Jaume I

El Rey de la Gamba €€

Prawns and mussels, served the traditional way with cured ham, are the speciality of this large, much-extended Barceloneta restaurant. At weekends, the place gets packed, but if you can find a free table, sit outside, watch the world go by and enjoy the wonderful view of the city back across the harbour.

196 C1 Passeig Joan del Borbó 48 93 221 83 10 Daily noon–midnight Barceloneta

Rodrigo €

Although full meals are not served in the evening, there is still an extensive choice of hot and cold snacks and sandwiches on offer. The home-cooked food, especially the daily dishes, the low prices and lively, slightly chaotic interior combine to make this a popular lunchtime choice. It is also one of the best places in the area for Sunday eating.

196 C3 Carrer de l'Argentaría 67 93 310 78 14 Daily 1–4 (also 8:30–midnight Fri–Tue) Jaume I

Senyor Parellada €€
Fifty years' experience has earned this bright Catalan *taberna*, with tables and benches around a covered patio, a solid reputation for reliable home-style cooking. Details include colourful menus wrapped in the linen napkins, and a paper cone filled with tiny black olives to nibble while you wait for lamb chops with whole garlic or salt cod with honey.

193 E2 · Carrer de l'Argenteria 37 · 93 310 50 94 · Mon–Sat 1–3:45, 8:30–11:45 · Jaume I

Les Set Portes €€€
If you eat only one paella in Barcelona, eat it here. The huge, historic restaurant opened its "seven doors" in 1836, and ever since has been serving a legendary selection of different paellas daily. The shellfish paella is classic, but varieties made with squid ink, rabbit or sardines are also available. There is also a wide choice of fish dishes and savoury casseroles. The standard of cooking is high, service is fast and prices surprisingly reasonable.

193 E1 · Passeig d'Isabel II 14 · 93 319 29 50; www.7portes@mhp.es · Daily 1–1 · Barceloneta

Vascelum €€€
The modern Catalan cooking here is presented in a stylish setting overlooking Santa Maria del Mar. Prices tend to be high, although there is a cheaper lunch and slightly more expensive evening set menu. It's a lovely place to eat, especially on a Sunday.

193 E2 · Plaça de Santa Maria 4 · 93 319 01 67 · Wed–Mon 12:30–4, 8–midnight · Jaume I

BARS AND CAFÉS

Café de la Ribera €
Sit outside on the peaceful, traffic-free square and snack on reasonably priced tapas any time from breakfast until the early hours of the morning. Lunchtimes can be busy; a daily special menu is supplemented by salads and pizzas.

193 E2 · Plaça de les Olles 6 · 93 319 50 72 · Daily Mon–Sat 8:30 am–1 am · Barceloneta

L'Hivernacle €
The fabulous Modernist greenhouse in the Ciutadella park (➤ 86) is the setting for this airy bar-café. Drinks and light meals are served among refreshing fronds.

197 D3 · Parc de la Ciutadella · 93 295 40 17 · Daily 10–1 · Arc de Triomf

Palau Dalmases €
Occupying the converted ground floor of a beautiful courtyard palace, this is more of a film set than a bar. The interior is decorated in baroque style and is suitably palatial, with period paintings, ornate furnishings, religious icons and spectacular displays of fruit and flowers. Your drink will be expensive, but the experience is one that you'll remember long after you have left Barcelona.

193 E2 · Carrer de Montcada 20 · 93 310 06 73 · Tue–Sat 8 pm–2 am, Sun 6–10 pm · Jaume I

Tèxtil Café €
This is an oasis of calm in the courtyard of the Museu Tèxtil i de la Indumentària and Museu Barbier-Mueller d'Art Precolombí (➤ 86). There are simple, light lunches and snacks and shady tables.

193 E2 · Carrer de Montcada 12–14 · 93 268 25 98 · Tue–Sun 10 am–midnight · Jaume I

El Xampanyet €
This tiny bar is an essential stop on any *cava* and tapas trail. The décor of coloured tiles has changed little since the 1930s. *Cava* and cider are specialities. Tapas include superb anchovies and *tortilla*.

193 E2 · Carrer de Montcada 22 · 93 319 70 03 · Tue–Sat noon–4, 6:30–11:30, Sun noon–4; closed Aug · Jaume I

Where to... Shop

La Ribera bursts with irresistible showrooms, galleries and traditional little shops. Jewellery, a wide range of crafts and tempting food shops are the district's main specialities. For the latest information on the shops and buzzing bars and restaurants in the area, pick up a copy of the *Born Circuit*, a widely available multilingual leaflet.

MARKETS

Every Monday, Wednesday, Friday and Saturday, the colourful **Els Encants** flea market sets up shop on the Carrer Dos de Maig near the Plaça de les Glòries (Metro: Glòries). From 9 am to 8 pm you can sift through the junk and, who knows, happen upon an antique or at least some item that takes your fancy.

ART AND CRAFTS

Galeria Maeght (Montcada 25, tel: 93 310 42 45, Metro: Jaume I) is perhaps the city's most exclusive art gallery, housed in a truly remarkable Renaissance palace. The adjoining bookshop has a splendid selection of publications on 20th-century art, architecture, design and photography, as well as an array of quality posters and reproductions. For something more accessible, check out the pottery and glass at stylish **1748** (Placeta de Montcada 2, tel: 93 319 54 13, Metro: Jaume I). **Aspectos** (Rec 28, tel: 93 319 52 85, Metro: Barceloneta) is another contemporary gallery confirming Barcelona's reputation as one of the world's design capitals, while **Ici et Là** (Plaça Santa Maria 2, tel: 93 268 11 67, Metro: Jaume I) specialises in accessories by local designers. The papier-mâché figures of dragons and Gaudí-inspired monsters at **Kitsch** (Placeta de Montcada 10, tel: 93 319 57 68, Metro: Jaume I) make for unusual souvenirs, while **Montcada Taller** (Placeta de Montcada 10 bis, tel: 93 319 15 81, Metro: Jaume I) has some exquisite and innovative glassware by local artists – many talented craftsmen and women start their careers here.

FASHION AND ACCESSORIES

The fine silver bangles and rings adorning the windows of **0,925 Argenters** (Montcada 25, tel: 93 319 43 18, Metro: Jaume I) will tempt you inside. Don't forget the **Botiga Tèxtil** (Carrer de Montcada 12, tel 93 268 25 98, Metro: Jaume I) at the Museu Tèxtil i de la Indumentària (➤ 86) – it's a goldmine of up-to-the-minute clothes and other items, such as silk sleeping-bags! Those looking for luggage will be in their element at **Casa Antich** (Carrer Consolat del Mar 27–31, tel: 93 310 43 91, Metro: Barceloneta). Finally, the stylish new mini shopping mall **Café de la Princesa** (Carrer Flassaders 21, tel: 93 268 15 18, Metro: Jaume I) has a slogan *Et Volem* (We Want You) – once you've seen its delightful boutiques selling jewellery, textiles and items for the home, the feeling will be mutual.

FOOD AND WINE

Casa Gispert (Carrer Sombrerers 23, tel: 93 319 75 35, Metro: Jaume I) sells roasted hazelnuts, walnuts, almonds and pistachios, by the sackful. Equally aromatic is **El Magnifico** (Carrer Argenteria 64, tel: 93 319 60 81, Metro: Jaume I) where a magnificent range of coffee beans, including the Blue Mountain variety from Jamaica, perfumes the air. Exclusive tea merchant **Sans & Sans Colonials** (Argenteria 59, tel: 93 319 60 81, Metro: Jaume I) is run by the same people. Quite different scents waft out of **Tot**

Formatge (Passeig del Born 13, tel: 93 319 53 75, Metro: Barceloneta) – literally "all cheese". You may not be able to find every type of cheese here, but the selection is vast, and all the best Catalan goat cheeses and *mató* (cottage cheese) are on sale. Complement your purchase with a bottle of something from **Vila Vinateca** (Carrer Agullers 7–9, tel: 93 310 19 56, Metro: Jaume I) – one of the city's leading wine-sellers.

MISCELLANEOUS

This is the seaside part of town so you'd expect to find a shop selling fishing tackle: **Casa Calico** (Plaça de les Olles 9, tel: 93 319 18 18, Metro: Barceloneta) is a traditional establishment serving fishermen and sports anglers alike for decades. **La Casa del Feltre** (Carrer Canvis Vells 8, tel: 93 319 39 00, Metro: Barceloneta) makes wonderful fancy-dress costumes out of felt (its speciality). Brighten up your life with a lamp from **Matarile** (Passeig del Born 24, tel: 93 315 02 20, Metro: Jaume I) – old and new, some recycled, some made from scratch, the lighting on sale here is always unusual.

Comics fans will need to be torn away from **Norma Comics** (Passeig de Sant Joan 9, tel: 93 245 45 26, Metro: Arc de Triomf) – in addition to a gallery displaying historic comics and a special Tintin store, the shop stocks thousands of comic books from Europe, North America and Japan. Budding magicians and would-be wizards should spirit themselves to **El Rei de la Magia** (Carrer Princesa 11, tel: 93 319 39 20, Metro: Jaume I), one of the city's most offbeat shops (which is saying something). Barcelona's Cuban connection comes up with the goods at the aromatic **L'Estanc de Via Laetana** (No 4, tel: 93 310 10 34, Metro: Jaume I), another institutional shop where Havana cigars star among a variety of luxury tobacco items.

Where to... Be Entertained

Although La Ribera, and the fashionable Born district in particular, remains lively at night, the focus of Barcelona's night-life has shifted to the sea-front, and the new Olympic city. Nightclubs there are not subject to any time or noise restrictions and have become some of the city's most popular clubbing haunts.

SPORT

Water sports are a major activity, as you might expect, though you're better off at Sitges, Castelldefels and the Costa Brava for windsurfing, yachting and kayaking. At the **Base Nautica de la Mar Bella** (tel: 93 221 04 32, Metro: Selva de Mar), at one of the beaches along the Avinguda Litoral, you can hire windsurfing and snorkelling equipment and small craft, and even learn to sail. Alternatively, you can just have a dip in the sea at the nearby beaches – they offer some of the cleanest city sea-bathing anywhere in Europe (➤ 90).

MUSIC

The **Palau de la Música Catalana** (➤ 78–79) may not have the world's best acoustics, but a concert in its extravagant auditorium is an unforgettable experience. Try to attend a performance by the amateur **Orfeó Català** choir, the institution for which it was originally built, or by its professional cousin, the **Cor de**

Cambra del Palau de la Música, or chamber-choir; one or the other gives a concert at least once a week during the season. The box office (tel: 93 268 10 00) is open Monday–Saturday 10–9, and one hour before Sunday concerts; also try Servi-Caixa (➤ 42).

The **OBC** (National Catalan Orchestra) now plays at the new **L'Auditori** (Carrer Lepant 150, Metro: Marina). It seats 2,300 in the Sala Simfònica, while chamber music and recitals are given in the rather smaller Sala Polivalente. It is modern, not to say clinical, in style, and some conservative concert-goers have boycotted it, but the programming is impressive. The box office (tel: 93 247 93 00) is open daily 10–9; look out for the Sunday lunchtime concerts. After evening concerts the **Bus de les Arts** will whisk you back to the Plaça de Catalunya. The splendid **Basílica de Santa Maria del Mar** (➤ 80–81) also makes a stunning setting for occasional classical concerts.

On quite a different note is **Magic** (Passeig de Picasso 40, tel: 93 310 72 67, Metro: Barceloneta), a weekend venue for live rock, pop and other modern music concerts. **Penúltimo** (Passeig del Born 19, tel: 93 310 25 96, Metro: Jaume I) plays host to jazz, flamenco, tango and other Latin sounds in the heart of the Born. Across towards Poble Nou, a formerly burned-out zone being relentlessly gentrified, **Zeleste** (Carrer Almogavers 122 and Pamplona 88, tel: 93 486 44 22, Metro: Marina) is a popular rock club open Thursday to Saturday.

CINEMA

The state-of-the-art **Icària Yelmo Cineplex** (Carrer Salvador Espriu 61, tel: 93 221 79 12, Metro: Ciutadella-Vila Olímpica) in the Olympic village houses 15 screens, many of which show English-language films. Half the films on average are blockbusters but there's also a decent programme of more serious, independent cinema, too. It is one of the few cinemas in Barcelona with wheelchair access.

THEATRE

Unless you understand Catalan, the government-sponsored **Teatre Nacional de Catalunya** (Plaça de les Arts 1, tel: 93 306 57 00, Metro: Glòries) is unlikely to be of interest, but dance is frequently staged here, too.

NIGHTCLUBS

The Born continues to be one of the heartlands of Barcelona nightlife. Try **Magic/Magic in the Air** (Passeig de Picasso 40, tel: 93 310 72 67, Metro: Barceloneta), a somewhat cramped club where the music – groovy, funky and up-to-date – pulls in the crowds. On Saturday nights **Foro** (Carrer Princesa 53, tel: 93 310 10 20, Metro: Jaume I), an extremely popular restaurant and nightclub complex, is overseen by in-tune DJs. **Astin** (Carrer Abaixadors 9, tel: 93 300 00 90, Metro: Jaume I) is renowned for being at the vanguard of rock. If you need rest for your eardrums and a refreshing cocktail, dive into one of the many bars along Passeig del Born: **Miramelindo** (at No 15), the best, or **Berimbau** and **Trípode** (both at No 17).

Formerly known as "Woman Caballero", **República** (Avinguda Marquès de l'Argentera 6, tel: 936 300 50 50, Metro: Barceloneta), right next to the revamped Estació de França, throbs to the sounds of hard house, with live stage shows adding to the wild ambience at times.

While the plethora of discos – some downright outrageous – in the Olympic village continue to thrive, interesting night-spots have sprung up in the Poblenou district. The gigantic **Razzmatazz**, for example (Carrer Almogávers 122, tel: 93 272 09 10, Metro: Marina), hosts national and international rock bands, with plenty of room in the converted factory space for all-night weekend dancing.

The Eixample

Getting Your Bearings

Spacious and orderly where the Old City is cramped and chaotic, the Eixample is home to Barcelona's prosperous middle classes. At its heart is the "Golden Square", a core of elegant streets studded with art nouveau wonders, two of them by architect Gaudí. A magical park and the world's most innovative cathedral are thrown in for good measure.

When the city expanded beyond its medieval walls 150 years ago, the new district, the Eixample, was laid out in a perfect chequerboard pattern of square blocks (*illes* or *manzanas*) separated by wide, tree-lined streets, ideal for gentle strolling. Its main thoroughfare, the Passeig de Gràcia, chic and aloof, offers row upon row of smart restaurants and even smarter boutiques. The most impressive block on the Passeig de Gràcia, known as the Manzana de la Discordia, is a showcase for the three greatest Modernist architects, among them Gaudí.

As the avenue slopes towards Gràcia, a bohemian village stubbornly refusing to be swallowed up into the city proper, you pass another example of Gaudí's genius, Casa Milà. This part of the city is also home to Gaudí's fairy-tale Parc Güell.

Wending your way back into the Eixample, you can see the Sagrada Família, Gaudí's unfinished masterpiece and the city's most celebrated sight.

Previous page: Gaudí's wrought-iron palm leaves adorn the gates at Casa Vicens

Above: A detail of the Hospital de la Santa Creu i de Sant Pau

Right: Shoppers pausing for a break on the Passeig de Gràcia

Left: Avinguda Portal de l'Angel

★ Don't Miss

- **1** **Manzana de la Discordia** ➤ 102
- **5** **Casa Milà** ➤ 105
- **7** **Gràcia** ➤ 108
- **8** **Parc Güell** ➤ 110
- **10** **La Sagrada Família** ➤ 113

At Your Leisure

- **2** Fundació Antoni Tàpies ➤ 118
- **3** Museu Egipci ➤ 118
- **4** Fundació Francisco Godia ➤ 119
- **6** Casa-Taller Durancamps ➤ 120
- **9** Hospital de la Santa Creu i de Sant Pau ➤ 120

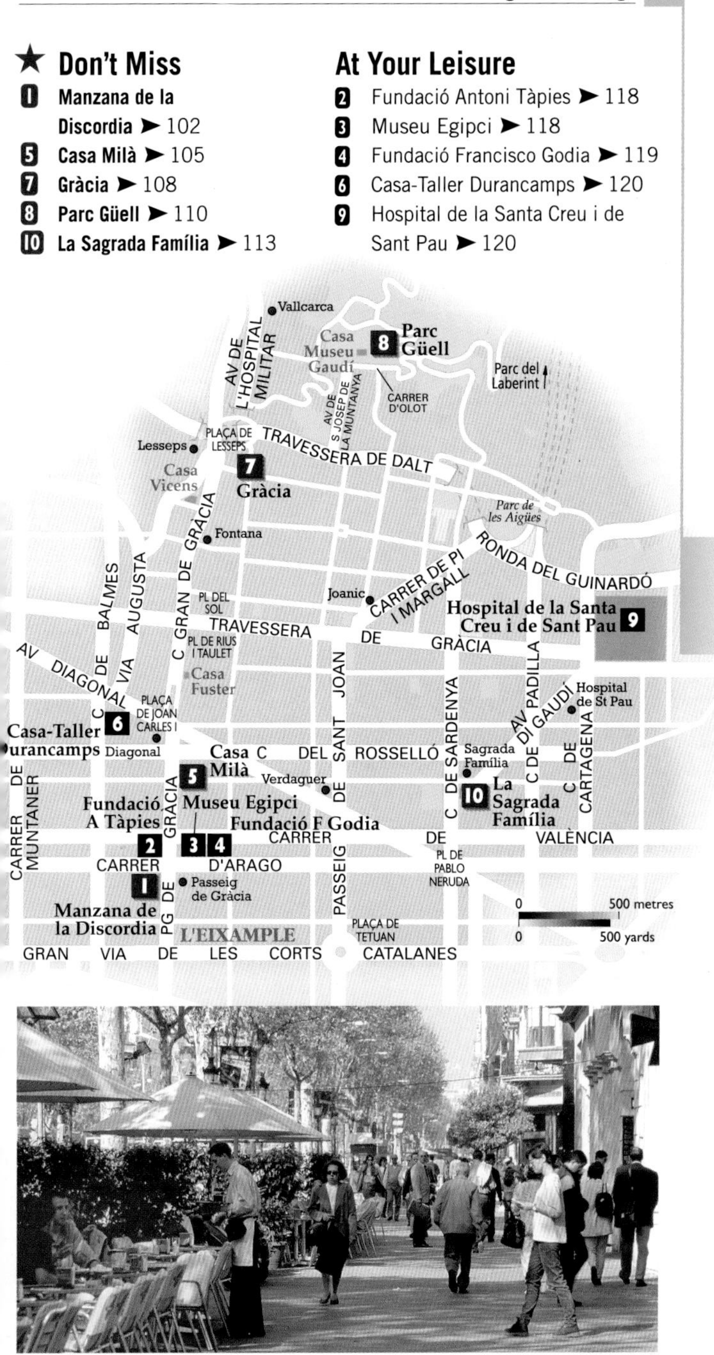

The extraordinary architecture of Gaudí and other Modernists makes for a full day of unforgettable sightseeing: a trio of incredible façades, a hallucinatory park and a cathedral that's not a cathedral...

The Eixample in a Day

9:00 am

The Eixample offers plenty of choice for an early-morning cup of coffee. Choose either the Bracafé (Carrer de Casp 2), for a robust *tallat* (a small coffee with milk, called a *cortado* in Spanish), or Laie Llibreria-Café (Carrer de Pau Claris 85), for a delicious cappuccino.

9:30 am

Stroll a short way up the Passeig de Gràcia to the 1 **Manzana de la Discordia** (left, ➤ 102–104). Three very different Modernist façades make up the block. Afterwards, spend some time at the nearby 2 **Fundació Antoni Tàpies** (➤ 118) or 4 **Fundació Francisco Godia** (➤ 119), depending on whether you like conventional or contemporary art. Both can be visited in under an hour.

11:30 am

Continue your gentle ascent of the Passeig de Gràcia – the extraordinary Modernist bench-cum-lampposts are perfect for resting on while you study the 5 **Casa Milà**, known as La Pedrera (➤ 105–107). Then go inside, enjoy the views from the roof-top (right), and visit the exhibition on the first floor, if it's to your taste.

1:00 pm

Now it's time to think about lunch in the *barrio* of 7 **Gràcia** (left, ➤ 108–109), with its villagey atmosphere and simple eateries. To get there, keep going up the Passeig de Gràcia until it narrows to become Carrer Gran de Gràcia. Branch off into one of the neighbourhood's little squares, such as Plaça Rius i Taulet or Plaça del Sol, where the *menú del dia* should give you energy for the afternoon.

3:30 pm

From Plaça Lesseps, at the top of Carrer Gran de Gràcia, turn along the Travessera de Dalt and follow the signs to 8 **Parc Güell** (➤ 110–112), up Avinguda del Santuari de Sant Josep de la Muntanya, and along Carrer d'Olot. Allow at least an hour to explore the park in depth and take in the wonderful views.

5:30 pm

Make your way back down to 10 **La Sagrada Família** (right, ➤ 113–117) in time to see it at its best – the panoramas from its towers are remarkable as the sun goes down. You can take a taxi or use public transport. For the latter, take the 24 bus or subway to Diagonal Metro, and then continue on to the Sagrada Família by Metro.

8:30 pm

The Eixample has plenty to offer in the evening: dinner at a fashionable restaurant, cocktails at a designer bar, a movie at an art-house cinema or all-night dancing at a the-place-to-be-seen night-spot. Rooftop entertainment at Casa Milà (➤ 105–107) is a great option on summer weekends.

0

Manzana de la Discordia

Casa Lleó Morera, Casa Amatller and Casa Batlló stand almost side-by-side in a single block on the Passeig de Gràcia, forming one of the most famous architectural ensembles in Barcelona. Built by three leading Modernist rivals, the houses are wildly disparate in style – hence the name.

Block of Discord

The name Manzana de la Discordia is a clever play on words. Manzana means both "block" and "apple" in Spanish, so the name means both Block of Discord and Apple of Discord (a reference to Greek mythology). The play on words doesn't translate well into Catalan as the words for block and apple differ. In Barcelona you may see references to the Illa de la Discordia – the true Catalan name.

Casa Lleó Morera

At the corner of Carrer del Consell de Cent (Passeig de Gràcia 35) is Casa Lleó Morera, Lluís Domènech i Montaner's 1905 ornate remodelling of an existing building, commissioned by local tycoon Albert Lleó i Morera. The orgy of stone carvings on the neo-Renaissance double façade reveals infinite symbolism, but the recurring themes to look for are the lion (*lleó*) and the mulberry tree (*morera*) and its leaves. The main entrance on the side street is decorated with exquisite green ceramics and, inside the circular oriel at the corner, is a marble column – in fact only the visible section is marble: the rest is of cheaper stone. It is not open to the public.

---

200 B1
Passeig de Gràcia 35–45
Passeig de Gràcia
7, 16, 17, 20, 22, 24, 28, 43, 44

Casa Amatller
93 488 01 39 Mon–Sat 10–7, Sun 10–3
Moderate

Casa Batlló
93 216 03 06; www.casabatllo.es Mon–Sat 9–2, Sun 9–8 Expensive

Casa Amatller

Casa Amatller at No 41, built in 1900, predates Casa Lleó Morera, and its architect Josep Puig i Cadafalch took quite a different approach. He attempted to create for his client, Antoni Amatller, a fanciful version of a Dutch or Flemish step-gabled house. He threw in fashionable Gothic details, such as gargoyles, twisted columns and coats of arms carved in stone, plus a fake marble column later copied in the Casa Morera. Catalonia's nationalism is symbolised by a carving of St George slaying a dragon, clinging to a column by the medieval-looking doors. The subtle sgraffito decoration (made on wet plaster to show a different surface underneath) on the main façade is set off by extravagant ceramic motifs. As for the windows and the shape of the house itself, they form stylised letter As, Antoni Amatller's initials.

Casa Amatller and Casa Batlló doing their best not to harmonise along the Passeig de Gràcia

Left: St George killing the dragon outside Casa Amatller

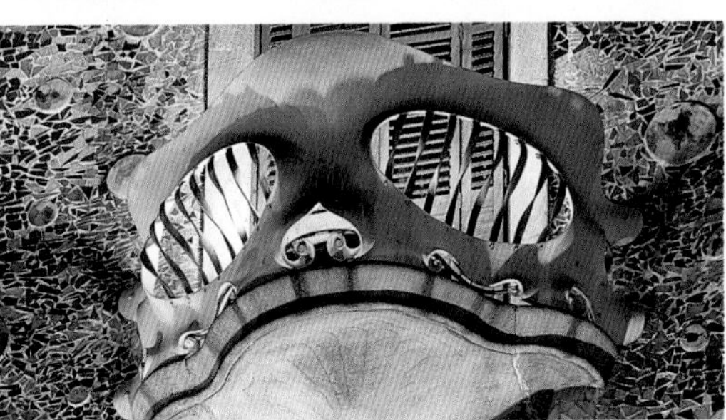

Right: One of the skull-like balconies at Casa Batlló

Casa Batlló

Finally, you come to Casa Batlló, one of the city's Modernist gems. The awe-inspiring building was designed by Gaudí for the textile industrialist Josep Batlló i Casanovas. The design deliberately clashes with that of other buildings in the block, jutting out several metres above them, and when it was built in 1907 it exceeded the official height limit in the area.

The exterior illustrates the legend of St George (the city's patron saint). The blue-and-green ceramic cladding on the walls is reminiscent of a dragon's scaly skin, the curved rooftop its crested back, the balcony railings and pillars the skulls and bones of its victims – earning it the nickname the House of Bones.

Inside, you can admire more undulating forms – the mushroom-shaped fireplace is a gem. Telephone-style audiguides (in several languages) are included in the price, though the cascade of excited superlatives can become tiresome.

In readiness for Casa Batlló's centenary celebrations, the elliptically arched attics and the **roofs**, adorned with multicoloured, tile-coated chimney-stacks, have been opened to the public – for a sizeable additional entrance fee.

Gaudí's curvaceous main staircase at Casa Batlló

TAKING A BREAK

The Passeig de Gràcia is lined with restaurants offering tapas, snacks and light meals. **Quasi Queviures** (Passeig de Gràcia 24, tel: 93 317 45 12), however, is one of the best, with a wide selection of Catalan charcuterie.

MANZANA DE LA DISCORDIA: INSIDE INFO

Top tips Avoid high noon on sunny days – you'll be blinded by the sun when trying to take in the detail of the buildings.

- The Ruta del Modernisme has its main offices in the middle building, the Casa Amatller; **staff can fix you up with multilingual guides** who'll describe the Manzana in detail.

One to miss The **next block up the Passeig de Gràcia** is another contender for the title "block of discord", with its horrendous metal-and-glass façades.

Hidden gem Keep a look out for the **lift in the Casa Batlló** – another Modernist wonder in shiny wood.

5

Casa Milà

This other-worldly apartment block designed by Gaudí is officially called the Casa Milà, after the dilettante politician Pere Milà who commissioned it nearly a century ago. More commonly known as La Pedrera (the Quarry), it has become one of the icons of the city

The undulating forms of La Pedrera's cliff-like silhouette dominate a corner of the elegant Passeig de Gràcia. The strange but beguiling exterior, remarkable for its pock-marked creamy limestone curves, tangled wrought-iron balconies and spider's-web main doorway, caused much controversy when it was completed in 1912. The building was described variously as a petrified aquarium, a hangar for airships and even an earthquake preserved in sculpture. In the 1920s, French president Georges Clemenceau was said to have been so disturbed by the sight of the building that he cut short a lecture tour to Barcelona; back in Paris he was quoted as claiming that in Barcelona they were building homes for dragons.

Controversial when it was built, Casa Milà is now recognised as an architectural masterpiece

---

200 B2 Passeig de Gràcia 92 and Carrer de Provença 261–5
93 484 59 95; www.caixacat.es/cccc
Daily 10–7:30 Diagonal 7, 16, 17, 22, 24, 28, N4
Espai Gaudí, attic and roof (joint ticket). Moderate

Did You Know?

- A wrought-iron grating from the basement was sold to an American for $60,000 in the 1970s and used as a bedhead until it was donated to the Museum of Modern Art, New York.
- Originally, the ramps inside the building were to be wide enough to allow horse-drawn carriages – and subsequently motor-cars – to drive all the way to the top, but this plan was modified. Amazingly, lifts were left out of the blueprint, and weren't installed until years later.

Shimmering walls, mottled ceilings and crooked banisters in the stunning stairwell at Casa Milà

The apartment block was one of Gaudí's final works before he dedicated himself to La Sagrada Família (➤ 113–117), and its sleek lines, smooth surfaces and curvaceous forms go beyond pure Modernisme. It is a triumph of aesthetics over practicality. When one of the tenants complained that it was hard to fit a piano into the curved rooms, Gaudí is reputed to have advised them to take up the violin instead. The building was also far bigger than had originally been envisaged. Barcelona City Council ordered Milà to knock down the top floor or pay a 100,000 peseta fine, a sum now roughly equivalent to a million dollars. Milà could not afford to pay the fine but was let off the hook; the city authorities eventually caved in, acknowledging that the building was a work of art. In 1984, UNESCO declared it a World Heritage Site – it was the first 20th-century building to achieve the honour.

Exhibitions and the Roof

On the first floor, reached from the entrance on Passeig de Gràcia 92, major **temporary art exhibitions** dedicated to artists such as Goya and Chagall are run by the Caixa Catalunya savings bank. The staircase rises from one of the fabulous inner courtyards, with its grotto-like decoration.

The other entrance, at Carrer de Provença 261–5, takes you to the **Espai Gaudí**, an exhibition about the origins of Casa Milà with a film, a reconstruction of a 1920s apartment and explanations of the architecture. From here, stairs lead to the fantastic brick-lined **attic**, with its labyrinth of elegant parabolic arches. Here you can see an interesting display of models of Gaudí buildings.

The grand finale to any visit, however, is stepping out onto the wonderful undulating **roof** (reached from the attic), with its forest of shard-encrusted chimney-stacks. The vistas of the city from here are breathtaking.

Originally, a huge statue of the Virgin Mary was to have perched on the top of the building but this idea was vetoed by Milà, who was wary of attracting anti-religious attacks by the Anarchists then dangerously active in the city.

TAKING A BREAK

La Bodegueta (Rambla de Catalunya 100, tel: 93 215 48 94) serves some of the best tapas and wines in the neighbourhood as well as *cava* by the glass. Ham, charcuterie, cheese and *pa amb tomàquet* (► 40) are all excellent and prices are reasonable. You may find you have to eat standing up as it is always crowded.

Two Gaudí masterpieces for the price of one: stunning views of the Sagrada Família from the rooftops of Casa Milà

CASA MILÀ: INSIDE INFO

Top tips Entrance to the Caixa Catalunya exhibitions is free.
- One ticket purchased at the Carrer de Provença 261–5 entrance includes the Espai Gaudí, the attic and the roof.
- It is worth coming back to **see the building at night**, when it is beautifully lit.
- During the summer (July to September, Friday and Saturday 9 pm–midnight) you can **listen to opera arias or flamenco singers** while sipping a glass of ice-cold *cava* on the amazing rooftop ("La Pedrera de Nit").

Hidden gem Some of the **original furniture** from Casa Milà is on display at the Museu Nacional d'Art de Catalunya (MNAC) (► 136–139).

One to miss The **film** about the history of Casa Milà, in the sixth-floor video-room, is most uninspiring.

7

Gràcia

Gràcia is Barcelona's bohemian quarter; artists, writers and students have long been drawn to its narrow streets and shady squares. Once a separate township with a reputation for radical politics, it has even been known to declare itself an independent republic. Although Gràcia has seen gentrification in recent years, it remains a place apart, with low-rise buildings and a villagey feel that contrasts sharply with the grid plan of the Eixample.

Gràcia is above all a place for strolling, pausing to shop at local markets or to absorb the atmosphere of the lively little squares. It begins at the top of Passeig de Gràcia, just beyond Avinguda Diagonal. This is where you will find **Casa Fuster**, a Modernist apartment block built by Lluís Domènech i Montaner and his son Pere, with a Venetian-style white marble façade. It has been converted into a five-star hotel. There are more Modernist houses as you continue up the hill along the main street of the district, Carrer Gran de Gràcia.

Above: Modernist Casa Fuster in Passeig de Gràcia

Carrer Moya to your right leads to **Plaça de Rius i Taulet**, Gràcia's unofficial heart. The square is popularly known as Plaça del Rellotge, after the mid-19th-century clock tower that stands some 30m (100 feet) high; at the time of publication the tower was undergoing renovation. During the 19th century the tower was a symbol of liberty and a rallying point for revolutionary demonstrations. The former town hall nearby is a reminder that Gràcia was Spain's ninth largest city until it was annexed by Barcelona in 1897.

Left: The clock tower in Plaça de Rius i Taulet

Across Travessera de Gràcia, **Plaça del Sol** is another typically lively, friendly plaça, successfully remodelled in the 1980s. There

200 C4 · Fontana, Joanic · 22, 24, 25, 27, 28, 31, 32

Gràcia is a village within the city

are several bars and night-spots, and the café terraces are great vantage points for watching impromptu soccer matches, *sardana* dances and *castell* rehearsals. Not far from here, reached across Carrer Gran de Gràcia, is **Mercat de la Llibertat** (1893), a magnificent Modernist market hall designed by Gaudí's assistant Francesc Berenguer.

Gràcia's most celebrated sight, **Casa Vicens** (Carrer de les Carolines 24), is situated a little way up the main street. It was one of Gaudí's first commissions in Barcelona, built between 1883 and 1888 as a summer house for the tile manufacturer Manuel Vicens. When Gaudí first visited the site, he found a yellow zinnia flower and adopted it as the motif for the thousands of tiles that clad the exterior of the Moorish-style building. A palm leaf, also discovered on the ground, inspired the fantastic iron railings that fence in the courtyard (and which were also used to great effect in Parc Güell). The house is now privately owned and the interior cannot be visited, though you may be able to peek through the windows at the lavish smoking room.

The tile-clad Casa Vicens was Gaudí's first commission in Barcelona

TAKING A BREAK

The food is as no-nonsense as the formica-and-leatherette décor at the extremely popular **Envalira** (Plaça del Sol 13, tel: 93 218 58 13). Fish and seafood cooked to Catalan, Basque and Galician recipes loom large on the reassuringly predictable menu. The generous portions of rice-based dishes come highly recommended, as do the salads and sausages. Prices are moderate and service is brisk.

GRÀCIA: INSIDE INFO

Top tips If you want an itinerary to see the best of Gràcia, follow the Gràcia walk ➤ 173–175.

- The **Festa Gran de Gràcia**, a week-long festival, starts on 15 August. The streets are decked out with thematic decorations and Graciencs party the night away. The opening ceremony is a colourful and noisy spectacle of *castells* (where young men stand on each other's shoulders to create a human tower), giants and other traditional Catalan festivities.

8

Parc Güell

Built as part of an idealistic dream, Parc Güell bristles with Gaudí's secretive symbolism and daring devices, a showcase for his inventiveness.

In 1900, Eusebi Güell, inspired by the garden-cities that had sprung up in London's suburbs, commissioned Gaudí to work on a design for a new residential area away from the city centre. Güell's plan for an estate with recreational areas and 60 houses, the design of which was to be entrusted to other architects, was snubbed by wealthy locals. Only a couple of the proposed houses, including the one where Gaudí briefly lived (now the Casa Museu Gaudí), were ever built, leaving the park as an expensive ornament later bought by the city.

The ceremonial staircase leading from the park's main entrance to the Sala Hipóstila

201 D5
Carrer d'Olot
Daily 10–9; closes 8 pm, Apr and Sep; 7 pm, Mar and Oct; 6 pm, Nov–Mar
Lesseps, Vallcarca
24, 25

Casa Museu Gaudí
201 D5
Parc Guell, Carrer del Carmel
93 219 38 11
Daily 10–8, May–Sep; 10–6, rest of year
Moderate

Inside the Walls

The 15ha (37-acre) park has several gates (the original intention was to have seven, like the ancient city of Thebes), but the most dramatic is the **main entrance** on Carrer d'Olot, most conveniently reached by bus 24 and 25. The tremendous iron railings of the gate are built to the same palm-leaf design as those at the Casa Vicens (► 109), and there are two fairy-tale **gatehouses** at the entrance: one is shaped like an elephant, with four thickset pillars for legs and a howdah of ceramic roof-tiles perched on top. One of its chimneys could be the elephant's trunk, held upright, while another is modelled on a hallucinogenic toadstool, the fly agaric; other stacks are the spitting image of the morel, a delicacy in Catalonia.

The Sala Hipóstila was designed as a market-place

Inside the gates, a **ceremonial staircase** leads up towards the Sala Hipóstila, the park's centre-piece. The brightly coloured, crenellated stairway is dominated by two colourful fountains: a salamander – symbolising alchemy – dribbles water from its mouth while, above it, a bronze-horned serpent's head, representing the staff of Aesculapius, the Greek god of healing, leers out from the Catalan flag's red and yellow stripes. At the top of the staircase is a bench in the form of a tile-rimmed gaping mouth. Designed so that it is shady in the summer and sunny in the winter, it is the perfect place to stop and look down upon the park's incredible entrance.

Signs and Symbols

The wavy edge of the Sala Hipóstila's upper terrace forms a series of benches

Gaudí intended the **Sala Hipóstila** to be the garden-city's market-place. Eighty-six Doric columns support the roof, which is decorated with four sun-shaped disks, composed of kaleidoscopic shards of tile, bits of bottle and fragments of stone, representing the four seasons. Encircling them are smaller circles representing the moon in various phases. Figures from Greek mythology, Christian emblems, Sanskrit script, Egyptian symbols and Old Testament characters are among the embellishments.

Forming a parapet around the edge of the open space above the market-place are the distinctive **wavy benches**; their multicoloured curves form niches like theatre-boxes, making a perfect spot to enjoy the fabulous views of the park and city stretching to the sea below.

Gaudí's gurgling salamander fountain, an unmissable feature of the ceremonial staircase

Equally impressive is the labyrinth of **serpentine viaducts and porticoes** that hugs the wooded hills on which the park is built. The organic-looking columns holding them up are shaped like crinkly palm trunks or twisted-stemmed champagne glasses.

Salavador Dalí once wrote: "At the Parc Güell we entered grottoes through gates shaped like ox livers". He adored the surreal park and one of his favourite photographs of himself was taken in 1933 by the stupendous undulating bench. You'll want to follow suit.

The elaborate gatehouses at the entrance to Parc Güell

TAKING A BREAK

Although the bar on the main terrace is an essential stop for a drink and a sit-down while you take in the fabulous view, for more substantial refreshment it is worth taking a cab the short ride to **Can Travi Nou** (Carrer Jorge Manrique, tel: 93 428 03 01), an old Catalan farmhouse that is difficult to reach by public transport. Here you can enjoy traditional food in the shady garden or elegant interior: *mar i muntanya* dishes (meat and fish combined) are a speciality. It's hugely popular with family groups on Sundays.

PARC GÜELL: INSIDE INFO

Top tips **Avoid Sunday afternoons and public holidays** when the park is crowded.
• Views from the park are superb, so try to go on a clear day.

Hidden gem The **Capelya**, part Mallorcan watch-tower, part Druids' shrine, is a typical Gaudíesque folly. It lies slightly off the beaten track, to the left from the main entrance. You can't go inside but it's worth taking a look.

One to miss Unless you have plenty of time, don't bother with the **Casa Museu Gaudí** on the Carretera del Carmel, housing Gaudí memorabilia and some of his own furniture.

10

La Sagrada Família

Part hermit's grotto, part futuristic tower of Babel, the Temple Expiatori de la Sagrada Família (Expiatory Temple of the Holy Family) has to be seen to be believed. Salvador Dalí found the cathedral's cigar-shaped turrets as sensual as a woman's skin, French film director Jean Cocteau called it an "idea-scraper" as opposed to a sky-scraper, while English novelist George Orwell described it as one of the most hideous buildings he had ever set eyes upon. Decide for yourself who was right.

201 E2 Plaça de la Sagrada Família
93 207 30 31; www.sagradafamilia.org
Daily 9–8, Apr–Sep; 9–6, rest of year Sagrada Família
10, 19, 33, 34, 43, 44, 50, 51, 101
Moderate

EXCELSIS
HOSANNA

A Life's Work

In 1883 the young Antoni Gaudí took over from the original architect, Francisco de Villar, who had planned a run-of-the-mill neo-Gothic pile. Gaudí, a fervent Catholic and iconoclastic young architect, had other ideas: he envisaged a "people's cathedral", a project more ambitious and original than anything hitherto conceived. He devoted the rest of his life to the cathedral's construction and was still working on the plans when he was run over by a tram in 1926. Almost a century later, his great project is still a long way from completion. Many locals and visitors feel that the cathedral should have been left alone when Gaudí died, while others are pleased that Gaudí's vision is continuing and evolving. The jury is still out.

Left and previous page: The Sagrada Família, Gaudí's visionary project, is still a work in progress

Grand Plans

During Gaudí's lifetime, only the crypt, apse, Nativity Façade and one of the bell-towers were completed. After his death, controversy raged over whether or not the work should continue. Since 1952 the Passion Façade has been added and there are now eight towers, clad in ceramic mosaics which spell out the Latin prayer *Sanctus, Sanctus, Sanctus, Hosanna in Excelsis* (Holy, Holy, Holy, Glory to God in the Highest). The plans include four more spires and a colossal central tower, 170m (560 feet) tall, representing Christ. Four domes at each corner will symbolise the Evangelists, and the nave will be filled in, making it probably the only cathedral to be built inside-out. Finally, the west façade, dedicated to the Celestial Glory, will be linked by a bridge across Carrer de Mallorca to an open atrium – once an entire block of houses has been demolished to make way for it.

Nativity Façade

For the best views of the Nativity Façade, the cathedral's *pièce de résistance*, do not enter the cathedral site but cross Carrer de la Marina to reach the small park in Plaça Gaudí. The façade is dedicated to the birth and early life of Christ. Its three doorways – representing Faith, Hope and Charity – resemble those of a Gothic cathedral that has melted in a furnace. They drip with detail, more like the natural

The footbridge linking two towers of the Nativity Façade affords great views of the site

Gaudí's Nativity Façade (top) literally drips with detail, while Subirachs's Passion Façade (above) is an exercise in straight lines

excrescences of a cave than the ornaments of a church. Above the central Nativity scene, look out for the wingless angels with their elongated bronze trumpets; they are said to have been modelled on guardsmen practising near the cathedral site. High above the doorway and nestling between the towers is the Tree of Life, a green ceramic cypress studded with white doves. Beneath it is an equally striking white pelican feeding its young. At least 36 different birds and 30 species of plants have been identified in the mosaic of the façade.

Passion Façade

The entrance to the cathedral is at the opposite end of the site to the Nativity Façade, facing Plaça Sagrada Família. It leads straight to the Passion Façade, completed in 1990 by the modern Catalan sculptor Josep Maria Subirachs. The towers are built to Gaudí's design, but the statues below (which tell the story of Christ's Passion and death, from the Last Supper to the crucifixion) are angular and rigid in contrast to Gaudí's flowing, organic style. The façade has created much controversy, with some people likening the figures to characters from a science-fiction film. Many argue, though, that Gaudí would have approved and that he always intended the cathedral to be built by different generations in changing styles.

A detail from the post-Gaudí Passion Façade

Inside the Church

Much of the interior still resembles a building site, as work continues to complete La Sagrada Família before the centenary of Gaudí's death in 2026. You can see some of the plans in the cathedral museum, which is situated in the crypt and reached from an entrance beside the Passion Façade. In one of the chapels, dedicated to Our Lady of Carmen, Gaudí's simple slab tomb lies at the feet of a statue of Mary, inscribed pithily in Latin: *Antonius Gaudí Cornet, Reusensis* (from Reus, the town where he was born in 1852).

TAKING A BREAK

For great views of the Sagrada Familia try any of the many **bars and pizzerias** with a terrace along Avinguda de Gaudí. None of them stands out, but you can feast your eyes on Gaudí's most celebrated building as you snack.

Gaudí's provocative crooked pillars in the crypt

LA SAGRADA FAMÍLIA: INSIDE INFO

Top tips Do **climb one of the towers**, either by lift or a long spiral staircase, for a close-up view of the spires. These multicoloured pinnacles have been compared to everything from hock bottles to billiard cues and are one of Barcelona's most emblematic sights. **Arrive early**, though, to have any chance of climbing the staircase in the Nativity Façade.

- Don't forget to **bring binoculars** to get a better look at the finer detailing, especially the pinnacles of the spires.
- There are **two lifts**, one at either end of the building, though the views are better from the Nativity Façade.

Hidden gems True to character, Gaudí slipped in hundreds of **symbols and private jokes**. Look at the base of the two main columns on the Nativity Façade; **a turtle** with flippers bears the seaward pillar and **a tortoise** with paws the landward one. **Chameleons**, among Gaudí's favourite creatures, can be seen carved in the stonework all over the cathedral.

At Your Leisure

2 Fundació Antoni Tàpies

This wonderful red-brick building, built for the Montaner i Simon publishing house in the 1880s by Modernist master Lluís Domènech i Montaner, houses the contemporary art foundation set up by Antoni Tàpies (➤ 27). The ornate façade is crowned by one of his sculptures, *Nuvol i Cadira* (Cloud and Chair), which looks as though he went berserk with a tonne of barbed wire. Inside, the immaculate galleries are hung either with Tàpies's own paintings – he has dominated Catalan art ever since Miró's death – or temporary exhibitions of guest artists. Tàpies himself favours huge canvases, mostly painted in earthy colours.

200 B1 · Carrer d'Aragó 255 · 93 487 03 15 · Tue–Sun 10–8 · Passeig de Gràcia · 7, 16, 17, 20, 22, 24, 28, 43, 44 · Moderate

3 Museu Egipci

The treasures at Spain's only museum devoted to Egyptian art span more than 4,000 years, from simple Predynastic vases to the striking *Golden Lady*, a stucco-and-goldleaf artefact dating from Roman times. Statuettes are the privately-owned museum's forte, made of a variety of materials including wood, bronze and limestone. They depict a pantheon of deities and sacred mammals and birds such as jackals, ibises and baboons. The mummy collection features cats, falcons and a baby crocodile as well as humans, while a set of wooden and terracotta funerary masks and sarcophagi will no doubt catch your eye. Among the gorgeous jewellery on show, the fabulous golden head of Osiris stands out – a bronze statue of the same goddess is equally remarkable.

Tàpies's work *Nuvol i Cadira* (Cloud and Chair) crowns the Fundació Antoni Tàpies

The golden head of the goddess Osiris at the Museu Egipci

The museum has an excellent shop, a bright terrace café and interesting temporary exhibits. The host of activities it organises include evening animations in which costumed actors bring the whole place to life.

200 B1 Carrer de València 284 93 488 01 88; www.fundclos.com Mon–Sat 10–8, Sun 10–2. Guided visits in English Fri 5 pm Passeig de Gràcia 7, 16, 17, 20, 22, 24, 28, 39, 43, 44, 45, 47 Moderate

4 Fundació Francisco Godia

Opened in 2000, the Fundació Francisco Godia is a welcome addition to Barcelona's already rich variety of museums. Francisco Godia (1921–90), local playboy and Formula One racing-driver, thought "driving fast was the most beautiful thing in the world", but he also had an excellent eye for paintings and sculpture. The result is this impeccably displayed collection.

In the first room as you enter the museum you can see a short video about the man dubbed "Paco, the Gentleman Driver". You'll also see a collection of memorabilia, consisting essentially of cups and driving gloves.

Beyond are Gothic masterpieces, such as the 14th-century *Virgin of Humility* attributed to Llorenç Saragossa, and 20th-century paintings and sculptures by Julio González and Antoni Tàpies. The cabinet of Spanish ceramics is dominated by the 15th-century Islamic-influenced plates from Manises. *At the Racecourse* (1905) by Ramon Casas, in the last room, encapsulates the Noucentisme movement.

200 B1 Carrer de València 284 93 272 31 80; www.fundacionfgodia.org Wed–Mon 10–8. Guided visits noon Sat and Sun Passeig de Gràcia 7, 16, 17, 20, 22, 24, 28, 39, 43, 44, 45, 47 Moderate

Five Beautiful Modernist Doorways

- **Casa Comalat** at Avinguda Diagonal 442 (corner of Carrer de Córsega).
- **Casa Jaume Forn** at Carrer de Roger de Llúria 52 (corner of Carrer de València).
- **Casa Ramon Casas** at Passeig de Gràcia 96.
- **Farmàcia Bolós** at Rambla de Catalunya 77 (corner of Carrer de València).
- **Farmàcia Puigoriol** at Carrer de Mallorca 312.

A portrait of Francisco Godia, one of the works at the Fundació Francisco Godia

8 7 9 6 5 10 2 3 4 1

The chapel-like entrance of the Hospital de la Santa Creu i de Sant Pau

6 Casa-Taller Durancamps

Rafael Durancamps (1891–1979) was one of Catalonia's leading 20th-century painters, and this small museum reproduces his workshop and, through its permanent collection and temporary exhibits, offers an overview of his elegant work. In the 1920s he settled in Paris where he met Picasso, but his style remained one of unadulterated realism, with the still life, notably depicting food (fish, lard and sprouting onions are just three of the more unusual subjects), at the heart of his production. Artistically conservative, he was undoubtedly influenced by Tintoretto, in his use of tones, and Cézanne, in the clarity of the forms. The stylish salon of his Paris apartment is also reproduced, adding a human touch to the exhibit.

200 B2
Avinguda Diagonal 407, entresol 1a
93 415 39 11
Tue, Thu–Sat 10–1:30 **Diagonal**
6, 7, 15, 16, 17, 22, 24, 27, 28, 32, 33, 34
Free

For Kids

- Two of Gaudí's spectacular creations, **Parc Güell** (► 110–112) and **La Sagrada Família** (► 113–117).
- The **Festa Gran de Gràcia** in mid-August (► 109).

9 Hospital de la Santa Creu i de Sant Pau

Definitely in the running for the world's most beautiful hospital, this marvellous garden-city infirmary was begun by Lluís Domènech i Montaner in

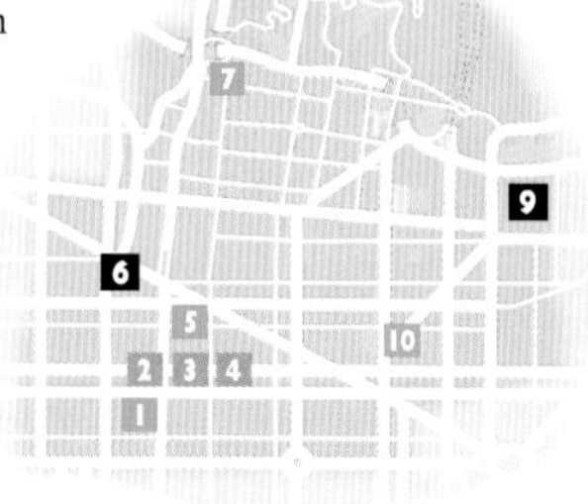

1901 and was eventually completed by his son Pere in 1930. The concept behind the design was that hospitals could be functional without being depressing or uncomfortable. It replaced the Antic Hospital de la Santa Creu in El Raval, where Gaudí died in 1926. Each of the 30-odd mosaic-covered pavilions is unique in design and designated as a specialist ward. The main reception building is a masterpiece of stone, ceramics and stained glass; wander around the park, admiring the Modernist craftsmanship and incredible detail.

Since the hospital doesn't meet the requirements of 21st-century medicine, departments are gradually being relocated to a new building. However, given its UNESCO World Heritage Site status, the building's future is guaranteed.

201 off F3 Carrer de Sant Antoni Maria Claret 167 93 291 90 00 Hospital de Sant Pau 15, 19, 20, 35, 45, 47, 50, 51, 92, N1, N4

Off the Beaten Track

A luxuriant cypress maze, with a statue of Eros at its centre (above), is the central element of romantic **Parc del Laberint**, tucked away in the northwestern Horta district of the city. Begun at the end of the 18th century by the eccentric Marquis of Llúpia, the park was designed to symbolise the game of frivolous love. The sumptuous neo-Mozarabic mansion, an unusual moss garden, a romantic canal with a rustic bridge, and a magnificent panorama of the city add to the appeal of the gardens. Note that amorous couples often take advantage of the privacy afforded by the maze.

(off 201 F5, Carrer del Germans Desvalls, open daily 10–9, in summer; 10–6, in winter; 10–7, in spring and autumn, Metro Montbau, admission inexpensive. Free on Wed and Sun).

Where to... Eat and Drink

Prices
Expect to pay per person for a meal, excluding drinks
€ under €15 €€ €15–35 €€€ over €35

Botafumeiro €€€
Mariscos Botafumeiro are an unforgettable experience at this legendary and madly expensive Galician seafood restaurant. Plate after plate of the best shellfish in Spain are placed before you by the white-jacketed staff, who wait on tables both in the bar and in the series of elegant dining rooms to the rear. Patronised by the international business community and by Spanish royalty, the establishment prides itself on the quality and freshness of its fish and seafood, much of which is flown in daily from Galicia and stored live in holding tanks near the restaurant's entrance. There is a lengthy list of fish dishes on the menu, plus a few token meat dishes.

200 B3 Carrer Gran de Gràcia 81 93 218 42 30 Daily 1–1; closed three weeks in Aug Fontana

Flash Flash €
Students of 1960s design will be in their element at Barcelona's pioneer designer bar. The décor is still all-white with leatherette booths and curvaceous corners. *Tortillas* (omelettes) are the house speciality, available in more than 50 varieties, savoury and sweet. A choice of burgers, salads and sandwiches completes the menu.

200 B3 Carrer de la Granada del Penedès 25 93 237 09 90 Daily 1 pm–1 am Diagonal

El Glop €€
The name means "The Sip". This lively Catalan taverna with a sliding roof serves traditional chargrilled meat as well as salads and seasonal vegetables. Specialities include snails as well as chorizo in wine. Wine is cheap and powerful. El Glop has become so successful that there are now two other branches; **El Nou Glop** in Carrer de Montmany, is just along the street.

201 D3 Carrer de Montmany 46 93 213 70 58 Tue–Sun 1–4 pm, 8 pm–1 am Joanic

El Nou Glop
201 D3 Carrer de Montmany 49 93 219 70 59

El Glop de la Rambla,
200 B1 Rambla de Catalunya 65 93 487 00 97

L'Illa de Gràcia €
You need to book on weekends to get a table at this cheap-and-cheerful vegetarian restaurant. Specialities include pancake with mushrooms, cream and pepper, as well as a good range of salads, omelettes and pasta and rice dishes.

200 C3 Carrer de Sant Domènec 19 93 238 02 29 Tue–Fri 1–4, 9–midnight, Sat–Sun 2–4, 9–midnight; closed late Aug Fontana

Jean-Luc Figueras €€€
Jean-Luc Figueras is a Frenchman of Catalan descent, and his modern cooking combines the best of both traditions. In the elegant setting of a spacious 19th-century villa, you can choose from an inspired menu. Dishes include tuna with caviar and vanilla oil or leg of Les Landes duck with pears and liquorice.

Leave room for one of the outstanding desserts. The Gourmet Menu is probably the best way to sample this inventive cuisine.

200 C2 Carrer de Santa Teresa 10 93 415 28 77 Mon–Fri 1:30–3:30, 8:30–11:30, Sat 8:30–11:30 Diagonal

Laurak €€€

Sophisticated Basque cuisine is on offer at this discreet restaurant, accompanied by an outstanding wine list. Whereas the service and ambience could be described as frosty, the food is faultless, with main dishes such as steak with cabbage, black pudding and apple sauce, and delicious desserts, including a memorable Idiazábal cheese mousse with quince and cider coulis. If the choice proves too baffling you can always go for the *menú degustación*, leaving the selection to the chef.

200 B3 Carrer de la Granada del Penedès 14–16 93 218 71 65 Mon–Sat 1–4, 9–11:30 Diagonal

L'Olivé €€

Don't expect to turn up for dinner without booking at this very popular Catalan restaurant. Frequented by office workers at lunchtime, it specialises in seafood such as rice in squid ink, and in mountain specialities including rabbit with mushrooms. Soberly garbed in grey, the waiters are helpful and extremely efficient. The house wine is very drinkable and the *crema catalana* (➤ 14) commendable.

200 B1 Carrer de Balmes 47 93 452 19 90 Mon–Sat 1–4, 8:30–midnight, Sun 1–4 Universitat

Roig Robí €€€

Mercè Navarro is not just one of Barcelona's few women chefs, and a self-taught one at that, she is one of the best in a city that takes its eating as seriously as its design. She serves imaginative food in a pair of flower-filled dining rooms. In summer, the glass doors open onto a shady courtyard, a perfect place for outdoor eating. Writers, artists and politicians are among the regulars who come to eat seasonal, market-fresh dishes such as lobster with rice and chicken, stuffed with foie gras. Prices are high but the value is exceptional.

200 B3 Carrer de Sèneca 20 93 218 92 22; email: roigrobi@mhp.es Mon–Sat 1:30–4, 9–11:30 Diagonal

La Valenciana €

This famous *orxateria* and *torroneria* (nougat shop) is one of the few places left which serves a malt-flavoured *granizado*, a traditional drink sipped through crushed ice, as well as *orxata*, a cold drink made with crushed tiger nuts. You can choose from a selection of light snacks and then indulge in excellent homemade ice creams. An inexpensive special lunch is also served in relaxed surroundings.

196 A5 Carrer d'Aribau 16 bis 93 317 27 71 Mon–Sun 8:30 am–10:30 pm, Fri–Sat 9 am–2 am. Opening times may vary Universitat

BARS AND CAFÉS

La Gran Bodega €

At this inexpensive, popular tapas bar you can test your skills by drinking with the *porrón*, a glass jug with a long spout, which (if your aim is good) pours the wine down your throat.

200 A2 Carrer de València 193 93 453 10 53 Daily 8:30 am–1 am Passeig de Gràcia

Laie Llibreria Cafè €

The comfortable, informal café on the floor above the well-stocked Laie Llibreria bookshop has its own entrance. This was Barcelona's first bookshop-café, and you can sit and read, or linger and chat over cakes, coffee and a good-value lunch. In fine weather there is verandah seating and occasionally in the evenings you can hear live jazz.

196 C5 Carrer de Pau Claris 85 93 302 73 10 Mon–Fri 9 am–1 am, Sat 10 am–1 am Urquinaona

Where to... Shop

The Eixample – in particular the Passeig de Gràcia, and the Rambla de Catalunya, running parallel to it – is *the* place to come for a truly extravagant shopping session. Craftspeople and designers turn precious materials into wondrous creations, some of them exclusive to this designer-mad city. Good traditional grocers' shops somehow manage not to look out of place amid this luxury thanks to their sumptuous Modernist fronts.

FASHION

Ready-to-wear clothes for all ages and both sexes, by local and international designers from Armani to Zegna can be found at **Gonzalo Comella** (Passeig de Gràcia 6, tel: 93 416 66 00, Metro: Catalunya), while Galician designer Adolfo Domínguez, "inventor" of the casually crumpled look for linen suits and cotton shirts, has his smart flagship outlet at Passeig de Gràcia 32 (tel: 93 487 41 70). **Vermont** (Rambla de Catalunya 64, tel: 93 215 19 43, Metro: Passeig de Gràcia) specialises in ladies' sandals. For charming babywear try **Jacadi** (Rambla de Catalunya 79, tel: 93 487 58 40, Metro: Passeig de Gràcia). **Santacana** (Rambla de Catalunya 90–94, tel: 93 215 04 13, Metro: Diagonal) is *the* place for lingerie and swimwear. **Groc** (Rambla de Catalunya 100, tel: 93 215 01 80, Metro: Diagonal) is an outlet for Miró's design clothing but also displays some fabulous silver jewellery. Barcelona hero **Antoni Miró** has his own shop at Carrer Consell de Cent 349 (tel: 93 487 06 70, Metro: Passeig de Gràcia), selling his flatteringly loose-fitting jackets and figure-hugging cocktail dresses, while **David Valls** (Carrer de València 235, tel: 93 487 12 85, Metro: Passeig de Gràcia) does a lovely line in New Age knitwear. **Muxart** (Carrer Rosselló 230, tel: 93 488 10 64, Metro: Diagonal) sells some highly sophisticated leather goods, as well as great shoes for men and women. Plunge into **Bulevard Rosa**, a modern shopping mall at Passeig de Gràcia 53 (Metro: Passeig de Gràcia): here you will find **Diesel**, **Vertigo Cometas**, **Joiell** and **Ona**, selling trend-setting clothing, colourful kites and silver jewellery. Some of the best footwear in the city is to be found at **Lottusse** (Rambla de Catalunya 103, tel: 93 215 89 11, Metro: Diagonal), but **Joan Sagrera** (Rambla de Catalunya 104, tel: 93 215 43 86, Metro: Diagonal) is a very close rival. Still on shoes, try **Camper** (Rambla de Catalunya 122, tel: 93 217 23 84, Metro: Passeig de Gràcia) for fashionable and ultra-comfortable slip-ons and lace-ups.

BOOKS, BANGLES AND BAGS

If you fancy reading more about Barcelona, try the comprehensive travel bookstore **Altaïr** (Gran Via de les Corts Catalanes 616, tel: 93 342 71 71, Metro: Universitat). **Crisol** (Carrer Consell de Cent 341, tel: 93 315 21 31, Metro: Passeig de Gràcia) is good for English-language books and press – the international press stand is conveniently open on Sundays and holidays. All manner of publications are sold alongside records and endless cups of cappuccino at **Laie Llibreria** (➤ 123). The store stays open until 1 am and sometimes hosts evening jazz sessions. Seek out the other browser-friendly branch at the CCCB (➤ 64). Splendid surroundings by Josep Lluís Sert (1934) set off the extra-special jewellery at **Roca** (Passeig de Gràcia 18, tel: 93 318 32 66, Metro: Passeig de Gràcia). **Bagués** (Passeig de Gràcia 41, Metro: Passeig de

Gràcia), housed in Puig i Cadafalch's Casa Amatller, is another well-located jeweller. On the ground floor of the nearby Casa Lleó Morera (➤ 102) is the prestigious national chain **Loewe** (Passeig de Gràcia 35, tel: 93 216 04 00, Metro: Passeig de Gràcia), well known for expensive leather.

In the **Bulevard dels Antiquaris**, a cavernous mall at Passeig de Gràcia 55 (Metro: Passeig de Gràcia), you'll find everything from art nouveau furniture to crystal chandeliers. It shares a building with the **Centre Català d'Artesania**, a showroom for up-and-coming and well-established Catalan designers alike. **Bd Ediciones de Diseño** (Carrer de Mallorca 291, tel: 93 458 69 09, Metro: Passeig de Gràcia, Diagonal, Provença), suitably housed in a fabulous building by Domènech i Montaner, is yet another place selling designer goods. There's even an amusing **Museu del Perfum** (perfume museum) at **Regia** (Passeig de Gràcia 39, tel: 93 216 01 21, open Mon–Fri 10:30–1:30, 4:30–7:30, Sat 11–1:30, Metro: Passeig de Gràcia), where among other sweet-smelling exhibits is a scent bottle designed by Salvador Dalí.

FOOD AND DRINK

Colmado Quílez (Rambla de Catalunya 63, tel: 93 215 23 56, Metro: Passeig de Gràcia) is a fabulous grocer – come here for wine, ham and cheeses. **La Taste** (Rambla de Catalunya 75, tel: 93 487 15 68, Metro: Passeig de Gràcia), stocks everything from ceramics to wine. Equally luxurious are the delicatessen, cakes and ice-creams tempting you at **Pastisseria Maurí** (Rambla de Catalunya 102, tel: 93 215 10 20, Metro: Diagonal, Provença). Last but not least, **Queviures Múrria** (Carrer Roger de Llúria 85, tel: 93 215 57 89, Metro: Passeig de Gràcia) is not only a great looker on the outside, but also serves up farm cheeses and selected wines with style.

Where to... Be Entertained

Despite the area's outwardly staid appearance, night-life in the Eixample and Gràcia is anything but dull. You'll find some of the city's most sophisticated nightclubs here, plus some outstanding cinemas screening English-language films with subtitles. This is also where Barcelona's vibrant gay life is focused. In the area around Consell de Cent (where it is crossed by Casanova and Muntaner), there are so many gay venues that the area has been dubbed the "Gayxample". For the latest information about what's on, check out *Nois* magazine (www.revistanois.com) available at Rambla kiosks.

NIGHTCLUBS

In Gràcia, one of the liveliest nightspots is **Blue** (Carrer Madrazo 49, tel: 93 415 88 84, Metro: Fontana). Blue is indeed the colour here, a mix of marine-hued seating and turquoise décor, but the mood is definitely upbeat every day of the week. **KGB** (Alegre de Dalt 55, tel: 93 210 59 06, Metro: Joanic) pounds to the sound of house till dawn in a converted warehouse, but it's also a great venue for avant-garde pop and rock gigs. The slick but fun nightclub **Otto Zutz** (Carrer Lincoln 15, tel: 93 238 07 22, Metro: Fontana) is one of Gràcia's old favourites, but dress smartly to get in. Live jazz is an occasional extra; closed Sunday and Monday.

In the Eixample, **Salsa Buenavista** (Carrer Rosselló 217, tel: 93 237 65 28, Metro: Diagonal) is the place to hear and dance to salsa from Wednesday to Sunday; on weekdays you can even learn for free from 10 pm onwards. **La Cova del Drac** (Carrer Vallmajor 33, tel: 93 200 70 32, FGC: Muntaner, buses: 14, 58, 64, Nitbus 8) is more jazz-oriented, with the odd jam session usually on Wednesday, and more pop or folk sounds on other nights. Two big names in Eixample nightlife are **Luz de Gas** (Carrer Muntaner 246, tel: 93 209 7711, buses: 6, 7, 15, 58, 64, Nitbus 8) and **Nick Havanna** (Carrer Rosselló 208, tel: 93 215 65 91, Metro: Diagonal): the former serves up concerts and disco in slightly kitsch surroundings, while Row Club is perhaps Barcelona's most famous designer bar and disco. Opened in the late 1980s, it remains elegant and intriguing, with smartly attired staff, banks of TV screens and all manner of special effects. Techno and house dominate the music. Located in the basement at Hotel Omm (➤ 38), **Ommsession** has quickly risen to the top of Barcelona's night-spot charts and is worth checking out. Finally, if the foxtrot or jive are your kind of rhythms, cha-cha-cha your way to the **Sala Cibeles** (Carrer Corsega 363, tel: 93 457 38 77, Metro: Diagonal).

Gay Nightlife

The stylish **Ouí Café** (Carrer Consell de Cent 247, Metro: Universitat) or **Punto BCN** (Carrer Muntaner 63, tel: 93 453 61 23, Metro: Universitat) are good places to start the evening. Later, head for **Arena Madre** (Carrer Balmes 32, Metro: Universitat), a popular gay venue, or its more mixed sibling **Arena VIP** (Gran Via de les Corts Catalanes 593, tel: 93 487 83 42, Metro: Universitat). **Ambar** (Carrer Casanova 71, tel: 93 323 10 00, Metro: Urgell) is one of the newest on the block and is usually packed to overflowing, while **Martins** (Passeig de Gràcia 130, tel: 93 218 71 67, Metro: Diagonal) is the grand old doyen of gay discos – its three floors still become packed every weekend. **Metro** (Carrer Sepúlveda 158, tel: 93 323 52 27, Metro: Universitat) is another megadisco, open all night, every night.

The drag-show restaurant is a quintessentially Barcelona experience. Of several dotted around the Eixample, the two best are the **Miranda** (Casanova 30, tel: 93 453 52 49, Metro: Universitat) – just look for the leopard-skin façade – and the **Diva** (Carrer Diputació 172, tel: 93 454 63 98, Metro: Universitat).

CINEMA

The **Casablanca** (Passeig de Gràcia 115, tel: 93 218 43 45, Metro: Diagonal) screens offbeat films, often English-language, with subtitles, and the **Meliès** (Carrer Villaroel 102, tel: 93 451 00 51, Metro: Urgell) runs great retrospectives dedicated to themes or directors.

Gràcia's **Verdi** remains one of the city's leading movie-houses. The original branch (Carrer Verdi 32, tel: 93 237 05 16, Metro: Fontana) and the newer four-screen **Verdi Park** (Carrer Torrijos 49, tel: 93 238 79 90, Metro: Fontana) show a blend of golden oldies and recent releases, with a high proportion of English-language films.

OTHER ENTERTAINMENTS

CAT (Travessera de St Antoni 6–8, tel: 93 218 44 85, Metro: Fontana) hosts home-grown and international folk music. The **Teatre Lliure – Lliure de Gràcia** (Carrer Montseny 47, tel: 93 218 92 51, Metro: Fontana) is an institution. Although the company moved into brand new surroundings on Montjuic (➤ 144), the old theatre is still used for smaller productions.

If you're in the city in the summer months, don't miss **La Pedrera de Nit** (➤ 107); you can listen to music, admire the cityscape and drink *cava* on the rooftop of the Casa Milà.

Montjuïc to Sants

Getting Your Bearings

Montjuïc, a steep, landscaped bluff looming to the south of the city, revels in the nickname of Magic Mountain – a survivor from Celtiberian and Roman times when a fort and temple to Jupiter crowned its heights. For centuries Montjuïc isolated Barcelona from the rest of the world and, with its cemetery and awe-inspiring castle from which Spanish troops subjugated their colony, it had grim associations. Since the 1929 International Exhibition, however, its outlook has been far brighter: designer pavilions stand cheek-by-jowl with exhibition palaces, and Olympic stadiums with concert halls.

One of the finest approaches to Montjuïc is by funicular railway, accessed from the Avinguda Paral.lel Metro station. The Drassanes, the city's medieval shipyards, lie to the east of Montjuïc at the port end of the Ramblas, close to the station and make a convenient place to start your day's sightseeing. The Drassanes have been transformed into Barcelona's highly acclaimed Museu Marítim, which provides a fascinating testimony to the city's seafaring past.

Once on Montjuïc, you'll find two of the city's greatest art museums, one dedicated to Joan Miró and his colourful works, the other showing off a world-renowned collection of Catalan Romanesque frescoes, rescued from decaying Pyrenean churches.

Previous page: Miró's *Dona i Ocell* statue at the Parc de Joan Miró

Below: Views from the Castell de Montjuïc

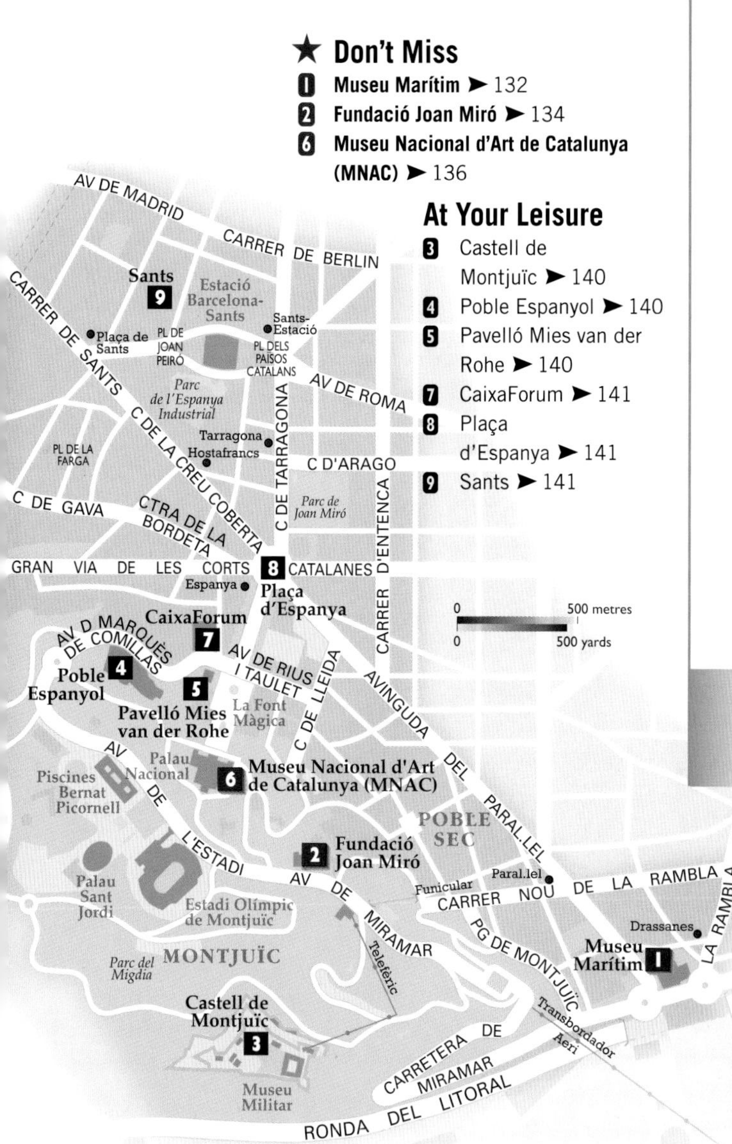

The Sants neighbourhood lies on the northern side of Montjuïc. Barcelona's main train station is located here, making the district the arrival point for many visitors to the city. Once highly industrialised, Sants has been the scene for some interesting urban-development projects (some more successful than others). Instead of factories and workshops, outdoor art, spacious squares and down-to-earth cafés await you, along with a pleasant laid-back atmosphere.

Travel up a mountain and down the other side for Romanesque and Gothic masterpieces, modern art and architecture, and an insight into Barcelona's maritime and military history. Be sure, though, to leave enough time to do justice to the superb collection of art at MNAC.

Montjuïc to Sants in a Day

9:30 am

After a leisurely start, wander down to the Drassanes (medieval royal shipyards) and the delightful café-restaurant, La Llotja (➤ 133), for a coffee-and-croissant breakfast. Then visit the outstanding 1 **Museu Marítim** (➤ 132–133), where Barcelona's seafaring history is laid out.

11:30 am

Exit the Drassanes along Carrer de Portal, past Columbian artist Fernando Botero's massive bronze of a podgy cat, *El Gat*, and continue up Avinguda del Paral.lel to the Metro station. Down in the subway you'll find the entrance to the funicular railway, which speeds you up to the 2 **Fundació Joan Miró** (➤ 134–135). An hour or so should suffice to see Joan Miró's works (right) and any temporary exhibition that is on. Either stop for lunch at the lovely café, or forge on to the Poble Espanyol for a choice of regional specialities – you might like to travel by bus (50 or 61).

1:00 pm

After a lazy lunch, explore the 4 **Poble Espanyol** (Spanish Village, ➤ 140). The many workshops here (right) provide a fertile hunting ground if you are looking for souvenirs to take home.

3:00 pm

Avinguda del Marquès de Comillas curves gracefully towards the city's fair and exhibition halls. Nip into the 5 **Pavelló Mies van der Rohe** (left, ➤ 140–141) for some Zen-like tranquillity, then head up the steps or escalators to the Palau Nacional, which houses the 6 **Museu Nacional d'Art de Catalunya** (MNAC, ➤ 136–139).

4:00 pm

The day's highlight, MNAC houses five major art collections: the pride and joy are the Romanesque frescoes. Leave time for the Gothic masterpieces, the Cambó Bequest, the Thyssen-Bornemisza Collection, or the modern section of 19th- and 20th-century artwork. It's impossible to see the whole lot in one go, so choose what takes your fancy.

7:00 pm

If you have any energy left over, head down to 8 **Plaça d'Espanya** (➤ 141) and explore 9 **Sants** (➤ 141), a great place for some pick-me-up tapas or a welcome drink. You could stay in Sants for the evening. In summer, don't miss the spectacular **Font Màgica** (➤ 141). Follow on with a Montjuïc nightclub or a concert at the **Palau Sant Jordi** (➤ 143).

0

Museu Marítim

Housed in the former royal shipyards, this is one museum which is worth a visit for the building alone. Built in the 13th century at the height of Catalonia's maritime power, the Drassanes Reials are both a triumph of civic Gothic architecture in Barcelona and the best surviving example of a medieval shipyard anywhere in the world. With soaring arches, elegant aisles and cavernous stone vaults, these remarkable medieval warehouses have all the appearance of a secular cathedral.

The yards were built to supply ships for the Catalan-Aragonese fleet at a time when the Crown of Aragón was expanding into a major Mediterranean empire. While other great seafaring cities such as Venice and Palermo destroyed their medieval shipyards, Barcelona continued to use them right up until the 18th century, and even as late as the Civil War, when they were put to use as an arsenal. Now brilliantly restored and under a single roof, the shipyards have housed the city's maritime museum since 1941.

The items on display cover the full history of seafaring, from ancient maps and compasses to models of fishing boats and actual vessels, such as the ***Flying Dutchman***, a racing sloop that helped Spain win a gold medal at the Barcelona Olympics. The exhibits are laid out in a logical sequence, but if time is short it is best to head for the central aisle, where there is a replica of

Above: The replica of the 16th-century warship *La Real*

Right: One of the antique figureheads on display on the upper floor

192 A1 · Avinguda de les Drassanes s/n · 93 342 99 20; www.diba.es/mmaritim
Daily 10–7; closed 1 and 6 Jan, 25 and 26 Dec · Drassanes
14, 18, 36, 38, 57, 59, 64, 91 · Top-rate café-restaurant · Moderate

La Real, the royal galley built here for John of Austria in 1568. It was this vessel, the flagship of the Christian fleet, that enabled the Holy League (Spain, Venice, Malta and the Papal States) to defeat the Ottoman Turks at the critical Battle of Lepanto on 7 October, 1571 – a battle which is seen as a turning point in the fortunes of the various Mediterranean empires. The replica, built in 1971 on the 400th anniversary of the battle, measures 60m (200 feet) in length and includes lifesize models of the 236 oarsmen needed to power the original. With its golden figurehead depicting Neptune astride a dolphin and its lavish gilt decoration, *La Real* looks more like a baroque altarpiece than a battleship.

For a close-up look at *La Real* follow **The Great Sea Adventure**, a free audio tour available in various languages. It includes a simulated sea storm and a reconstruction of the prototype submarine built by the Catalan inventor Narcís Monturiol.

The museum charts the history of navigation from primitive dug-outs to sophisticated sailing yachts

TAKING A BREAK

The museum's lofty arches are the inspired setting for **La Llotja** (tel: 93 302 64 02), and, in keeping with the period, you might find a few medieval-style dishes on the menu. The two-course set menu is good value for money.

MUSEU MARÍTIM: INSIDE INFO

Top tip Come here **early in the morning** before the museum gets crowded out by parties of school children.

Hidden gem Don't miss the **upper floor display** of a dozen or so carved figureheads, mostly from the 18th and 19th centuries.

2

Fundació Joan Miró

Joan Miró's playful sculptures and brightly coloured paintings are given the perfect setting in this purpose-built gallery. The building commands dreamy views across the city, and its white walls, terracotta flagstones and elegantly curved roofs lend it a pleasing Mediterranean aspect that complements Miró's work.

With his simple, bold designs and childlike use of primary colours, Joan Miró (1893–1983) seems to embody the artistic spirit of Barcelona. His works can be seen all over the city, from the mural at the airport to the pavement mosaic on the Ramblas (➤ 51) and the sculpture that dominates Parc de Joan Miró (➤ 135). Catalans have taken him to their hearts, perhaps because unlike Picasso he was actually born in the city. His striking abstract images have become symbols of the city, seen on everything from T-shirts and ashtrays to the branches of La Caixa bank, for whom he designed the logo.

A Spectrum of Work

This extensive collection, much of it donated by Miró himself, provides an excellent introduction for anyone unfamiliar with his work. In addition to 200 paintings, 150 sculptures and a series of vivid tapestries, the collection includes more than 5,000 sketches and all of his graphic works. Although there are large gaps, especially around the mid-life period, it is

The outdoor sculptures are one of the Fundació Joan Miró's main attractions

194 C3 ✉ Plaça de Neptú, Parc de Montjuïc
☎ 93 443 94 70; www.bcn.fjmiro.es ⏲ Tue–Sat 10–8, Sun and public holidays 10–2:30, Jul–Sep; Tue–Sat 10–7, rest of year; open till 9:30 pm on Thu all year round. Guided tours 12:20 Sat and Sun
Ⓜ Paral.lel plus Funicular de Montjuïc 🚌 50, 55, Bus Turístic (Blue)
🍴 Café-restaurant, excellent bookshop and giftshop ✋ Moderate

possible to trace Miró's artistic development from his childhood etchings and youthful experiments with Cubism to the emergence of his highly personal and instantly recognisable style, a blend of surrealism and abstract art.

The best of the early works are found in the Sala Joan Prats, named after Miró's friend and patron. These include ***Street in Pedralbes*** (1917) and ***Portrait of a Young Girl*** (1919), as well as the disturbing ***Man and Woman in Front of a Pile of Excrement*** (1935). His familiar themes start to emerge in paintings such as ***Morning Star*** (1940), though at the same time he was also working on ***Barcelona*** (1944), a powerful series of black-and-white lithographs inspired by the Civil War.

Strong colours and bold designs characterise Miró's work

The Sala Pilar Juncosa, named after Miró's wife, contains many of his later works, produced after he moved to Mallorca in 1956. Among the paintings here are ***Figure Before the Sun*** (1968) and ***Woman in the Night*** (1973), large canvases with simple lines and bold yellows and reds. This gallery also contains some of his best-known sculptures, including ***Sunbird*** (1968), in sparkling white Carrara marble. There are more sculptures on the rooftop terrace and in an adjoining sculpture garden.

TAKING A BREAK

After touring the gallery, most people make a beeline for its shady courtyard restaurant and café. Alternatively, walk back to the **Miramar Bar** (Avinguda Miramar 93, tel: 93 442 31 00) by the Funicular de Montjuïc. It serves basic snacks only, but you can take in the majestic vista across the port.

FUNDACIÓ JOAN MIRÓ: INSIDE INFO

Top tip From July to September an excellent **series of concerts** is held in the auditorium (➤ 144).

In more detail One of Miró's most famous sculptures can be seen in Parc de Joan Miró, across the Plaça d'Espanya at the foot of Montjuïc. On the site of the former *escorxador* (slaughterhouse) – hence the square's other name, Parc de l'Escorxador – the park is dominated by the gigantic ***Dona i Ocell*** (Woman and Bird), a tile-encrusted obelisk that has become one of the city's landmarks.

6

MNAC

The Museu Nacional d'Art de Catalunya (MNAC) has one of the finest collections of medieval art in Europe, boosted in late 2004 when two major art collections were moved here from other venues in the city: the Thyssen-Bornemisza collection of European masterpieces and a huge display of 19th- and 20th-century Catalan paintings, sculptures and furniture. All are housed in the Palau Nacional, a mock-baroque palace with an impressive dome built for the 1929 Exhibition.

Together with some fine examples of Catalan Gothic art, two priceless collections of old European masterpieces, and an exhibition of more modern creations, vivid Romanesque frescoes salvaged from crumbling Pyrenean churches are displayed in the museum's great galleries. These were stunningly laid out by Gae Aulenti – the Italian architect who metamorphosed an old Paris train station into the acclaimed Musée d'Orsay. An added attraction is the breathtaking view from the terrace, across Plaça d'Espanya and the city roofs to the mountain of Tibidabo.

Romanesque Galleries

You should start chronologically with the Romanesque galleries, divided into *ambits*, or areas, rather than rooms. In each *ambit* is an informative plan locating each church, with scale models, photos and ample explanations in English as well as Catalan.

Romanesque art is remarkable for its simplicity. In medieval times, many Catalan villagers were illiterate and the church walls would become a colourful story book, a "poor man's Bible" adorned with childlike images. Take, for example, the **apse from Santa Maria d'Àneu** (Ambit III), recovered from a remote Pyrenean valley: the all-knowing eyes on the stylised angel's wings are powerful symbols of God's power. The undoubted highlight, though, is the **set of murals from Sant Climent de Taüll** (Ambit V), which date from 1123 but remain as vivid as when they were painted. The figure of Christ in Majesty in the central apse is wonderfully expressive, with wide eyes, flowing hair and a book in his left hand, inscribed with the words *Ego Sum Lux Mundi* (I am the light of the world).

The12th-century apse mural from Sant Climent de Taüll is one of the museum's treasures

194 C4

Palau Nacional, Parc de Montjuïc

93 622 03 75; www.mnac.es

Tue–Sat 10–7, Sun and public holidays 10–2:30

Espanya

9, 13, 30, 50, 55, 57, 65, 91, 109, 157, 165

Moderate. Free first Thu of the month

Gothic Galleries

On the opposite side of the central hallway are the Gothic galleries, also divided into *ambits*. First are some colourful murals, more like medieval comic strips, recording the Catalan capture of Mallorca in 1229. They were rescued from several palaces along Barcelona's Carrer de Montcada, now home to the Museu Picasso (► 82–85). The subsequent rooms contain items ranging from chests and statues to coins and cabinets, along with a fine collection of mostly religious paintings from Catalonia and elsewhere in Europe.

One of the highlights, the **retable of St Barbara**, attributed to Gonçal Peris Sarrià (Ambit VIII), is a magical riot of colour and gold leaf, with fairytale castle turrets adding to its charm. The saint's quill pen and delicate crown are portrayed with the finest of brush strokes. In Ambit XII, look for Jaume Huguet's **retable of St Michael**, regarded as one of the finest examples of Gothic art. The richness of the archangel's attire and his insect-like wings make him a striking if somewhat disturbing figure. In the lower right-hand corner, you can make out bits of the dragon he's just killed.

Above: *The Virgin and Child with St Ines and St Barbara* is among the works by Jaume Huguet on display in Ambit XII

Must-sees

The five outstanding treasures in this treasure-trove of a museum are:

- The **apse from Santa Maria d'Àneu** (Romanesque, Ambit III).
- The **paintings from Sant Climent de Taüll** (Romanesque, Ambit V).
- Fra Angelico's tempera ***Madonna of Humility*** (Thyssen-Bornemisza collection).
- Jaume Huguet's **retable of St Michael** (Ambit XII).
- **Furniture** designed by Gaudí (19th- and 20th-century art, Rooms X–XIII).

Fra Angelico's Madonna of Humility alone makes a visit to MNAC worthwhile

Thyssen-Bornemisza Collection and Cambó Bequest

During the 1920s and 1930s, German industrialist Baron Heinrich amassed an outstanding collection of European art. In 1993, the Spanish State acquired the collection from his son, the Baron Hans Heinrich Thyssen-Bornemisza de Kaszon. Most of it went to Madrid, but part was kept in Barcelona, at first at the Monestir de Pedralbes (➤ 150–153) from where it was moved in late 2004.

The most important paintings – along with a few choice Gothic sculptures – belong to the Italian Trecento (14th century), though there are also some fine examples from the 15th and 16th centuries. Fra Angelico's tempera ***Madonna of Humility*** (*c*1435) is notable; in this majestic yet delicate work, the harmony of the composition, Mary's blue robes and the fine lily, a symbol of purity, offered to her by the infant Jesus, are simply perfect. The ***Nativity*** (1325) by Taddeo Gaddi, and the ***Madonna and Child*** (1340–5) by Bernardo Daddi, a pupil of Giotto, are both wonderful examples of the simplicity of 14th-century Italian art, albeit with the lavish use of gold paint. Lorenzo Monaco's harmonious tempera panel ***Madonna and Child Enthroned with Six Angels***

(1415–20) conveys intense emotion, while Veronese's ***Annunciation*** (1570) is a decoratively lyrical work that sums up the triumphant monumentalism of the 16th century. Among the handful of baroque paintings by artists from Italy, Holland, Flanders and Spain, Francisco de Zurbarán's intense ***Christ on the Cross*** (1630) stands out.

A smaller, but no less significant, collection of paintings was bequeathed to Barcelona by the influential **Cambó** family, and includes works by **Tiepolo, Goya and Rubens**. The collection is housed in its own galleries at the end of the Gothic galleries.

Art of the 19th and 20th centuries

Spanning the period from 1800 to the Spanish Civil War, and ranging from neo-classicism to Modernisme and Noucentisme, a return to classical forms as a backlash against the decadence of Modernisme, the collection includes paintings by great Catalonian artists such as bohemian Santiago Rusiñol (1861–1931) and Ramon Casas (1866–1932), who led the early Modernist painters with their evocative Parisian works, ***Laboratory at La Galette*** (1890) and ***Plein Air*** (1890), respectively (Room VI). Casas's beige-toned painting of himself and Pere Romeu ***On a Tandem*** (1897) has become an icon of late 19th-century art in Barcelona. Josep Clarà (1878–1958) was the finest exponent of Noucentiste sculpture. His ***Repose***, a marble with the purest of forms, was sculpted for the International Exhibition in 1929 (Room XIX). There are also some fabulous pieces of furniture and ornaments by **Gaudí** and Puig i Cadafalch that once graced the interiors of Casa Milà (➤ 105–107) and the Manzana de la Discòrdia (➤ 102–104) (Rooms X–XIII). Don't miss Gaudí's undulating wooden sofa from the Casa Batlló.

Ramon Casas and Pere Romeu riding their tandem at MNAC

TAKING A BREAK

There is a **café** in MNAC, but you may prefer to walk down to the far better one at the gleaming new CaixaForum complex (➤ 140; open 10–8 except Mon). The reasonably priced special menu includes a choice of Catalan dishes and a drink.

MNAC: INSIDE INFO

Top tips It is impossible to see this huge mass of great art all in one visit. Especially if time is short, concentrate on the **Romanesque frescoes**, which can be described as the truly world-class element of the museum.

Hidden gem The **temporary art exhibitions** sometimes held downstairs are worth investigating if you have time.

At Your Leisure

3 Castell de Montjuïc – Museu Militar

The trip to the 18th-century castle by *telefèric* (cable car) is exhilarating and the views from its battlements are splendid. The fortress has a sinister history that many Catalans would prefer to forget. It was here that Catalan president Lluís Companys was executed by one of Franco's firing squads in 1940.

The castle houses the Museu Militar (Military Museum), which, although in need of a face-lift, contains some fascinating exhibits. In one echoing chamber you'll find medieval tombstones from the nearby Jewish cemetery, precious vestiges of the city's Hebraic past.

194 C2 93 329 86 13 Tue–Sun 9:30–8, Mar–Oct; 9:30–5, rest of year Paral.lel, plus Funicular and Telefèric de Montjuïc (➤ 182) 50 Inexpensive

4 Poble Espanyol

There are more than 100 buildings illustrating Spain's architectural and cultural diversity in the Poble Espanyol – even the attractive Plaza Mayor (main square) combines different styles. The "village" was built for the 1929 International Exhibition but, long resented by Catalan nationalists, it went into decline until an admirable refurbishment in the 1990s revived its fortunes.

Some of the finest buildings on the site are replicas of houses and palaces from around Catalonia – for example Gerona, Lleida and the Pyrenees. There are many shops on the site, where resident artisans sell their wares, and many offer crafts of very high quality (➤ 143). You can also eat well in the variety of bars and restaurants: choose from Andalucian or Basque, Castilian or Galician specialities. At night, entertainments are plentiful.

194 B4 Avinguda del Marquès de Comillas s/n 93 325 78 66; www.poble-espanyol.com Mon 9–8, Tue–Sat 9 am–2 am, Sun 9 am– midnight; Fri and Sat 9 am–4 am, Jul and Aug Espanya 13, 50, 61 Expensive

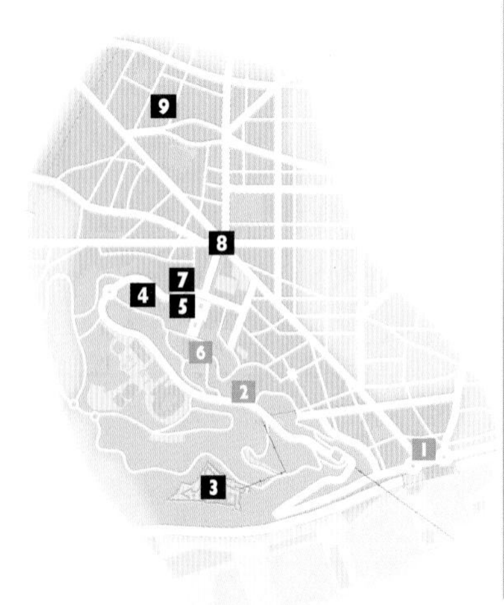

5 Pavelló Mies van der Rohe

Pioneering architect Mies van der Rohe designed this functionalist structure (also known as the Pavelló Barcelona) as the German pavilion for the 1929 International Exhibition. The pavilion was reconstructed in the 1980s as a tribute to the architect on the centenary of his birth. The building is characterised by clean lines and simple forms, and its combination of sleek marble, granite and glass, and still pools of water create a calm, meditative atmosphere – the perfect escape from the busy city.

Among the exhibits of the architect's life and work on display is the Barcelona Chair, which he designed especially for the pavilion. Ever since, the square-shaped leather-and-steel seat has been a favourite in office waiting rooms.

The clean lines of the Pavelló Mies van der Rohe contrast sharply with the city's Modernist architecture

194 B4 Avinguda del Marquès de Comillas s/n 93 423 40 16 Daily 10–8, Apr–Oct; 10–6:30, rest of year Espanya 13, 50, 100 Inexpensive

7 CaixaForum

Castle-like Casaramona, a whimsical brick textile mill, built in 1911 by Puig i Cadafalch, stood empty for decades until the Fundació La Caixa had the brilliant idea of transforming it into their new arts centre, opened in 2002. Japanese architect Arata Isozaki respectfully but daringly turned it into one of Barcelona's sleekest, most rewarding exhibition spaces. In addition to the permanent collection of contemporary art – with works by, for example, Miquel Barceló, Anish Kapoor, Tony Cragg, Joseph Beuys and Jannis Kounellis – outstanding temporary exhibits are held. So far these have included Lucian Freud's paintings and Rodin's sculptures. A children's section, workshops, concerts, an excellent gift shop and a smart cafeteria are added attractions.

194 B/C4 Avinguda Marquès de Comillas 6–8 93 476 86 00 Tue–Sun 10–8, Apr–Oct; 10–6:30, rest of year Espanya 9, 13, 27, 30, 37, 50, 56, 57, 65, 79, 91, 105, 106, 109, 157, 165 Free

8 Plaça d'Espanya

This monumental "square", guarded by two majestic red-brick Venetian style campaniles, was designed as a grand entrance to the 1929 International Exhibition. Your gaze is drawn upwards by a series of staircases and escalators towards the ostentatious Palau Nacional. On summer evenings, the row of fountains in the middle of the staircase come to life as **La Font Màgica**, a spectacular but tacky sound and light show.

194 C5 Espanya

9 Sants

For many people Sants is little more than an arrival point – Barcelona's main train station is in the neighbourhood. Yet it's a lively place, with some interesting urban-development projects, some decent restaurants (➤ 142) and a character all of its own. Sants used to be full of factories and workshops, many of which have been closed or converted into arts centres. The Parc de l'Espanya Industrial (➤ 23), turned into a park after years of neglect, is typical of the area's avant-garde approach to urbanism.

The area comes into its own during the Festa Major in late August. Events such as the traditional *corre-foc* (fire-walking), *castells*, *sardanes* and general partying take place in the main squares – Plaça del Centre, Plaça de la Farga and Plaça de Joan Peiro.

198 B2 Hostafrancs, Plaça de Sants, Sants-Estació

For Kids

- The futuristic technology and historic ships at the **Museu Marítim** (➤ 132–133).
- The funicular and cable car rides up and down **Montjuïc** (➤ 182).
- The bright colours and imaginative forms at the **Fundació Joan Miró** (➤ 134–135).
- **La Font Màgica** above the Plaça d'Espanya (➤ 141).
- Souvenir hunting at **Poble Espanyol** (➤ 140).

Where to... Eat and Drink

Prices
Expect to pay per person for a meal, excluding drinks
€ under €15 €€ €15–35 €€€ over €35

Bar Primavera €
This shady, outdoor bar halfway up Montjuïc provides a convenient recuperation point for a drink or sandwich for those who have chosen to make the climb on foot.
195 D3 Carrer Nou de la Rambla 192 93 329 30 62 Daily 8 am–10 pm; closes at 5 pm in winter Paral.lel

La Bodegueta €€
One of the best restaurants along a pedestrian street, this converted wine cellar – still stacked with atmospheric barrels – serves mouth-watering open sandwiches plus a range of barbecued meats, accompanied by an outstanding house wine. Start with a refreshing vermouth or sherry.
197 off F2 Carrer Blai 47 93 442 08 46 Tue–Sun 1:30–4, 8:30–midnight Poble Sec

Cervecería Jazz €
Live jazz and great German and Belgian beer are the winning formula at this stylish Poble Sec bar. Sandwiches are better than they sound – try the *frankfurt a la cerveza*, frankfurter in beer, an odd but curiously successful combination. Note that the bar does not have a telephone.
195 D1/E1 Carrer de Margarit 43 Mon–Sat 6 pm–2 am Paral.lel

La Parra €€€
Few restaurants have as much atmosphere as this former coaching inn, hidden away in a little back alley. This is country cooking at its most exuberant; huge chunks of lamb, rabbit or pork that have been cooked on the wood-fired grill are served on wooden boards along with *alioli* and excellent *escalivades*. Everything is washed down with local wine. Other specialities include roast duck and gilt-head bream baked in salt. There are tables outdoors in summer, but booking is always advisable as this is a favourite family restaurant.
198 B1 Carrer de Joanot Martorell 3 93 332 51 34 Tue–Sat 8:30–12:30, Sat–Sun 2–4:30; closed Aug Hostafrancs

El Peixerot €€€
This branch of a well-known seafood restaurant in Vilanova i la Geltrú, the largest port between Barcelona and Tarragona, gets the pick of the day's catch. Explore the excellent wine list while you enjoy the *arròs a la marinera* (a seafood and rice dish), the paella, or freshly grilled fish.
198 C1 Carrer de Tarragona 177 93 424 69 69 Mon–Sat 1–4, 8:30–11:30, Sun 1–4; closed Sat pm and Sun in Aug Sants-Estació

Quimet & Quimet €–€€
In this special little bodega the tapas are prepared before your eyes. The quality of the ingredients is superb – try cured shoulder of pork, air-dried tuna or tiny sardines. Wine is sold by the glass, and there are up to a dozen special beers available. The house vermouth is served in the traditional way, with soda water.
195 D1/E1 Carrer del Poeta Cabanyes 25 93 442 31 42 Tue–Sat 11:30–4, 7–10:30, Sun 11:30–4 Paral.lel

Where to... Shop

MUSEUM SHOPS

Montjuïc and Sants are not the most fertile shopping districts in the city. That said, the gift shops at the Museu Marítim (➤ 132–133), Fundació Joan Miró (➤ 134–135), MNAC (➤ 136–139) and the Poble Espanyol (➤ 140) are excellent. In addition to directly related souvenirs – model ships, Miró reproductions and signed prints, books on Gothic painting, and crafts from the regions of Spain – you'll also find all manner of souvenir items, mostly of a frivolous nature.

The **Museu d'Arqueologia** in Poble Sec also has an excellent shop (Passeig de Santa Madrona 39–41, tel: 93 423 21 49, open 9:30–7 Tue–Sat, 10–2:30 Sun, Metro: Poble Sec). It sells remarkable reproductions of ancient artefacts, including Visigothic ceramics. You don't have to visit the museum to shop here.

CRAFTS

The workshops at the purpose-built **Poble Espanyol** (➤ 140) produce a comprehensive range of goods, including stained glass, pewterware, lace and jewellery. They are worth investigating, as the quality can be exceptionally high. Be warned, though, some shops just sell the usual touristy trinkets.

FOOD AND DRINK

Some of the little food shops in **Sants** offer unbeatable bargains. **El Celler de Gèlida** (Carrer Vallespir 65, tel: 93 339 26 41, Metro: Sants-Estació) is one of the best wine shops in the city. It stocks an array of Catalan and other Spanish wines – if you have a doubt as to what to choose, just ask.

Where to... Be Entertained

SPORT

In Montjuïc, the entertainment emphasis is firmly on sport, whether spectator or participatory. The attractive **Piscines Bernat Picornell** swimming pool (Avinguda de l'Estadi, tel: 93 423 40 41, Metro: Espanya) is part of the Anella Olímpica, or Olympic complex, but unless the pool is being used for local or national championships, you can use it daily from 7 am–midnight on weekdays; it closes at 9 pm at weekends. While the **Festival del Grec** (➤ right) is on, the pool is used for various events including evening film-and-swim sessions, with a huge screen at one end of the pool (naturists take it over on Saturday night).

Nearby **Palau Sant Jordi**, a masterly feat of modern architecture, doubles up as an indoor sports venue, used for basketball and athletics, and a giant concert hall; it hosts most of Barcelona's mega rock concerts – look around for posters.

The **Estadi Olímpic de Montjuïc**, which incorporates a stadium built in 1929 by Mila and Correa, was the major venue for the 1992 Olympics and is now the home of Espanyol, Barcelona's second soccer club and Barça's bitter rival.

THEATRE

The annual **Festival del Grec** takes place from the end of June to mid-August. Events are staged at venues throughout the city, including the

Teatre Grec, the elegant Greek-style amphitheatre on Montjuïc that gives the festival its name. Theatre, both mainstream and avant-garde, dominates, but there's also dance, jazz, flamenco and rock, plus a short-film festival and street performers. If you can, try to catch a performance at the Teatre Grec itself (Metro: Poble Sec). Here, against a fabulous backdrop of cypress trees, you can see open-air productions of plays in Catalan and other languages and the festival's major dance spectacles. For more information, consult the website www.bcn.es/icub or contact the city's tourist offices (➤ 34).

Not far away, lies the **Teatre Mercat de les Flors** (Plaça Margarida Xirgu, Carrer Lleida 59, tel: 93 426 18 75, Metro: Poble Sec), a converted flower market, whose massive, hangar-like halls lend themselves to large-scale productions of a less conventional kind. Next door the Teatre Lliure (tel: 93 289 27 70) occupies a futuristic space designed by Fabià Puigserver, inside the 1929 Palace of Agriculture, part of the Ciutat del Teatre. Drama and dance of a very high standard alternate here.

CONCERTS AND SHOWS

From July to September, usually on Thursday evenings, the auditorium at the **Fundació Joan Miró** hosts a series of concerts of world contemporary music. Contact Tel-entrada (➤ 42) or the box office (tel: 93 329 19 08) for more information and to book tickets.

For **flamenco**, look no farther than **El Tablao de Carmen** (Carrer dels Arcs 9, tel: 93 325 68 95, Metro: Espanya), up at the Poble Espanyol. Foot-tapping shows take place from Tuesday to Sunday at 9:30 pm and 11:30 pm. It's not cheap, but you can choose between the dinner and glass of champagne options, and the quality of the musicians, singers and dancers is invariably high.

From May to September, Thursday to Sunday and public holidays, from 8 pm till midnight (earlier during the rest of the year), you can witness the astounding spectacle of the **Font Màgica** (➤ 141), a free sound-and-light show. It takes place along the sloping avenue linking the Plaça d'Espanya to the Palau Nacional.

NIGHTCLUBS

Amid a pinegrove just behind the Poble Espanyol lies **La Terrrazza** (Avinguda Marquès de Comillas, tel: 93 423 12 85, Metro: Espanya), one of the city's most celebrated and outrageous nightspots. Despite its huge open spaces it gets packed. To see it at its most glorious don't show up before 3 am, when the orgy of music, ostentation and frenzied dancing reaches its peak; summer weekends only. Another hot spot, **Torres de Ávila** (tel: 93 424 93 09) is actually located at the main gates of the Poble Espanyol. Designed by Mariscal (➤ 27) during the city's Olympic spree, it is one of Barcelona's most beautiful night-clubs. Seven bars, a roof-top terrace affording magical views and a techno dance area are what you get for your money – plus one drink – but you're also treated to a sumptuous setting and beautiful people to watch. **Nitsaclub** (aka **Sala Apolo**, Carrer Nou de la Rambla 113, tel: 93 441 40 01, Metro: Paral.lel), in Poble Sec, is a converted ballroom where you can rave to electronica, house and techno on weekends.

The whole of Avinguda del Paral.lel used to be lined with sleazy, Moulin Rouge-style cabarets. There are still one or two of them left; their clientele mainly comprises members of stag and hen parties set on humiliating their friends. Finally, **Tinta Roja**, a late-night bar just off Avinguda Paral.lel (Carrer Creu dels Molers 17, tel: 93 443 32 43, Metro: Poble Sec), is a small tango haunt doubling up as an art gallery.

Pedralbes and Tibidabo

Getting Your Bearings

Barcelona's outlying districts lay claim to some of its top destinations. Beyond walking distance they may be, but the city's efficient public transport will whisk you there in no time.

In the western neighbourhood of Pedralbes sits the splendid royal monastery of the same name. The monastery's cool cloisters, resounding with the trickle of a fountain and the gentle murmur of nuns singing in the chapel, are the perfect place to escape the bustle of the city.

South of the monastery, just off the Avinguda Diagonal, lies the Palau Reial de Pedralbes, a royal palace that now houses a museum of ceramics and a museum of decorative arts. The section of the Avinguda Diagonal that cuts through the district of Les Corts, between the Palau Reial de Pedralbes and Plaça de Francesc Macià, is mostly lined with offices, banks and high-rise apartment buildings, though several ultra-modern megamalls have recently been built, making it a popular place for shoppers.

To the south is FC Barcelona's mammoth stadium, Camp Nou, where football fans flock to the temple-like stands to see their team in action. To the west are Barcelona's ultramodern science museum, CosmoCaixa, and Tibidabo, where you can ride on roller-coasters with the whole city laid out spectacularly before you.

Left: Monestir de Pedralbes, a beautiful convent in Barcelona's leafy southern district

Previous page: View from Tibidabo of the Torre de Collserola, designed by architect Lord Foster for the 1992 Olympics

★ Don't Miss

At Your Leisure

Torre de Collserola
Sagrat Cor
Parc d'Atraccions
PLAÇA DEL TIBIDABO
6 Tibidabo
Funicular al Tibidabo
PL DEL DOCTOR ANDREU
RONDA DE DALT
CosmoCaixa
5
CARRER DEL CISTER
AV DEL TIBIDABO
Tramvia Blau
PG DE SANT GERVASI
BONANOVA
Av del Tibidabo

Above: Detail from the Pavellons de la Finca Güell

Below: The spectacular view from Tibidabo; on a clear day you can see all the way to Mallorca

This trip has something to please everyone: football or ceramics, science and a funfair with a panoramic view. Perhaps take a picnic with you as eating options are limited at lunchtime.

Pedralbes and Tibidabo in a Day

9:00 am

This day needn't be rushed. Linger over breakfast wherever you choose, and then make your way out to the 1 **Monastir de Pedralbes** (➤ 150–151) by Metro, FGC, regular bus, or maybe the Bus Turístic. Be warned: there are no café facilities to speak of there. Be at the gates of the convent when it opens at 10 am, to enjoy the cloisters (below) in the gentle morning sunlight.

11:00 am

Go down the sloping Avinguda de Pedralbes, either by bus (the Bus Turístic comes this way) or on foot, past the magical entrance to the 2 **Pavellons de la Finca Güell** (➤ 156); pause to look at Gaudí's wrought-iron dragon, half-horror, half-wonder.

12:00 noon

Next, visit either the ceramics (detail left) and design museums in the aristocratic 3 **Palau Reial de Pedralbes** (➤ 156–157) or join the crowds of football pilgrims at 4 **Camp Nou** (➤ 157–158). If you're quick you could do both. To get to Camp Nou, cross Avinguda Diagonal at Plaça de Pius XII and go down Avinguda de Joan XXIII.

Alternatively, go on a shopping spree along Avinguda Diagonal (➤ 160).

1:30 pm

Enjoy a picnic in the gardens of the Palau Reial de Pedralbes or take a taxi to have lunch at La Balsa restaurant (➤ 153). Then find your way to Barcelona's exciting new science museum, 5 **CosmoCaixa** (right; ➤ 152–153).

5:00 pm

This is the time to set your sights on 6 **Tibidabo** (➤ 154–155). Public transport will get you there easily – a big part of the fun are the Tramvia Blau (Blue Tram) and the funicular railway that hauls you up to the top. It will take 30–45 minutes in all, so leave plenty of time and make sure you're there before sunset – the views over the city are marvellous.

8:00 pm

You can stay up here all evening. Pre-dinner drinks are top-rate at the Mirablau (➤ 155), next to the tram terminus – either on the garden-terrace or inside the bar. Alongside, on the Plaça del Doctor Andreu, is the fabulous La Venta restaurant (➤ 159), which doesn't take advantage of its location with high prices. And Partycular (➤ 159), just below at Avinguda del Tibidabo 61, is one of the city's classiest nightspots.

0

Monestir de Pedralbes

This 14th-century monastery was built for a Catalan queen. Its exquisite cloisters and garden retain their regal majesty 700 years later.

Pedralbes (from the Latin *petrae albae*) means "White Stones". The monastery was founded here in 1326 for the nuns of the Order of St Clare by Elisenda de Montcada, cousin and second wife of King Jaume II. The Montcadas were one of the most powerful noble families in 14th-century Catalonia and Montcada women in particular played a significant role in the kingdom's history. Having been widowed just two years after her marriage, Elisenda withdrew to the newly built convent. Thanks to her it grew rich and most of what you see there was built through her generosity. Today there are only 24 sisters in the community, who live in separate, specially built quarters.

The elegant **cloisters** consist of three tiers of galleries each supported by the slimmest of stone pillars. In the far left-hand corner of the central garden a Plateresque well-head, built around 1500, stands discreetly behind trees and beds of medicinal herbs.

Slender columns and elegant arches cast their shadows in the cloisters

202 C4
Baixada del Monestir 9
93 280 14 34
Tue–Sun 10–2
FGC Reina Elisenda
22, 63, 64, 75

Moderate (separate charges for convent and museum). Free first Sun of the month

Church

Daily 10–1, 5:30–8

You can see Giotto's influence on the 14th-century frescoes lining the Capella de Sant Miquel

Walk around the cloisters counterclockwise to the **Capella de Sant Miquel** (St Michael's Chapel), lined with frescoes executed in the 1340s by Ferrer Bassa, a student of Giotto di Bondoni. Oils and tempera depict the life of the Virgin and the Passion.

As you explore the cloisters you'll also see exquisitely painted **prayer cells** from the 14th century. The Cell of St Francis, the Cell of St Alexius and the Cell of St Joseph are on the ground floor, while the Cell of Our Lady of Montserrat, the Cell of Our Lady of the Snows and the Cell of the Holy Entombment are on the upper floor. The finest of all is the Cel.la de la Pietat on the ground floor, with its 16th-century retable of Mary as a child. Don't forget to go down to see some of the living quarters of the monastery: the cells and cellars, the beautiful **kitchen** and the infirmary give an insight into how the nuns lived.

TAKING A BREAK

Vivanda (Carrer Major de Sarrià 134, tel: 93 205 47 17) serves delicious Catalan food, inside or on a garden terrace.

MONESTIR DE PEDRALBES: INSIDE INFO

Top tip Remember the monastery is open **mornings only**; save yourself a wasted trip in the afternoon.

Hidden gem Although the adjacent **church** is a simple edifice, far less impressive than the monastery, it is worth visiting for the effigy tomb of Queen Elisenda – she died in 1364, and this alabaster masterpiece, to the right of the main altar, was made soon afterwards.

5

CosmoCaixa

Housed in an early 20th-century building, CosmoCaixa is definitely a science museum for the 21st century. Laying strong emphasis on evolution and ecology, it is designed to arouse interest in the world around us. Its interactive displays and fun activities will be a hit with younger visitors especially.

Visitors using the museum's spiral stairway get a close-up view of the Tree of Life, a tree trunk suspended by cables in the central well

CosmoCaixa ambitiously sets out to trace the history of existence from the Big Bang to modern telecommunications. Applying the motto "From a Quark to Shakespeare", its whole ethos is based on universality and environmental concerns. Language, writing and the whole complexity of human culture are also addressed in depth.

This humanistic ethos is also reflected in the museum **building**. Constructed as an asylum for the insane to an ornate Modernist design, it was completed by Josep Domènech i Estapà in 1909. Seven decades later the abandoned edifice was converted into Barcelona's Science Museum, but more than 20 years further on the Fundaciò La Caixa called on architects the Terradas brothers to thrust what was rather a dull museum firmly into the new millennium. In doing so they provided the city with Europe's most up-to-date museum of its kind. Shiny glass and metal prevail in the new structure, while all exhibits are accessible to young and old alike.

You can wander around a permanent display on the **History of Matter**. Divided into four parts – Inert, Living, Intelligent and Civilised Matter – it traces the development of planet Earth, explaining all phenomena from gravity to electricity by means of sophisticated hands-on exhibits.

202, off A5
Carrer de Teodor Roviralta 55
93 212 60 50
Tue–Sun and most public holidays 10–8
FGC Av del Tibidabo
17, 22, 58, 60, 73, 85
Moderate

The Foucault's pendulum is a sure-fire winner with small children

Looming over it all, like a hi-tech cliff, is the **Geological Wall**. Seven slices of rock – quarried around Spain and Brazil – allow us to interpret the world's geology, again thanks to graphic information panels (in English as well as Catalan and Spanish) and ingenious machines.

You can walk both through and beneath the centrepiece **Flooded Forest**. It re-creates an Amazonian rainforest habitat complete with enormous fish, turtles and anacondas, in a huge glasshouse-cum-aquarium whose steamy atmosphere full of jungle smells transports you to northern Brazil. More than 50 species of amphibians, insects, reptiles, mammals and birds have their home here – don't worry, though, none of the creatures you can come into contact with is harmful.

Two further dimensions are provided by a working **Foucault's pendulum** and a 136-seat **Planetarium** in which you can go on a journey through the history of the Universe.

An excellent **bookshop** by the entrance is a great place for souvenir hunting; naturally it specialises in all things scientific.

TAKING A BREAK

The museum has an attractive cafeteria serving snacks. Conveniently close by, however, is **La Balsa** (Carrer Infanta Isabel 4, tel: 93 211 50 48), a moderately priced restaurant in an attractive wooden building surrounded by lush gardens. Catalan fare includes hake in squid-ink sauce, and prawn and salt cod croquettes in a tarragon sauce. In August it is closed at lunchtime.

COSMOCAIXA: INSIDE INFO

Top tip You will find several sections specially for **kids**: their names – Touch Touch!, Clik, Flash and Bubble Planetarium – speak for themselves. Be warned: there is an additional entrance fee, and check for opening times.

Hidden gem Lifts take you up and down, but don't miss the stylish spiralling **ramp** for alternative inter-floor access. In its well dangles the desiccated trunk of an Amazonian tree that looks like a giant loofah.

6

Tibidabo

There are two main reasons for making your way to the summit of Mount Tibidabo, the highest peak of the wooded Collserola range that looms behind Barcelona: the stunning views and the old-fashioned fairground, the Parc d'Atraccions. The journey up, by tram and funicular, is part and parcel of the enjoyment.

Parc d'Atraccions

Few amusement parks in the world can claim better views from their helter-skelters, carousels and Ferris wheel than this one. Located near the top funicular station, the park is set in landscaped gardens spread over different levels on the mountainside. A highlight is the Hotel Krueger, a house of horrors of which even Alfred Hitchcock would have approved.

From the Ferris wheel at the Parc d'Atraccions you get breathtaking views of the city

Torre de Collserola

On a nearby ridge rises the elegant glass and steel Torre de Collserola, a beautiful example of modern architecture. The 268m (880-foot) tower was built by British architect Norman

200 off A5
FGC Av del Tibidabo, Tramvia Blau and Funicular
17, 22, 58, 73, 85

Parc d'Atraccions
Plaça del Tibidabo 3–4
93 211 79 42
10–6, late Mar to early Oct; noon–1 am, Jul–Aug; Sat and Sun noon–7 pm, only in winter
Expensive (children under 1.20m (4 feet) tall 9 Euros

Torre de Collserola
Wed–Fri 11–2:30, 3:30–8, Sat, Sun and holidays 11–8, Jun–Aug; closes at 7 pm, Sep–May. Closed Mon and Tue
Moderate

Getting There

Every bit as much fun as Tibidabo itself is the journey to get there. First take a No 17 bus or the FGC train from Plaça de Catalunya to Avinguda del Tibidabo. Look for the tram tracks, and you'll see the stop for the **Tramvia Blau** (Blue Tram) that trundles up to Plaça del Doctor Andreu (pay the conductor on entering). The tram runs daily the week before Easter, July to mid-September and around Christmas, 10–6 (8, in summer); Saturday and Sunday only, rest of year (10–6). Otherwise (or for quicker access) take Tibibus from Plaça de Catalunya. At Plaça del Doctor Andreu, take the funicular railway that storms to the top of Tibidabo. From June to September it runs daily every 15 to 30 minutes from 10:45 am to 10:30 pm (1:15 am on Friday and Saturday). In winter, Friday and Saturday only 10:45 to 7:15.

Foster as a telecommunications tower for the 1992 Olympics. From the top, reached by a glass lift, you can see back towards the mountains as well as across the city and out to sea. It is an experience not to be missed.

TAKING A BREAK

The **Mirablau** (Plaça del Doctor Andreu, tel: 93 418 58 79), at the end of the tram line, boasts the finest view in Barcelona; the entire port and city are seemingly at your feet. It's open till the early hours of the morning for drinks on the garden terrace or in the bar, which has huge floor-to-ceiling windows that give you an almost disorientating sensation of being suspended in space. Drinks are expensive and it can become very crowded, but a stop here is an essential Barcelona experience.

TIBIDABO: INSIDE INFO

Top tips Come only when **the weather is good**, preferably when there's not too much haze or smog.

- Time your visit for the early evening as the **sunsets** are unforgettable.
- For a touch of nostalgia, look out for the **Museu d'Automates del Tibidabo** inside the fairground. It houses a wonderful collection of coin-operated fairground machines in perfect working order, the oldest dating back to 1909.
- Funfair fans in search of **more modern, more extreme rides** might consider visiting Port Aventura, near Tarragona (ask at the city's tourist offices ➤ 34 for more information).

One to miss Above the fairground is the huge basilica of **Sagrat Cor** (the Church of the Sacred Heart), modelled on the Sacré-Coeur in Paris. Topped by a huge statue of Christ, it is a clearly visible landmark from nearly everywhere in the city but proves ugly on close inspection.

At Your Leisure

A detail of the dragon motif on Gaudí's magnificent wrought-iron gates at the entrance to the Finca Güell

2 Pavellons de la Finca Güell

The Moorish pavilions (gatehouses) of the Finca Güell (the Güell estate) were designed by Gaudí. Among his earliest achievements, they point to some of the extraordinary concoctions he dreamed up for the Parc Güell (➤ 110–112). But the pièce de résistance is without doubt the gate to the estate. Gaudí literally stretched the use of wrought iron beyond anyone else's imagination, and here the taut forms of the dragon, with its horrific jaws, make it look as though it is about to spring off the frame towards you.

202 B2 · Avinguda de Pedralbes 7 · Palau Reial · 7, 63, 67, 68, 74, 75

3 Palau Reial de Pedralbes

During the 1920s the handsome Palau Reial was created out of the Finca Güell summer residence at Pedralbes. It was supposed to be the official royal palace in Barcelona, but the Spanish royal family has hardly ever stayed inside its splendid yellow walls, although Franco did live it up there on a couple of occasions.

Within the great salons and halls are two permanent museums, the **Museu de la Ceràmica**, a huge collection of jars, plates and tiles, and the **Museu de les Arts Decoratives**, a smaller display of designer furniture and other decorative items. They can be visited separately or on a joint ticket, but if you're in a hurry the Museu de la Ceràmica is the better bet.

The collection at the Museu de la Ceràmica ranges from simple dishes and bowls to floor tiles and ceramic sculpture, with works by Picasso and Miró. The set of lustreware plates from Manises in southern Spain is particularly fine. One of the outstanding exhibits is a pair of sumptuous 18th-century panels, one depicting a refined bullfight and the other a genteel chocolate feast.

The collection at the Museu de les Arts Decoratives is eclectic, but sadly with far too little in the way of explanation. It starts in the Middle Ages, with Hispano-Arabic chests and Renaissance writing-desks, and takes you up to the 1980s with furniture made by some of Catalonia's leading designers, including Oscar Tusquets, Javier Mariscal and BKF. Modernisme obviously looms large and the early 20th-century glassware and lavishly decorated bedheads, which would have graced the sitting-rooms and bedrooms of the Eixample's finest homes, are particularly impressive.

The landscaped park surrounding the palace is slightly overgrown in places, but perfect for a relaxed picnic or a quiet pause in the day's sightseeing.

202 B3 · Avinguda Diagonal 686 · Museu de la Ceràmica: 93 280 16 21; Museu de les Arts Decoratives: 93 280 50 24 · Tue–Sat 10–6, Sun and holidays 10–3 · Palau Reial · 7, 63, 67, 68, 74, 75 · Inexpensive. Free first Sun of the month

4 Camp Nou – FC Barcelona

If soccer is your thing, then you should do your utmost to see a match at Camp Nou, home to FC Barça and the second biggest soccer stadium in the world, after Rio's Maracanã. Don't build up your hopes though – the stadium seats some 120,000 but there are even more members, including the late Pope John Paul II. Unless you book tickets in advance (➤ 21), your best bet is to turn up for a match and see

The handsome Palau Reial de Pedralbes now houses the Museu de la Ceràmica and the Museu de les Arts Decoratives

Barça playing at home in the palatial Camp Nou stadium

if anyone has a spare ticket (*carnet*). Be wary, though, of buying from anyone that looks as if they might be an unofficial ticket-seller, as this practice is illegal.

Entrance 9 will also get you into the **Museu del FC Barcelona** (Barça Museum), one of the city's most popular museums with more than half a million visitors every year. Cups and trophies are displayed alongside all kinds of memorabilia, including posters, photos and even antique table-football sets, with big names such as Johan Cruyff and Maradona looming large. Informative exhibits trace the club's history back to 1899, when it was co-founded and chaired by Englishman Arthur Witty and fielded four British players. The high point of the tour is a glimpse of the stadium – you can go out into a fenced-off section of the stands and survey the immaculate turf and the rows upon rows of red seats.

Camp Nou
202 B1
Carrer d'Aristides Maillol 7–9 93 496 36 00; www.fcbarcelona.es

For Kids

- One of the world's biggest football stadiums, **Camp Nou** (➤ 157–158), home to Barça.
- The wonderful wrought-iron dragon on the gates to the **Pavellons de la Finca Güell** (➤ 156).
- The hands-on exhibits at **CosmoCaixa** (➤ 152–153) were designed for youngsters.

Museu del FC Barcelona
Mon–Sat 10–6:30, Sun and holidays 10–2 Collblanc 15, 52, 53, 54, 56, 57, 75
Moderate

Where to... Eat and Drink

Prices
Expect to pay per person for a three-course meal, excluding drink
€ under €15 €€ €15–35 €€€ over €35

Arcs de Sant Gervasi €€
Enjoy Catalan cooking at this smart neighbourhood restaurant. Meals, typically, feature crab soup, then goat cutlets with wild mushrooms and a choice of traditional desserts such as *crèma catalana* (➤ 14).

199 F4 Carrer de Santaló 103 93 201 92 77 Tue–Sat 1–4:30, 9–midnight, Sun 1–4:30 Muntaner

Gaig €€€
Named after the family that has run the restaurant for more than a century, this elegant temple to Catalan haute cuisine is, for many, one of Barcelona's best restaurants. As in many leading dining rooms in the city you can opt for a *menú degustación*, leaving the choice of dishes to the chef, though you can negotiate minor changes to suit your taste. Each dish is served in delicate portions, with emphasis on blends of compatible but often unusual ingredients. Inevitably there are ideas influenced by master chef Ferran Adriá (➤ 27), such as layered desserts served in a shotglass.

201, off F5 Passeig Maragall 402 93 429 10 17 Tue–Sun 1:30–4, Tue–Sat 9–11 Horta

Neichel €€€
Every detail at Neichel, considered by many to be the best restaurant in the city, reflects the enormous care that Alsace-born chef Jean-Louis Neichel puts into his cooking. The interior has a look of subdued sophistication; the emphasis is on the plate. Dishes such as pheasant braised in its own juices with grapes and fresh quince are memorable and individual. The cheeses and changing array of desserts are also spectacular. The trendy location combined with immensely refined cooking are reflected in the sky-high prices, but you'll be paying for a true gastronomic experience.

200 C2 Carrer de Beltrán i Rózpide 16 bis 93 203 84 08 Mon–Fri 1:30–3:30, 8:30–11, Sat 8:30–11:30 Maria Cristina

La Venta €€€
This smart restaurant is well located in the square by the funicular up to Tibidabo. Innovative dishes are served either on the attractive terrace or in the glass conservatory. Booking is recommended.

200 off A5 Plaça del Dr Andreu s/n 93 212 64 55 Mon–Sat 1:30–3:15, 9–11:15 FGC Avda Tibidabo

BARS AND CAFÉS

Jamón Jamón €
The smart chrome-and-granite décor may be contemporary, but the tapas remain traditional. As the name implies, cured ham is the speciality, carved to order. No credit cards.

199 E4 Carrer del Mestre Nicolau 4 93 209 41 03 Mon–Sat 9 am–midnight Muntaner

Partycular €
It's almost impossible to get here by public transport, but it's worth a taxi ride to have a cocktail at the enormous bar and then wander through the spacious, romantic gardens.

200 off A5 Avda del Tibidabo 61 93 211 62 61 Wed–Sun 6:30 pm–2:30 am

Where to... Shop

In the upper reaches of the Avinguda Diagonal, amid the high-rise office blocks, you'll find some fashionable but rather soulless malls where you can shop at international chains plus Spanish big-names **Zara**, **Springfield** and **Mango**. Spain's megastore, **El Corte Inglés**, has another two mammoth branches at Avinguda Diagonal Nos 471–473 (tel: 93 419 20 20) and 617–619 (tel: 93 419 28 28); they're both reliable for ready-to-wear clothing, beach attire and shoes. The nearest Metro is Maria Cristina.

L'Illa (Avinguda Diagonal 545–557, tel: 93 444 00 00) is a vast mall, with international stores such as **Decathlon** (sportswear) and **Fnac** (books and records). **Prestige** (tel: 93 444 01 41) is a particularly trendy fashion boutique within its precincts. Metro Maria Cristina is nearby, while buses Nos 6, 7, 33, 34, 63, 66, 67, 68, 78 and the Bus Turístic and TomBus (➤ 33) all run out here.

Its main rival, the **Pedralbes Centre** (Diagonal 609, tel: 93 419 12 80), farther away from the city centre, is where you'll find **Escada** and **Macon**, for her and his fashion, **Madonna**, for pregnant women, and **Sharper Image**, for fun designer goods.

Two special shops worth tracking down nearby are **Jaime Tresserra** (Carrer Josep Bertrand 17, tel: 93 200 49 22, Metro: Maria Cristina), for its limited edition furniture, which has been featured in films such as *Batman* and Almodóvar's *The Flower of My Secret*; and **Oriol** (Carrer Bori i Fontesia 11, tel: 93 201 03 77, Metro: Maria Cristina), which sells candelabras and cigarette holders alongside mostly sterling silver contemporary jewellery.

Where to... Be Entertained

MUSIC

Jazz *aficionados* might like to make the long trek out to **La Boite** (Avinguda Diagonal 477, tel: 93 419 59 50), unassumingly tucked away in a basement behind a modern block. The night bus N12 could come in handy. Not exactly cheap (though a drink is included), this popular place, with a shiny interior and smart clientele, plays host to blues and Latin rhythms, and traditional and avant-garde jazz. Housed unexpectedly in the L'Illa shopping-centre is the **Winterthur** (tel: 93 290 10 90, Metro: Maria Cristina), a small auditorium, with just the right acoustics for chamber music, though it is rarely used for that purpose. Look out for the concerts in listings pages.

NIGHTCLUBS

Bikini (Carrer Déu i Mata 105, tel: 93 322 08 00, Metro: Les Corts) is renowned for rock and South American gigs. It's open late every night Tuesday to Saturday and dies down only at daybreak on weekends. The peaceful gardens at **Partycular** (➤ 159) are a delightful place to head for a drink when you're in the Tibidabo area.

CINEMA

At **Renoir (Les Corts)** (Carrer Eugeni d'Ors 12 , tel: 93 490 55 10, Metro: Les Corts), films are always shown in their original version with subtitles. English-language classics and recent releases loom large in the cinema's varied programming.

Excursions

Excursions

Barcelona is not just a great city, it also enjoys a fantastic location wedged between magnificent mountains and the Mediterranean. Should you feel like a break from the hectic circuit of museums and city cafés, you could take advantage of the highly efficient regional transport network to get away and see a bit more of what Catalonia has to offer.

Whether you head south along the coast to the resorts of the Costa Dorada or north to those of the famed Costa Brava, you'll happen upon enticingly sandy beaches. Although some parts of the Costa Brava have become over-developed, there are still some charming resorts. To the south lies the popular resort of Sitges, a picturesque fishing village and a sometimes outrageous holiday haunt.

Inland, there are just as many choices. The monasteries at Poblet and Santes Creus are outstanding, as is the holy site of Montserrat, set amid spectacular mountain scenery.

Southwest of the city lies the lush wine-growing region of Alt Penedès. *Cava* is the speciality here, and you can enjoy free tastings at wineries in Vilafranca, the regional capital, and at nearby Sant Sadurní d'Anoia. The traditional market town of Vic, not far to the north of Barcelona, gives you a taste of deepest Catalonia.

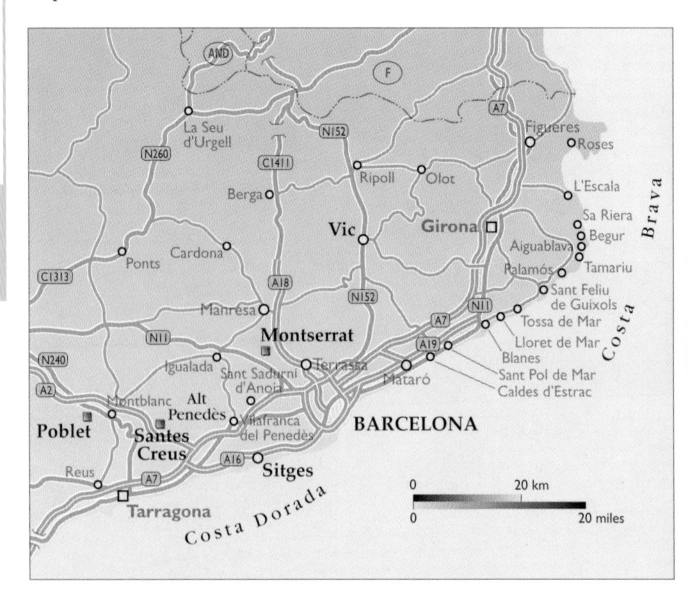

Sitges

Despite the fact that Barcelona has some wonderful beaches, it is worth taking a trip out to Sitges, a popular Costa Dorada resort some 30km (19 miles) to the southwest.

The lively resort of Sitges has several beaches from which to choose

The nine safe, sandy beaches here can get packed in the summer season, but that won't mar the friendly holiday atmosphere as locals mingle with the many visitors. Charming little hotels, fine restaurants and, above all, an unequalled nightlife are further reasons to visit Sitges.

Having started out as an artists' colony at the end of the 19th century, the town has always taken a tolerant, alternative view of life, and for years has been a favourite with gay tourists. Mardi Gras (February to March) is a time for outrageous dressing up and night-long raves in the picturesque whitewashed streets. If all this gets too much, hangover permitting, there are plenty of cultural activities, too.

The **Museu Cau Ferrat**, **Museu Maricel** and **Museu Romantic** are all worth a visit. Santiago Rusiñol, a local painter who made Sitges fashionable in the 1890s, used Museu Cau

Sitges station from Sants

Museu Cau Ferrat
Carrer Fonollar 93 894 03 64
Tue–Sun 10–2, 5–9, Jun–Sep; Tue–Fri 10–1:30, 3–6:30, Sat 10–7, Sun 10–3, Oct–May
Inexpensive (combined ticket moderate)

Museu Maricel
Carrer Fonollar see Museu Cau Ferrat

Museu Romantic
Carrer Sant Gaudenci 1
93 894 29 69
see Museu Cau Ferrat

A quieter side to Sitges: the baroque church

Ferrat as a hideaway. The nautical house, with superb sea views, displays an eclectic collection of paintings, religious artefacts and memorabilia. The Maricel, next door, is another collector's paradise, with all kinds of antiques and curios mingled with priceless objects and amusing junk. The high point of the tour of the Museu Romantic, a rather camp aristocratic villa that was once home to a wine magnate, is an international collection of dolls and dolls' houses.

The Costa Brava

If you're set on seeing the famous Costa Brava, to the north of Barcelona, or even considering basing yourself there for visits to the city, it's worth knowing what each resort offers.

Nearest to Barcelona, and strictly speaking on the Costa del Maresme, **Caldes d'Estrac** (popularly known as Caldetes) and **Sant Pol de Mar** boast some great beaches at great locations, with art nouveau architecture and quaint little fishermen's houses. Both can be reached by train from Plaça de Catalunya.

Blanes, which is easily accessible, including by train, and **Tossa de Mar** (right) are both fine if a bit built up, but avoid **Lloret de Mar** and **Palamos** if you can as they are overcrowded and polluted.

Sant Feliu de Guíxols is another picturesque little resort between Tossa and Palamos. The beach is sandy – whereas much of the coast is rocky – and the Museu de la Ciutat is worth a look.

Begur and **Sa Riera**, north of Palamos, reward the relative difficulty of getting there (roads can get congested and public transport is inconvenient), and are oases of good taste along a particularly nasty stretch of seaboard. **Aiguablava** (accessible from Begur) and **Tamariu** (reached from Palafrugell) each have a pristine sandy beach and the clearest water imaginable; their seafood restaurants are among the best along the coast.

The Cistercian Monasteries

The majestic Royal Monasteries of Poblet and Santes Creus, near the exquisite little town of Montblanc (with its dazzling white hilltop fortress, 110km (68 miles) west of Barcelona), are two of the finest monastic buildings you'll see anywhere, a fascinating combination of Romanesque and Gothic architectural styles. Their beautifully proportioned cloisters are near-perfect works of art, and both are idyllic havens of peace, the ideal getaway from the big-city frenzy.

Monestir de Poblet

The numerous coaches parked outside are proof that Poblet, a huge monastery just a few kilometres west of Montblanc, is one of Catalonia's most popular tourist destinations. The monastery was originally built to house the tombs of the Catalan and Aragonese kings and queens in the 12th century and was taken over by the Cistercian Order in the 15th century. The dissolution of the monasteries in the early 19th century and the Civil War both took their toll, and Poblet is now home to only a handful of monks. The buildings were stripped bare of many of their glorious decorations, but some fabulous lace-like stone carving and an evocatively meditative atmosphere linger on.

The restored 12th-century monastery at Poblet

You can visit the monastery only as part of an official tour, guided either by a member of the community or a professional guide (tours leave every 30 minutes or so). Highlights are the lavish high altar reredos – a miraculously preserved masterpiece finely carved in honey-hued alabaster – the gorgeous royal tombs with their lifelike effigies and the covered fountain in the middle of the lush garden-like cloisters.

Monestir de Santes Creus

Santes Creus, some 30km (19 miles) to the east and nestling in a staggeringly beautiful setting of poplars and hazel-trees, tends to be far quieter than Poblet and rather than being shepherded around on a guided tour, you're left to your own devices. The highly ornate baroque altarpiece, King Peter the Great's impressive tomb and some delicate frescoes remain, and many of the outbuildings are in an appealing state of semi-ruin. It simply oozes charm and monastic peace.

Monestir de Poblet

Poblet at L'Espluga de Francolí
977 87 00 89
Guided tours daily 10–12:30, 3–5:30 (6 pm Mar–Oct)
Moderate

Monestir de Santes Creus

95km (59 miles) west of Barcelona
977 63 83 29
Tue–Sun 10–1:30, 3–6 (7 pm Mar–Sep)
Moderate. Free Tue

The Wineries of the Alt Penedès

The chief reason for visiting the rolling countryside of the Alt Penedès, within striking distance to the west of Barcelona, is to go wine-tasting.

Catalonia's best wines and, above all, *cava* (Spain's answer to champagne) are produced by big-name wineries such as Freixenet and Codorníu. All the bodegas open their doors to the public and conduct tours of the presses and cellars before the wine-tasting. If you go to only one, make it **Caves Codorníu** for its marvellous grotto-like Modernist building designed at the end of the 19th century by Josep Puig i Cadafalch.

Both the regional capital, **Vilafranca del Penedès** (55km/ 34 miles), and nearby **Sant Sadurní d'Anoia** (44km/27 miles), are within easy reach of Barcelona by road and rail. With your own transport, you could combine the trip with a visit to **Poblet** or **Santes Creus** monasteries (▶ 165), or an afternoon on the beach at **Sitges** (▶ 163–164). If you're driving, be aware that the Spanish police are extremely strict with drink-driving. Both towns, especially Vilafranca, are pleasant places to wander around and have informative tourist offices (Carrer Cort 14 in Vilafranca and Plaça de l'Ajuntament 1 in Sant Sadurní).

Tour Operators

For guided tours of the region, also contact the Catalonia tourist office (▶ 34). Other specialist operators include:

Julià (Ronda Universitat 5, tel: 93 317 64 54)

Pullmantur Tours (Gran Via de les Corts Catalans 645, tel: 93 318 02 41).

The Caves Freixenet at Sant Sadurní d'Anoia, one of the many wineries in the Alt Penedès

Monestir de Montserrat, a place of pilgrimage since the 12th century

At the delightful **Museu del Vi,** the historic centre of Vilafranca, you can learn about wine-making in Catalonia since Roman times. Wine festivals are held in the region in late September and early October, coinciding with the grape harvest.

From Plaça de Catalunya and Sants, hourly trains take 40–50 minutes to reach Sant Sadurní and Vilafranca

Caves Codorniú

Sant Sadurní d'Anoia
93 818 32 32
Mon–Fri 9–5, Sat and Sun 9–1
Inexpensive

Caves Freixenet

Carrer Joan Sala 2 Sant Sadurní
93 891 70 00
Mon–Thu four tours daily, Fri 10 and 11:30

Museu del Vi

Plaça Jaume I, Vilafranca del Penedès
93 890 05 82
Tue–Sat 10–2, 4–8; Sun and holidays 10–2
Inexpensive

Montserrat

Montserrat (meaning Serrated Mountain), 40km (25 miles) north-west of Barcelona, has been an important place of pilgrimage since a monastery was founded on the mountainside to house the "Black Virgin" of Montserrat (*La Moreneta*), a wooden statue of the Madonna and Child with a smoke-blackened face. The statue was believed to have been made by St Luke and mysteriously turned up here in the 12th century. Today, *La Moreneta* is on display in the 16th-century basilica, the monastery's church – but be prepared for a long wait. In the nearby Museu de Montserrat, you can see a display of the many gifts left by pilgrims, including silver and gold, some paintings and even a couple of works by Picasso.

Dotted over the mountain are 13 hermitages, all still in use, and a signposted route takes you past them all with superb views along the way. Those that can be seen inside include the Hermitage of Sant Joan, which can be reached by funicular or a steep, 20-minute walk from the monastery, or the Hermitage of San Jeroni, at the mountain's peak.

The Saturday morning market at Vic takes place in the attractive Plaça Major

Though Montserrat figures highly in the Catalan psyche, visitors can be disappointed by the tacky souvenir shops and somewhat kitsch atmosphere. That said, part of the appeal of a visit to Montserrat lies in the stunning mountain scenery (strange, knobbly rocks that form the saw-toothed mountain look like melted wax from a giant candle) and in the journey to get there, which involves a tangle of hairpin bends or a stomach-churning cable car ride.

Getting to Montserrat

FGC from Placa d'Espanya to Aeri de Montserrat (cable car), every 2 hours, takes 1 hour; then cable car to the monastery and basilica, every 15 minutes all day. There is also a daily bus service from Estació Autobussos de Sants.

Montserrat
93 877 77 77 or 835 02 51

Basilica

7:30–8:30, Jul–Sep; 8–6:30, rest of year
Free

Museu de Montserrat

10–6, Mar–Dec; 10–4:45, rest of year
Moderate

Vic

Despite being way out in the heart of the Catalan countryside, 65km (40 miles) from Barcelona, Vic is a sophisticated city with a lively cultural agenda. The vibrant market that is held every Saturday morning is undoubtedly one of its main attractions. All kinds of local produce, plus mushrooms and fruit, hams and pâtés, are piled up on traditional stalls, and here you won't hear much Spanish being spoken. Vic is almost synonymous with sausages, especially its famous *fuet*, a mild salami-like creation sliced up as a topping for *pa amb tomàquet* (► 40), and is also renowned for its *botifarra*, grilled and served with white beans (*mongetes*). Sample these gastronomic delicacies in the beautiful Plaça Major, one of the finest main squares in the country.

The interior of the neo-classical cathedral is decorated with some thought-provoking 20th-century murals by Josep Lluís Sert, and the rest of the town is scattered with curious little churches and convents. A fine collection of medieval religious art at the **Museu Episcopal** (look out for the 13th-century altarpiece by Mestre de Soriguerola) and the remains of a Roman temple complete the picture; all of the central sights can be conveniently visited by following a well-signposted tourist route through a tangle of delightful medieval streets. Don't hesitate to drop in at the tourist office first.

From Plaça de Catalunya or Sants, direction Ripoll or Puigcerda, every 30–50 minutes; takes 1 hour to 1 hour 20 minutes

Tourist Office

Plaça Major 1 (tucked away in a corner)
93 886 20 91

Museu Episcopal

Plaça Bisbe Oliba 3
93 886 93 60
Tue–Sat 10–7, Sun 10–2, Apr–Sep; Tue–Fri 10–1, 3–6, Sat 10–2, rest of year
Inexpensive

Walks

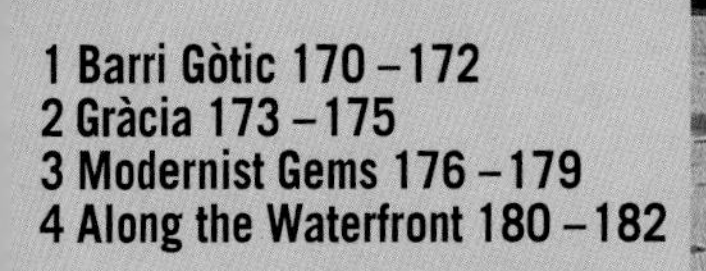

1 BARRI GÒTIC

Walk

DISTANCE 2.5km (1½ miles) **TIME** 2 hours
START POINT Plaça Nova Liceu or Jaume 1 193 D3
END POINT Plaça de l'Angel 192 A5

One of Barcelona's many slogans is "the past has a future". This walking tour takes you back to that past: shady little squares, quaint narrow streets, vestiges of Roman walls and Gothic churches galore. You'll get off the beaten track in the Barri Gòtic, without wandering around aimlessly or getting lost.

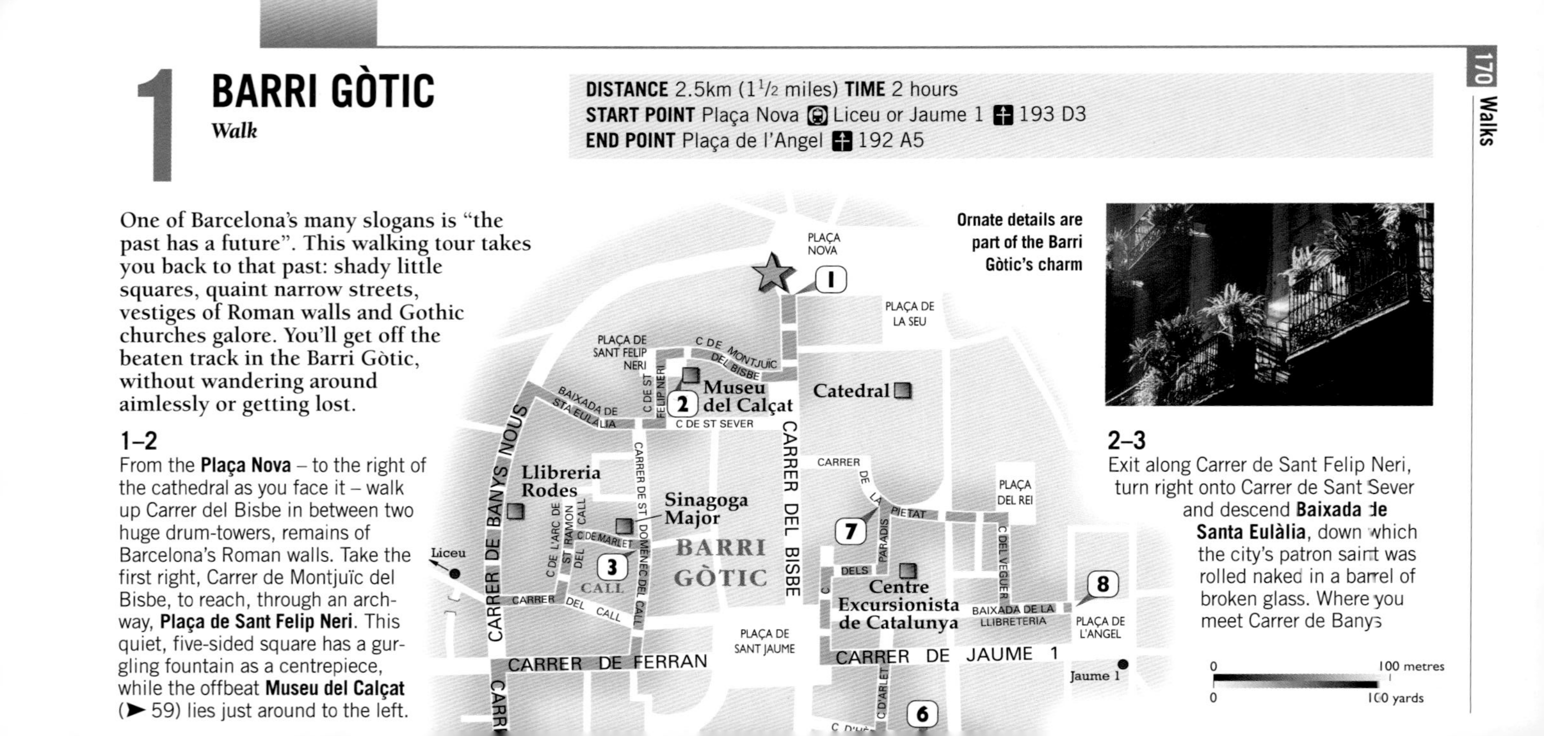

Ornate details are part of the Barri Gòtic's charm

1–2

From the **Plaça Nova** – to the right of the cathedral as you face it – walk up Carrer del Bisbe in between two huge drum-towers, remains of Barcelona's Roman walls. Take the first right, Carrer de Montjuïc del Bisbe, to reach, through an archway, **Plaça de Sant Felip Neri**. This quiet, five-sided square has a gurgling fountain as a centrepiece, while the offbeat **Museu del Calçat** (➤ 59) lies just around to the left.

2–3

Exit along Carrer de Sant Felip Neri, turn right onto Carrer de Sant Sever and descend **Baixada de Santa Eulàlia**, down which the city's patron saint was rolled naked in a barrel of broken glass. Where you meet Carrer de Banys

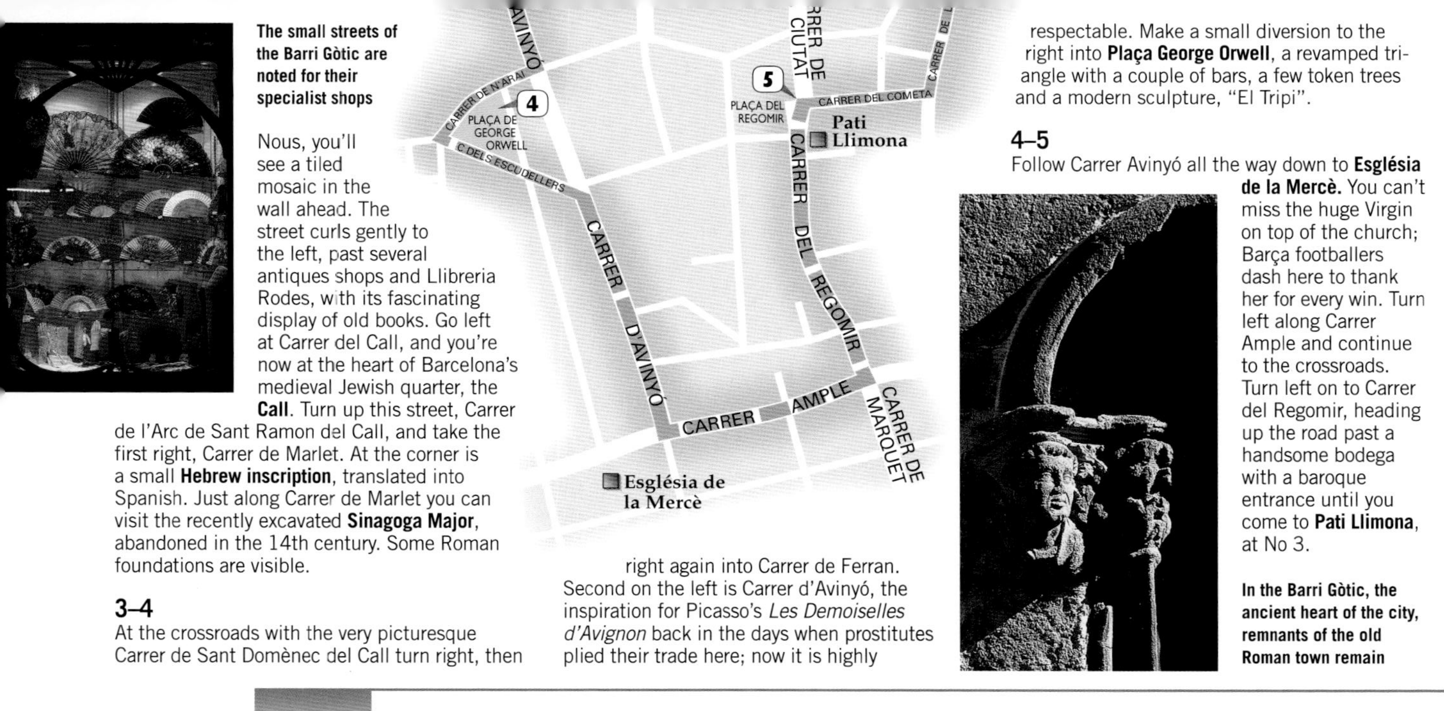

The small streets of the Barri Gòtic are noted for their specialist shops

Nous, you'll see a tiled mosaic in the wall ahead. The street curls gently to the left, past several antiques shops and Llibreria Rodes, with its fascinating display of old books. Go left at Carrer del Call, and you're now at the heart of Barcelona's medieval Jewish quarter, the **Call**. Turn up this street, Carrer de l'Arc de Sant Ramon del Call, and take the first right, Carrer de Marlet. At the corner is a small **Hebrew inscription**, translated into Spanish. Just along Carrer de Marlet you can visit the recently excavated **Sinagoga Major**, abandoned in the 14th century. Some Roman foundations are visible.

3–4

At the crossroads with the very picturesque Carrer de Sant Domènec del Call turn right, then right again into Carrer de Ferran. Second on the left is Carrer d'Avinyó, the inspiration for Picasso's *Les Demoiselles d'Avignon* back in the days when prostitutes plied their trade here; now it is highly respectable. Make a small diversion to the right into **Plaça George Orwell**, a revamped triangle with a couple of bars, a few token trees and a modern sculpture, "El Tripi".

4–5

Follow Carrer Avinyó all the way down to **Església de la Mercè.** You can't miss the huge Virgin on top of the church; Barça footballers dash here to thank her for every win. Turn left along Carrer Ample and continue to the crossroads. Turn left on to Carrer del Regomir, heading up the road past a handsome bodega with a baroque entrance until you come to **Pati Llimona**, at No 3.

In the Barri Gòtic, the ancient heart of the city, remnants of the old Roman town remain

5–6
Now go right along Carrer del Cometa, and left along Carrer dels Lleidó, lined with impressive stone buildings. You'll quickly reach Plaça de Sant Just: on the left-hand side, as you look at the church of **Sants Just i Pastor**, you'll notice a row of beautiful fountainheads still used by locals for their drinking water. The church has a fine, typically Catalan Gothic façade and a single, slender tower – but inside it's gloomy.

6–7
Next, turn left down Carrer d'Hercules, right into Carrer d'Arlet, and left again into **Plaça de Sant Jaume** (➤ 58). Head up Carrer dels Paradis; the street slopes steeply upwards before making a sharp turn to the right. Ahead of you at No 10 is the entrance to the **Centre Excursionista de Catalunya**; inside stand four fine Corinthian columns, all that remains of the Temple d'August, built at the highest point of the Roman city, 16.9m (55 feet) above sea level.

7–8
As Carrer dels Paradis twists around and enters Carrer de la Pietat, you're treated to splendid views of the **Catedral** and its gargoyles. Carry on down Carrer de la Pietat, turn right into Carrer Veguer, and left again into Plaça de l'Angel.

The interior of the church of Sants Just i Pastor

Places to Visit
Sinagoga Major
✉ Carrer de Marlet 5
🕐 Daily 11–2:30, 4–7:30 Free

Centre Excursionista de Catalunya
✉ Carrer Paradis 10
🕐 Tue–Sat 10–2, 4–8, Sun 10–2

Taking a Break
If you're in need of some light refreshment the atmospheric *orxateria* **La Granja** (Carrer dels Banys Nous 4) is the perfect place to stop. Alternatively, for something more substantial, try your luck at the ever-popular **Can Culleretes** (➤ 68), the oldest restaurant in the city.

When?
Go on a busy weekday or Saturday morning – otherwise the back streets are often quiet to the point of eeriness – and don't venture here alone at night.

2 GRÀCIA

Walk

DISTANCE 3km (2 miles) **TIME** 2½ hours
START POINT Plaça de Joan Carles 1 Diagonal 200 B2
END POINT Plaça Lesseps Lesseps 200 C5

Enticing little squares and narrow streets characterise the neighbourhood of Gràcia. Long a favourite haunt of artists and students, it has become smarter and more fashionable in recent years, yet retains its special, Bohemian charm.

1–2

The landscaped, open area in the middle of the Passeig de Gràcia, officially Jardins de Salvador Espriu, is popularly known as the **Jardinets**, or little gardens. On the right-hand side, where the street narrows to become Carrer Gran de Gràcia, is the **Casa Fuster** (Passeig de Gràcia 132), a Modernist masterpiece with lavish stone carving, built between 1908 and 1911 by Lluís Domènech i Montaner and his son, Pere. Immediately afterwards on the left, at Gran de Gràcia 15, is the superb **Casa Francesc Cama Escurra**, sporting beautiful stained-glass oriels. Opposite is Carrer de Gràcia, a typically narrow Gràcienc alleyway; turn along it, past the stern 19th-century façade of the church of **Santa Maria de Jesús**. Turn left into Carrer Sant Pere Martir and left again into Carrer de Jesús, to rejoin Carrer Gran de Gràcia.

Casa Fuster, noted for its combination of neo-Gothic and classical styles

2–3

Up on the left-hand side is the gorgeous sgraffito façade of **Casa Elisa Bremon** (Gran de Gràcia 61), another Modernist house, dating from 1904. Go up to the corner of Carrer Santa Eugènia to take a peek at the equally fine **Casa Francesc Cama**, at No 77. Its architect, Francesc Berenguer i Mestres, wasn't allowed to sign the façade when it was finished in 1905 as he had no university degree, so it bears his boss's signature: Miquel Pascual i Tintorer.

3–4

Now backtrack a few metres to **Travessera de Gràcia**, one of the neighbourhood's axes, lined with small shops, and turn left. Continue past a

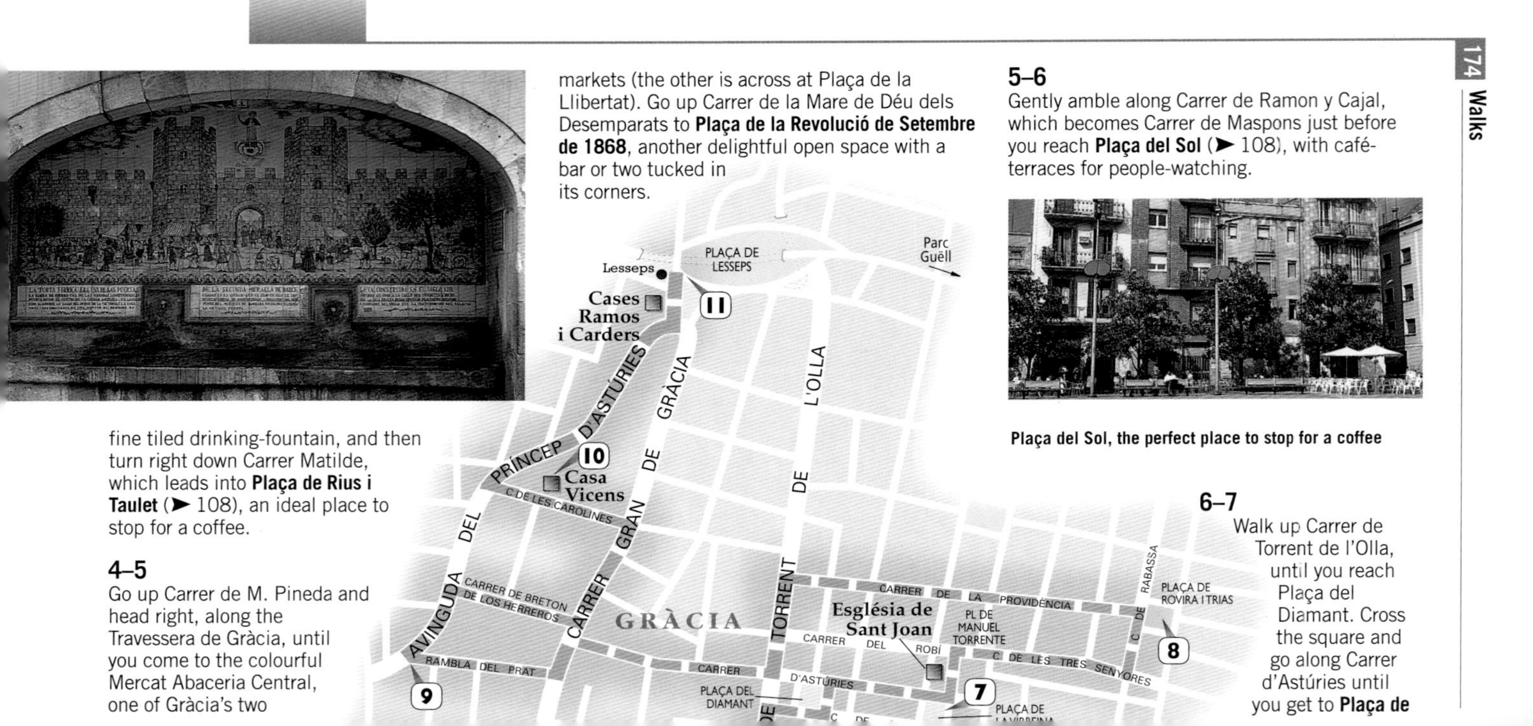

fine tiled drinking-fountain, and then turn right down Carrer Matilde, which leads into **Plaça de Rius i Taulet** (➤ 108), an ideal place to stop for a coffee.

4–5

Go up Carrer de M. Pineda and head right, along the Travessera de Gràcia, until you come to the colourful Mercat Abaceria Central, one of Gràcia's two markets (the other is across at Plaça de la Llibertat). Go up Carrer de la Mare de Déu dels Desemparats to **Plaça de la Revolució de Setembre de 1868**, another delightful open space with a bar or two tucked in its corners.

5–6

Gently amble along Carrer de Ramon y Cajal, which becomes Carrer de Maspons just before you reach **Plaça del Sol** (➤ 108), with café-terraces for people-watching.

Plaça del Sol, the perfect place to stop for a coffee

6–7

Walk up Carrer de Torrent de l'Olla, until you reach Plaça del Diamant. Cross the square and go along Carrer d'Astúries until you get to **Plaça de**

la Virreina. It boasts the *barrio's* finest church, **Sant Joan**. On the opposite side is the handsomely ornate Modernist façade of **Casa Rubinat i Planas** (1906–09), at Carrer de l'Or 44.

7–8

Via the Plaça Manuel Torrente, head along Carrer del Robí and Carrer de les Tres Senyores before going up Carrer de Rabassa to the attractively shady **Plaça de Rovira i Trias**. Look for the statue of Rovira i Trias, who came second in the competition to design the Eixample: a bronze map at his feet shows what it would have looked like if he had beaten Cerdà (➤ 24).

8–9

From here carry on along Carrer de la Providencia and turn left on to Carrer Torrent de l'Olla. Turn right on to Carrer de Astúries, cross Carrer Gran de Gràcia, and wander along the **Rambla del Prat**, one of the noblest of Gracienc streets, lined with a serried rank of Modernist houses.

9–10

Go up wide Avinguda del Princep d'Astúries and turn right on to Carrer Breton de los Herreros. At the intersection with Carrer Gran de Gràcia, turn left. Climb a short stretch, then turn left on to Carrer de les Carolines to see **Casa Vicens** (➤ 109).

10–11

Finally, make your way up Avinguda del Princep d'Astúries to the major transport interchange, **Plaça Lesseps**. On the corner of Carrer Gran de Gràcia, at Nos 30–32, you can admire three heavily ornamented houses called the **Cases Ramos i Carders**, built between 1905 and 1908 by the extravagant architect Jaume Torres i Grau. Their rich decoration and fantastic stained glass finish this walk around Gràcia with a flourish. Either go and visit Parc Güell (➤ 110–112) or catch the Metro or bus back.

Taking a Break

Gràcia is packed with cafés and down-to-earth eateries, clustered around all the main squares. **El Glop** (➤ 122) and **Can Punyetes** (Carrer Francisco Giner 8–10, tel: 93 217 79 46) are two of the few restaurants here open all day Sunday.

When?

Around lunchtime, to take advantage of the bars and restaurants. Or late afternoon, early evening, for the winding-down atmosphere – then stay for dinner.

3 MODERNIST GEMS
Walk

DISTANCE 4.5km (3 miles) **TIME** 3 hours
START POINT Els Quatre Gats, Carrer de Montsió 3 Ⓜ Catalunya ✚ 193 D4
END POINT Palau Robert, Passeig de Gràcia and Avinguda Diagonal Ⓜ Diagonal ✚ 200 B2

Although Gaudí is Barcelona's most famous Modernist architect, and his buildings tend to steal the limelight, there is a great deal of art nouveau architecture to be seen in the city besides his. Leading names in the movement include Lluís Domènech i Montaner, Puig i Cadafalch and Jujol i Gilbert.

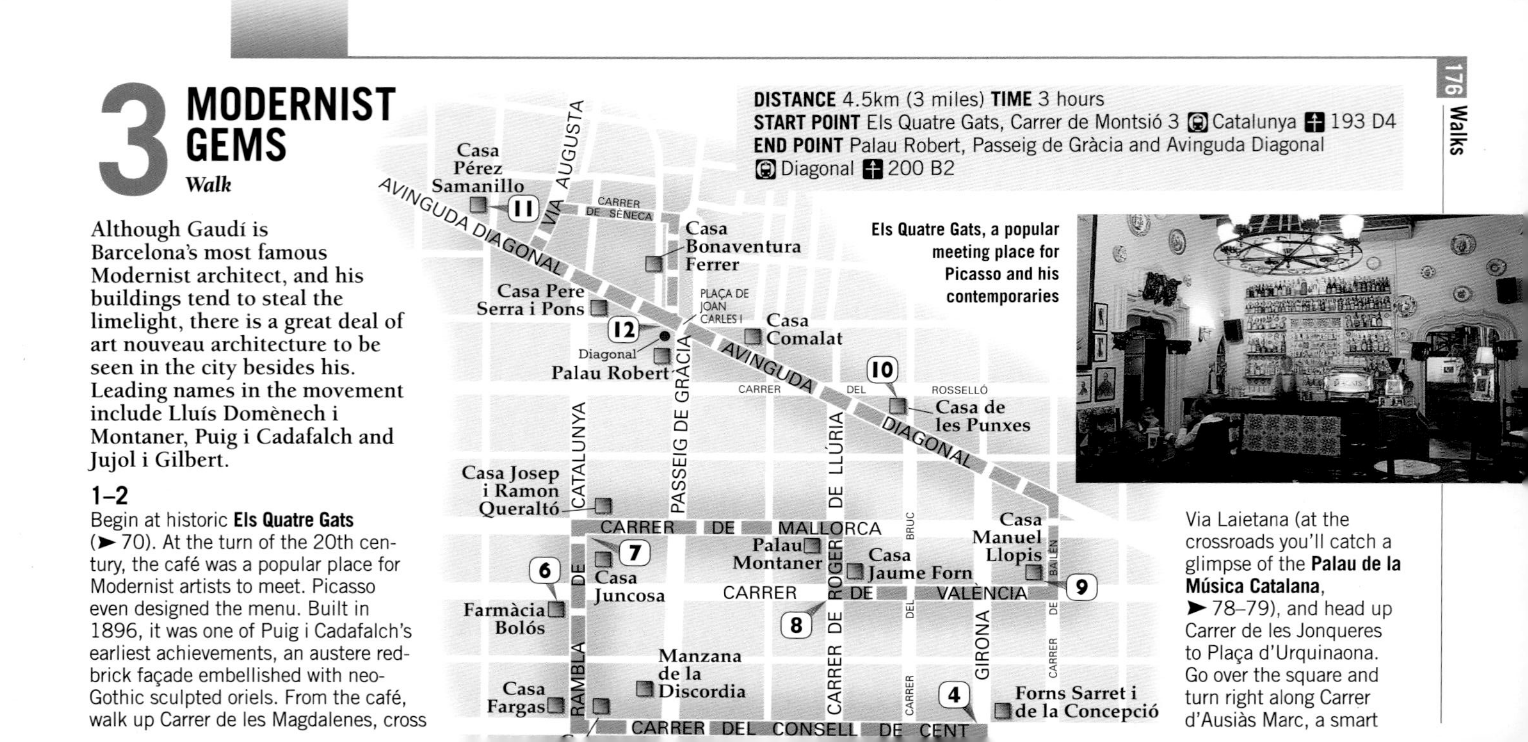

Els Quatre Gats, a popular meeting place for Picasso and his contemporaries

1–2

Begin at historic **Els Quatre Gats** (➤ 70). At the turn of the 20th century, the café was a popular place for Modernist artists to meet. Picasso even designed the menu. Built in 1896, it was one of Puig i Cadafalch's earliest achievements, an austere red-brick façade embellished with neo-Gothic sculpted oriels. From the café, walk up Carrer de les Magdalenes, cross Via Laietana (at the crossroads you'll catch a glimpse of the **Palau de la Música Catalana**, ➤ 78–79), and head up Carrer de les Jonqueres to Plaça d'Urquinaona. Go over the square and turn right along Carrer d'Ausiàs Marc, a smart

Art imitates life on the façade of Casa Antonia Burés

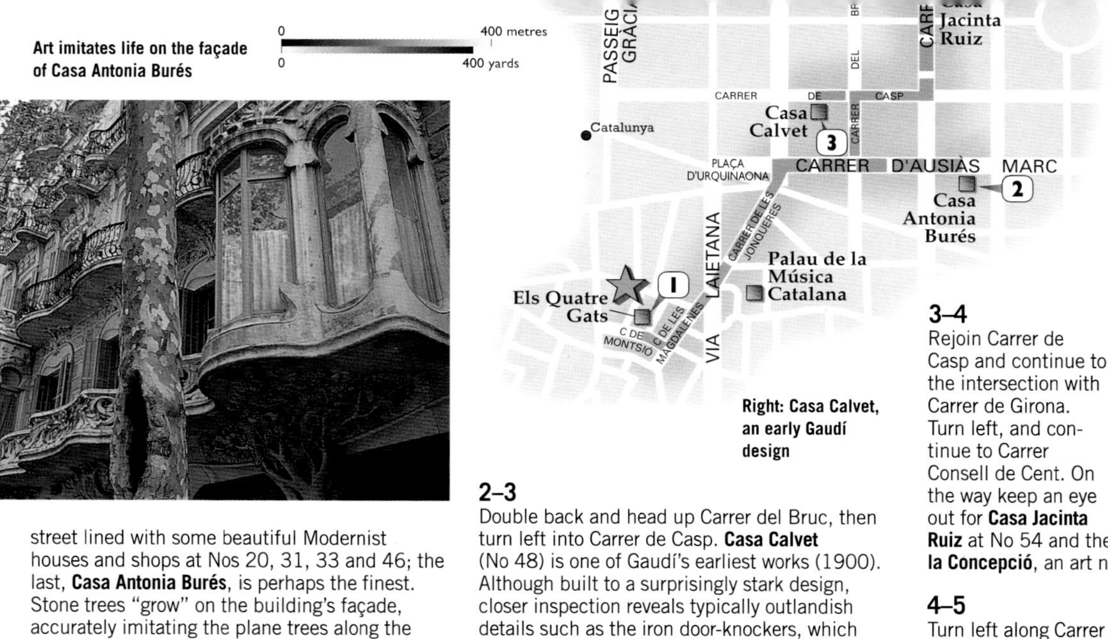

Right: Casa Calvet, an early Gaudí design

street lined with some beautiful Modernist houses and shops at Nos 20, 31, 33 and 46; the last, **Casa Antonia Burés**, is perhaps the finest. Stone trees "grow" on the building's façade, accurately imitating the plane trees along the roadside.

2–3

Double back and head up Carrer del Bruc, then turn left into Carrer de Casp. **Casa Calvet** (No 48) is one of Gaudí's earliest works (1900). Although built to a surprisingly stark design, closer inspection reveals typically outlandish details such as the iron door-knockers, which look as though they've melted.

3–4

Rejoin Carrer de Casp and continue to the intersection with Carrer de Girona. Turn left, and continue to Carrer Consell de Cent. On the way keep an eye out for **Casa Jacinta Ruiz** at No 54 and the charming **Forns Sarret i de la Concepció**, an art nouveau bakery at No 73.

4–5

Turn left along Carrer Consell de Cent; you cross Passeig de Gràcia at a wonderful vantage point,

Casa Batlló, part of the Manzana de la Discordia

with a side-on view of the **Manzana de la Discordia** (➤ 102–104). Notice also the street lamps with seats coated in white *trencadí* (ceramic shards), a much-photographed feature of the Passeig. They were designed by Pere Falqués i Urpí in 1906.

5–6

After cutting across the Passeig de Gràcia, turn right after one block into the equally elegant Rambla de Catalunya, with its wide central pavement. Here you're treated to a trio of wonders. First, **Casa Dolors Calm** at No 54, by Josep Vilaseca i Casanovas (who built the Arc de Triomf, ➤ 86), has a striking five-storeyed gallery jutting out over the street, inspired by houses in Seville. **Casa Fargas** at No 47 echoes the Casa Dolors gallery with a stone oriel, but the overall style is eminently sober, not unlike the buildings along the grand boulevards of Paris. Last but not least is **Farmàcia Bolós** at No 77; the tree-of-life stained-glass window, laden with ripe oranges, is breathtaking.

6–7

Now cross the Ramblas to No 78 to admire **Casa Juncosa**. This is an altogether more restrained affair, with its rough-hewn ashlars and symmetrical balconies, but the finely carved tympanum, with botanical motifs, gives it away as a Modernist building – it went up in 1909 to a design by Salvador Vinals i Sabater. Continue up the Rambla de Catalunya until you reach the intersection with Carrer de Mallorca.

7–8

Stop for a moment to look at **Casa Josep i Ramon Queraltó**, on the corner of the Rambla de Catalunya – the sgraffito work on the façade is particularly fine. Then continue down Carrer de Mallorca until you reach Carrer de Roger de Llúria. On the corner, to your right, stands **Palau Montaner** (Carrer de Mallorca 278), a masterpiece by Lluís Domènech i Montaner. The wrought-iron work in the gates and the glazed-tile mosaics are outstanding. Now turn right down Carrer Roger de Llúria to reach Carrer de València.

8–9

You can't miss the flamboyant **Casa Jaume Forn** on the left-hand corner at Carrer de València 285. This tour de force by Jeroni Granell i Manresa, built in 1909, has an almost plain chamfered corner façade with edges softened by semi-cylindrical columns filled in with delicately decorated stained glass. The wood and

wrought-iron of the central doorway is outstanding. Count three blocks along Carrer de València to the left until you come to the corner with Carrer de Bailèn. Here at No 339 stands the **Casa Manuel Llopis** (1903), by Antoni Gallissà i Soque, with sgraffito by Josep Maria Jujol, who also worked on several of Gaudí's projects.

9–10

Go up Carrer de Bailèn to Avinguda Diagonal, turn left and go along two blocks. Wonderful **Casa de les Punxes**, once described as a cross between a Flemish guildhall and one of mad King Ludwig's Bavarian castles, stands at Nos 416–420, on the corner of Carrer del Rosselló. Its official name is **Casa Bartomeu Terrades i Brutau**. It is really three houses in one: Terrades' three daughters each lived in one section. When it was built to a design by Josep Puig i Cadafalch in 1905 a pamphleteer described it as a "crime against the nation".

Palau Montaner (see page 178) was designed by architect Lluís Domènech i Montaner

10–11

Continue along the avenue, past **Casa Comalat** (No 442), a "harlequin's hat set in stone" (take a look at the fabulous doorway), and turn right up the Passeig de Gràcia. On the left-hand side look for **Casa Bonaventura Ferrer** (Passeig de Gràcia 113), an unassuming house with subtle wrought-iron balconies by Pere Falqués i Urpí, dwarfed by the Deutsche Bank next door. Turn left along Carrer de Sèneca then left again, down the lower reaches of Via Augusta, and turn right into Avinguda Diagonal. On the first corner is **Casa Pérez Samanillo**, a belvedere occupied by the Círculo Ecuestre (horse riding club), with a wonderful large oval window on the Avinguda Diagonal façade.

11–12

Cross over Avinguda Diagonal and backtrack to the corner with Passeig de Gràcia, where the Diagonal Metro station is located. On the way you'll recognise the exuberant style of Puig i Cadafalch in the splendid neo-Renaissance stone façade and mock-medieval turret of the **Casa Pere Serra** (Rambla de Catalunya 126).

Taking a Break

There is a wealth of cafés, tapas bars, restaurants and brasseries on the Passeig de Gràcia and the Rambla de Catalunya from which to choose. **Pastisseria Maurí** (Rambla de Catalunya 102, tel: 93 215 10 20), which serves delicious cakes, and **Café Torino** (Passeig de Gracia 59, tel: 93 487 75 71), where you can enjoy top-notch coffee in elegant Modernist surroundings, are particularly good.

When?

Aim for Sunday afternoons or Monday mornings, when nearly everything else in the city is closed.

4 ALONG THE WATERFRONT

Walk

TIME 3 hours
START POINT Castell de Montjuïc 194 C2
END POINT Port Olímpic 197 F1

Since the 1990s, the city has made a feature of its waterfront. Starting from a vantage point that gives excellent views of the harbour and the sea, the walk will take you past luxury marinas and along waterside promenades to reach sandy beaches.

1–2

You don't need to go inside the forbidding **Castell de Montjuïc** (➤ 140) to enjoy spectacular views of the city's new commercial harbour, to the south, and of the old port, now a pleasure marina, to the north: the terraces in front of the fortified walls offer splendid panoramas for free. From the castle, either swing down on the *telefèric* **cable cars** and follow the signs along the Avinguda de Miramar to the **Miramar** (Sea Lookout) itself, or walk down the Carretera de Montjuïc.

2– 3

From the Miramar you get closer views of the harbour and its maritime activity. If you have plenty of time and weather permits, amble around the delightfully landscaped **Jardins de Miramar** and wend your way down through the exotic cacti of the **Jardins de Mossèn Costa i Llobera**; otherwise catch the Transbordador cable car (➤ 182) to the **Torre de Sant Jaume I**, on the Moll de Barcelona. It looks scarier than it actually is, and the views down onto Port Vell are breathtaking.

Views of the city from the *telefèric* cable cars are superb

3– 4

Head for the **Moll de la Fusta**, or Timber Wharf, by aiming for the landmark **Monument a Colom** (➤ 52) – the statue of **Columbus** atop his lofty column – surrounded by official buildings such as the Duanes (Customs House), the **Drassanes** (➤ 132–133) and the Govern Militar (Military Governor's House). On the portside is the ticket-office for the double-decker **Golondrinas** pleasure boats (➤ 182); time permitting, take a ride around the harbour or even a short way along the coast. You can also disembark at Barceloneta (➤ 90).

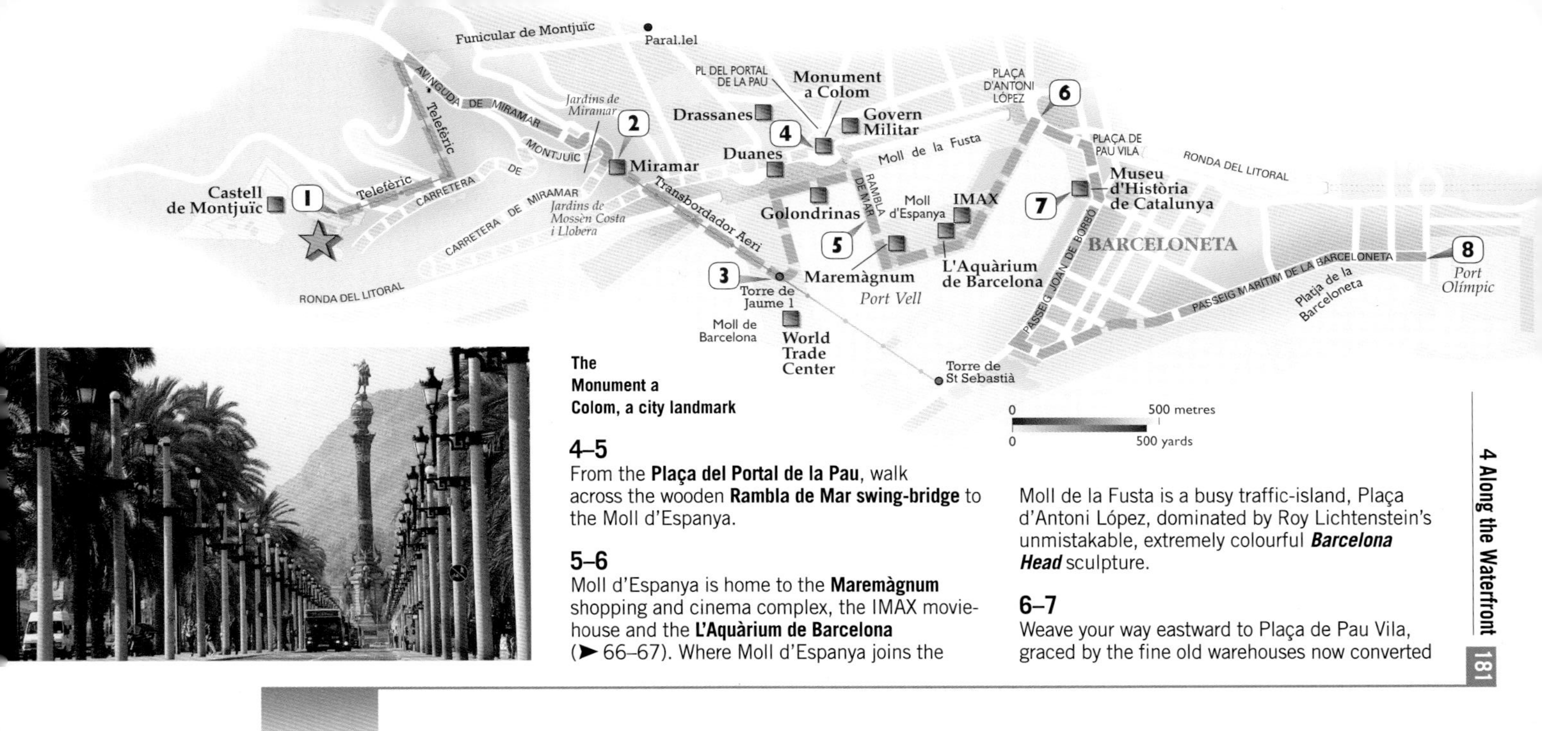

The Monument a Colom, a city landmark

4–5

From the **Plaça del Portal de la Pau**, walk across the wooden **Rambla de Mar swing-bridge** to the Moll d'Espanya.

5–6

Moll d'Espanya is home to the **Maremàgnum** shopping and cinema complex, the IMAX movie-house and the **L'Aquàrium de Barcelona** (➤ 66–67). Where Moll d'Espanya joins the Moll de la Fusta is a busy traffic-island, Plaça d'Antoni López, dominated by Roy Lichtenstein's unmistakable, extremely colourful ***Barcelona Head*** sculpture.

6–7

Weave your way eastward to Plaça de Pau Vila, graced by the fine old warehouses now converted

Cable car and Golondrinas Info

***Telefèric* Cable cars**
The cable cars up and down Montjuïc run from 11 to 8 in the summer, and from 11 to 7:30 in the winter, with a lunch break.
Hot tip: the wait for the upward ride from the Estació Funicular can get quite lengthy in the summer; get there early or take a taxi up.

Transbordador Cable cars
☎ 93 441 50 71
The cable cars across the harbour (often crowded) run daily from 11 to 8 in the summer, afternoons only from October to February.

Golondrinas
☎ 93 442 28 54
The boats run from 11 to 8:30 in the height of the summer, whittling down their hours to lunchtimes only in the winter. Closed 15 December to 1 January.

The return trip to the breakwater takes 30 minutes and the voyage to the Port Olímpic and back takes 90 minutes, but you can't disembark.

Redeveloped for the 1992 Olympics, Port Vell is now a sophisticated pleasure port

into the **Museu d'Història de Catalunya** (➤ 88–89). **Barceloneta** (➤ 89), with its tantalising seafood restaurants and characterful narrow streets, stretches before you; either make your way through it or walk round the edge of the peninsula to reach the Passeig Marítim de la Barceloneta.

7–8

The **Passeig Marítim de la Barceloneta** takes you behind Barceloneta's beach to the ever-bustling **Port Olímpic** (➤ 90), a marina that was built specially for the 1992 Olympiad. It's still a popular haunt with families and anyone looking for some frivolous fun or a tasty fish dinner. Beyond Port Olímpic is the seaside promenade where you'll compete for space with roller bladers and cyclists. If you feel inclined, you could round off the walk with a dip in the Mediterranean. For more information on Barcelona's new **beaches**, ➤ 90.

Taking a Break

Port Vell, Barceloneta and Port Olímpic are, as you'd expect, places to sample seafood of every description (➤ 91–93).

When?

You can do this walk any day of the week. To make the most of the views, the beaches and the bracing seaside air, go in fine weather.

Practicalities

GETTING ADVANCE INFORMATION

Websites
- City of Barcelona
www.bcn.es
- Tourist Authority
www.barcelonaturisme.com

In Barcelona
Tourist Information Office
Plaça de Catalunya
☎ 906 30 12 82

In the UK
Spanish Tourist Office
22–23 Manchester Square
London W1U 3PX
☎ (020) 7486 8077

BEFORE YOU GO

WHAT YOU NEED

- ● Required
- ○ Suggested
- ▲ Not required
- △ Not applicable

	UK	Germany	USA	Canada	Australia	Ireland	Netherlands	Spain
Passport/National Identity Card	●	●	●	●	●	●	●	●
Visa	▲	▲	▲	▲	▲	▲	▲	▲
Onward or Return Ticket	▲	▲	▲	▲	▲	▲	▲	▲
Health Inoculations (tetanus and polio)	▲	▲	▲	▲	▲	▲	▲	▲
Health Documentation (► 188, Health)	●	●	●	●	●	●	●	●
Travel Insurance	○	○	○	○	○	○	○	○
Driver's Licence (national)	●	●	●	●	●	●	●	●
Car Insurance Certificate	○	○	n/a	n/a	n/a	○	○	○
Car Registration Document	●	●	n/a	n/a	n/a	●	●	●

WHEN TO GO

Barcelona

High season   Low season

JAN	FEB	MAR	APR	MAY	JUN	JUL	AUG	SEP	OCT	NOV	DEC
14°C	15°C	17°C	19°C	22°C	25°C	29°C	29°C	27°C	23°C	18°C	15°C
57°F	59°F	63°F	66°F	72°F	77°F	84°F	84°F	81°F	73°F	64°F	59°F

Sun   Cloud   Wet   Sun/Showers

Temperatures are the **average daily maximum** for each month.
The best time to visit Barcelona is May to June or September to October, when the weather is fine but not too hot, and there is a lot going on in the city. July and August see an exodus of locals and many museums; restaurants and shops either close or reduce their opening hours; day-trippers from coastal resorts crowd the city; and the weather can be hot and sticky, with some violent thunderstorms. On the upside, there are plenty of fiestas and festivals to keep you entertained. Winters are cool but seldom cold, though it can snow; when skies are blue and visibility perfect, January and February can be good months of the year.

In the US (New York)
Tourist Office of Spain
666 Fifth Avenue
35th Floor
New York
NY 10103
☎ (212) 265-8822

In the US (Los Angeles)
Tourist Office of Spain
8383 Wilshire Blvd,
Suite 960
Beverly Hills
CA 90211
☎ (323) 658-7195

In Germany
Tourist Office of Spain
Myliusstrasse, 14
60323 Frankfurt Main
☎ (49) 69 72 50 38

GETTING THERE

By Air Barcelona has one airport, El Prat, 12km (8 miles) from the city centre.
From North America Non-stop flights are operated from New York by Iberia, in association with its partner in the Oneworld alliance, American Airlines. Other flights from North America involve a stop at Madrid or a change of planes, either at Madrid or one of the other leading European airports, notably Amsterdam, Frankfurt, Lisbon, London, Milan or Paris.
From the UK and Ireland There is intense competition – especially from London. The lowest fares are often on the no-frills airline easyJet, from Gatwick, Luton and Stansted. British Airways and its alliance partner, Iberia, fly from Gatwick, Heathrow, Birmingham and Manchester. British Midland (bmi) flies from Heathrow, and easyJet also flies from Liverpool to Barcelona. Iberia flies from Dublin, in association with its Oneworld partner Aer Lingus.
From Australia and New Zealand There are no direct flights to Spain from Australia or New Zealand; connections via London, Frankfurt or Paris are the most common.
Approximate flying times to Barcelona: London (1½ hours), Liverpool (2 hours), New York (8 hours).
Ticket prices Flight prices tend to be highest in spring and summer (Easter to September). A good way to solve the problem of finding somewhere to stay, especially at busy times, is to buy a city-break package that includes flights and accommodation. Check with airlines, travel agents, specialist tour-operators and the internet for current best deals.

By Rail The main regional, national and international rail station is Sants-Estació. Comfortable, fast, express trains connect the city to Paris, Madrid and Valencia.

TIME

Spain is on Central European Time, one hour ahead of Greenwich Mean Time (GMT +1). From late March, when clocks are put forward one hour, until late October, summer time (GMT +2) operates.

CURRENCY AND FOREIGN EXCHANGE

Currency Spain is one of the 12 European Union countries to use a single currency, the **Euro**. Coins are issued in denominations of 1, 2, 5, 10, 20, and 50 Euro cents and 1 and 2 Euros. Notes are issued in denominations of 5, 10, 20, 50, 100, 200 and 500 Euros.

Exchange You can change **travellers' cheques** at banks and savings banks (*caixes d'estalvis*), at *oficines de canvi* (including late-night bureaux de change along The Ramblas) and at stations and airports. Bureaux de change don't charge commission but apply (often far) less favourable rates.

Credit cards are widely accepted in shops, restaurants and hotels. Some shops require **proof of identity** (no copies). VISA, Mastercard, AMEX and Diners Club are the preferred cards, and they can be used to withdraw cash from widespread ATMs.

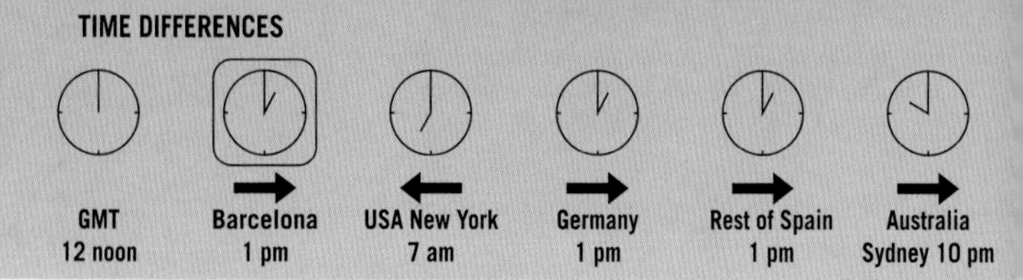

WHEN YOU ARE THERE

CLOTHING SIZES

UK	Spain	USA	
36	46	36	Suits
38	48	38	Suits
40	50	40	Suits
42	52	42	Suits
44	54	44	Suits
46	56	46	Suits
7	41	8	Shoes
7.5	42	8.5	Shoes
8.5	43	9.5	Shoes
9.5	44	10.5	Shoes
10.5	45	11.5	Shoes
11	46	12	Shoes
14.5	37	14.5	Shirts
15	38	15	Shirts
15.5	39/40	15.5	Shirts
16	41	16	Shirts
16.5	42	16.5	Shirts
17	43	17	Shirts
8	34	6	Dresses
10	36	8	Dresses
12	38	10	Dresses
14	40	12	Dresses
16	42	14	Dresses
18	44	16	Dresses
4.5	38	6	Shoes
5	38	6.5	Shoes
5.5	39	7	Shoes
6	39	7.5	Shoes
6.5	40	8	Shoes
7	41	8.5	Shoes

PUBLIC HOLIDAYS

1 Jan	New Year's Day
6 Jan	Epiphany
Mar/Apr	Good Friday and Easter Monday
1 May	May Day
May/Jun	Whit Monday
24 Jun	St John's Day
15 Aug	Assumption
11 Sep	Catalan National Day
24 Sep	La Mercè
12 Oct	Discovery of Americas
1 Nov	All Saints' Day
6 Dec	Constitution Day
8 Dec	Immaculate Conception
25 Dec	Christmas Day
26 Dec	St Stephen's Day

OPENING HOURS

Shops
Offices
Banks
Post Offices
Museums/Monuments
Pharmacies

8 am 9 am 10 am noon 2 pm 4 pm 6 pm 8 pm 9 pm

Day Midday Evening

Shops Apart from big department stores, most shops close on Saturday afternoons and don't open again until Monday or even Tuesday. Major stores and malls are open all day and are increasingly allowed to trade on Sundays. Many shops close or work shorter hours in August.

Banks Banks open 8:30–2 Monday to Friday. Many banks open on Saturdays in the summer. Savings banks are open all day on Thursdays.

Museums Most, but not all, museums close on Sunday afternoons and all day Monday. Opening hours vary wildly from one to another so check individual entries.

EMERGENCY 112

POLICE 091

FIRE 080

AMBULANCE 061

PERSONAL SAFETY

Petty crime is largely confined to The Ramblas. Report any thefts to the police or the special **Turisme-Atenció station** at La Rambla 43 (tel: 93 301 90 60 or 93 317 70 16). It is open daily 7 am–midnight, and until 2 am on Friday and Saturday nights.

To be safe:

- Watch out for suspicious behaviour and keep a firm hold of your belongings.
- Never leave any belongings in vehicles and keep valuables in the hotel safe.
- Avoid the narrow Old City streets and the bottom end of The Ramblas at night, especially if you're alone.

Police assistance:
091 from any phone

TELEPHONES

Calls from phones in bars and cafés are more expensive than those made from phone booths on the street.

The best place to make international calls is from *locutorios* (phone centres), chiefly found in the Raval district. International cheap rates apply from 8 pm to 8 am and all weekend.

Increasingly public phones require a phonecard (*tarjeta*). You can buy these from post offices, newsstands and *estancs* (tobacconists).

International Dialling Codes
Dial 00 followed by

UK:	**44**
USA / Canada:	**1**
Irish Republic:	**353**
Australia:	**61**
France	**33**
Germany:	**49**

POST

Post offices are identified by the yellow Correos sign, but it is often more convenient to buy stamps from *estancs* (tobacconists). The main post office, in a beautiful building at Plaça Antoni López, is open Mon–Sat 8:30 am–9:30 pm. Post boxes are yellow.

ELECTRICITY

The power supply in Barcelona is 220 volts. Plugs are two-round-pin (or increasingly three-round pin); visitors from the UK and North America will require an adaptor. A transformer is needed for appliances operating on 110/120-volts.

TIPS/GRATUITIES

Most people round up **restaurant**, **bar** and **taxi** charges, and the more generous add on 5–10 per cent, but tipping is not expected.

Hotel porters and **lavatory attendants** expect a small gratuity, but cinema and theatre ushers do not – and may even refuse a tip.

CONSULATES and EMBASSIES

UK	USA	Germany	Australia	New Zealand
☎ 93 366 62 00	☎ 93 280 22 27	☎ 93 292 10 00	☎ 93 330 94 96	☎ 93 209 03 99

HEALTH

Insurance EU citizens can get most medical treatment at reduced cost with the relevant documentation (Form E111 for UK and Irish nationals), although medical insurance is still advised. Health insurance is essential for non-EU nationals. If you need to see an English-speaking doctor, try the Centre Mèdic Assistencial de Catalunya (Carrer Provença 281, tel: 93 215 37 93, open Mon–Fri 8–8).

Dental Services Private dental care only is available and is not covered by EU agreements. The walk-in Centre Odontològic de Barcelona (Carrer Calàbria 251, tel: 93 439 45 00) is the most convenient place to go for help.

Weather In the height of summer – June to September – it can get very hot. Wear a hat and sunglasses, use a high-factor sunscreen and drink plenty of fluids. Avoid alcohol during the day.

Health Pharmacies *(farmàcies)* are distinguished by a green cross (night pharmacies by a red cross). They sell prescription and non-prescription drugs and medicines. The staff often speak English and can help with minor ailments.

Safe Water Tap and drinking-fountain water is safe (unless it says *no potable*), but most people prefer to drink bottled water.

CONCESSIONS

Students and Young People Holders of a valid International Student Identity Card (ISIC), the International Youth Travel Card or GO 25 card pay discounted admission to most museums and attractions. Children under a certain age may be allowed in free.
Senior Citizens Anyone over 65 can get discounts in museums and other attractions; ID must be shown.
The Articket covers MNAC, MACBA, Fundació Miró, Espai Gaudí, Fundació Tàpies and the CCCB. It can be purchased at any of them and represents a 50 per cent saving if you go to all six.
The **Ruta del Modernisme** gives reduced admission to the paying sights along the Modernist Route.

TRAVELLING WITH A DISABILITY

Some buses and the newest Metro line, L2, have wheelchair access, but most facilities and attractions lack special amenities. The newer museums, such as MACBA, have facilities.
For additional help call a special transport service (tel: 93 486 07 52), or contact the Municipal Institute for the Disabled (tel: 93 291 84 00).

CHILDREN

Children are welcome almost anywhere in Barcelona and often stay up late. Most attractions either offer reduced-price entrance for children, or allow them in free of charge.

LAVATORIES

Public facilities are rare, but nearly all places of interest have modern, clean lavatories. If you stop at a café, you may be expected to buy a drink.

CUSTOMS

The import of wildlife souvenirs from rare and endangered species may be either illegal or require a special permit. Before purchase you should check customs regulations.

PRONUNCIATION

Catalan pronunciation differs considerably from Spanish. Catalan is more closed and less staccato in sound than its Castilian cousin but, like Spanish, is nearly always phonetic, albeit with a few special rules of its own, summarised below:

au ow in wow
c ss or k (never th)
ç ss
eu ay-oo
g g or j (never h)
gu (sometimes) w
h silent
j soft j (never guttural)
ig ch at the end of a word: *vaig* (I go) sounds like "batch"
ll lli in million
l.l ll in silly
ny ni in onion
r at beginning and rr heavily rolled
s z or ss, depending on position
tx ch in cheque
tg/tj dge in lodge (*lotja* sounds like "lodger")
v b (*vi*, wine, sounds like "bee")
x sh in shake

SURVIVAL PHRASES

Yes/no **Sí/no**
Please **Si us plau**
Thank you **Gràcies**
You're welcome **De res**
Goodbye **Adéu-siau**
Good morning **Bon dia**
Good afternoon **Bona tarda**
Good night **Bona nit**
How are you? **Com va?**
How much? **Quant és/val?**
Sorry **Ho sento**
Excuse me **Perdoni**
I'd like **Voldria**...
Open **Obert**
Closed **Tancat**

Today **avui**
Tomorrow **demà**
Yesterday **ahir**
Monday **dilluns**
Tuesday **dimarts**
Wednesday **dimecres**
Thursday **dijous**
Friday **divendres**
Saturday **dissabte**
Sunday **diumenge**

DIRECTIONS

I'm lost **Estic perdut/a**
Where is...? **On és...?**
How do I get to...? **Per anar a...?**
  the bank **el banc**
  the post office **els correus**
  the telephone **el telèfon**
  the lavatory **els serveis**
  the station **l'estació**
Left **a l'esquerra**
Right **a la dreta**
Straight on **tot recte**
At the corner **a la cantonada**
At the traffic-light **al semàfor**
At the crossroads **a la cruïlla**

IF YOU NEED HELP

Help! **Ajuda!**
Could you help me, please
  Em podria ajudar, si us plau?
Do you speak English? **Parla anglès?**
I don't understand **No ho entenc**
I don't speak Catalan
  No parlo català
Please could you call a doctor?
  Podria avisar un metge, si us plau?

NUMBERS

1 **u/un/una**
2 **dos/dues**
3 **tres**
4 **quatre**
5 **cinc**
6 **sis**
7 **set**
8 **vuit**
9 **nou**
10 **deu**
11 **onze**
12 **dotze**
13 **tretze**
14 **catorze**
15 **quinze**
16 **setze**
17 **disset**
18 **divuit**
19 **dinou**
20 **vint**
21 **vint-i-un**
30 **trenta**
40 **quaranta**
50 **cinquanta**

ACCOMMODATION

Do you have a single/double room?
Té alguna habitació senzilla/doble?
With/without bath/lavatory/shower
amb/sense bany/lavabo/dutxa
Does that include breakfast?
Inclou l'esmorzar?
Could I see the room?
Podria veure l'habitació?
I'll take this room
Ens quedarem aquesta habitació
Thanks for your hospitality
Gràcies per la seva amabilitat

RESTAURANT

I'd like to book a table
Voldria reservar una taula
A table for two, please
Una taula per a dos, si us plau
Could we see the menu, please?
Podríem veure el menú, si us plau?
A bottle of/a glass of...
Una ampolla/copa (vas) de...
Could I have the bill?
El compte, si us plau

service charge included **servei inclòs**
breakfast **esmorzar**
lunch **dinar**
dinner **sopar**
table **taula**
waiter/waitress **cambrer/a**
starter **entrant**
main course **segón plat**
cover charge **cobert**
bill **compte** VAT **IVA**

a la planxa grilled
aigua water
albergínia aubergine (eggplant)
all garlic
amanida salad
ànec duck
anxoves anchovies
anyell lamb
arròs rice

bacallà salt cod
bistec steak
bolets mushrooms
botifarra spicy sausage
bou beef
bullabesa fish soup

caça game
calamar squid
canelons Catalan cannelloni
carn meat
ceba onion
cervesa beer
cigrons chickpeas
coca cake
col cabbage
conill rabbit
cranc crab
cru raw

embotit sausage
enciam lettuce
ensaïmades pastry spirals
escopinyes cockles
escalivada roasted vegetable salad
escudella meat and vegetable stew

farcit stuffed
fetge liver
fideuà paella made from noodles
fideus spaghetti
formatge cheese
fregit fried
fruita fruit
fuet salami

gall d'indi turkey
gambes prawns
gel ice
gelat ice-cream
julivert parsley

llagosta lobster
llet milk
llimona lemon
llonganissa salami sausage
mantega butter
marisc seafood
mel honey
mongetes beans
musclos mussels

oli oil
oliva olive
ostra oyster
ou egg

pa bread
pastanaga carrot
pastís cake
patata potato
pebre pepper
pebrot pepper (vegetable)
peix fish
pernil dolç cooked ham
pernil serrà cured ham
plàtan banana
pollastre chicken
poma apple
porc pork
postres dessert

raïm grapes
rap monkfish
rostit roast

sal salt
salsa sauce
salsitxa sausage
sec dry
sopa soup
suc de taronja orange juice
sucre sugar

tonyina tuna
tortilla omelette
truita omelette/trout

vedella veal
verdura vegetables
vi blanc/negre white/red wine

xai lamb
xocolata chocolate

Streetplan

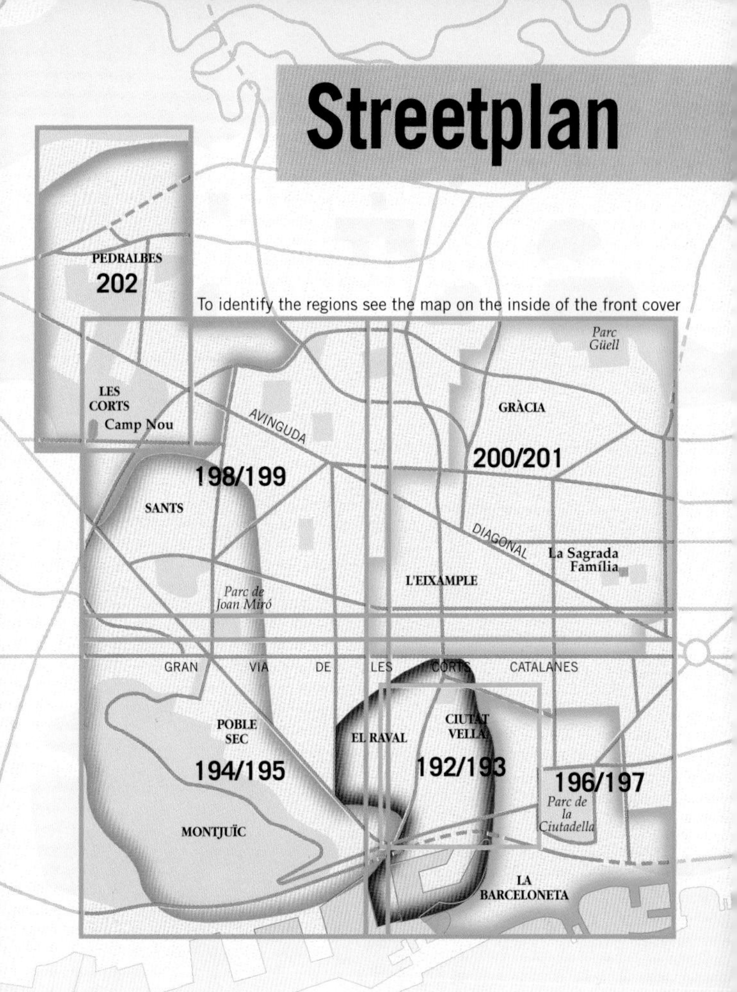

Key to Streetplan

- Main road
- Other road
- Rail line
- Cable car
- Park
- Important building
- Featured place of interest
- Metro station
- FGC station

192/193 — 0, 50, 100, 150, 200, 250 metres; 0, 50, 100, 150, 200, 250 yards

194-202 — 0, 100, 200, 300, 400, 500 metres; 0, 100, 200, 300, 400, 500 yards

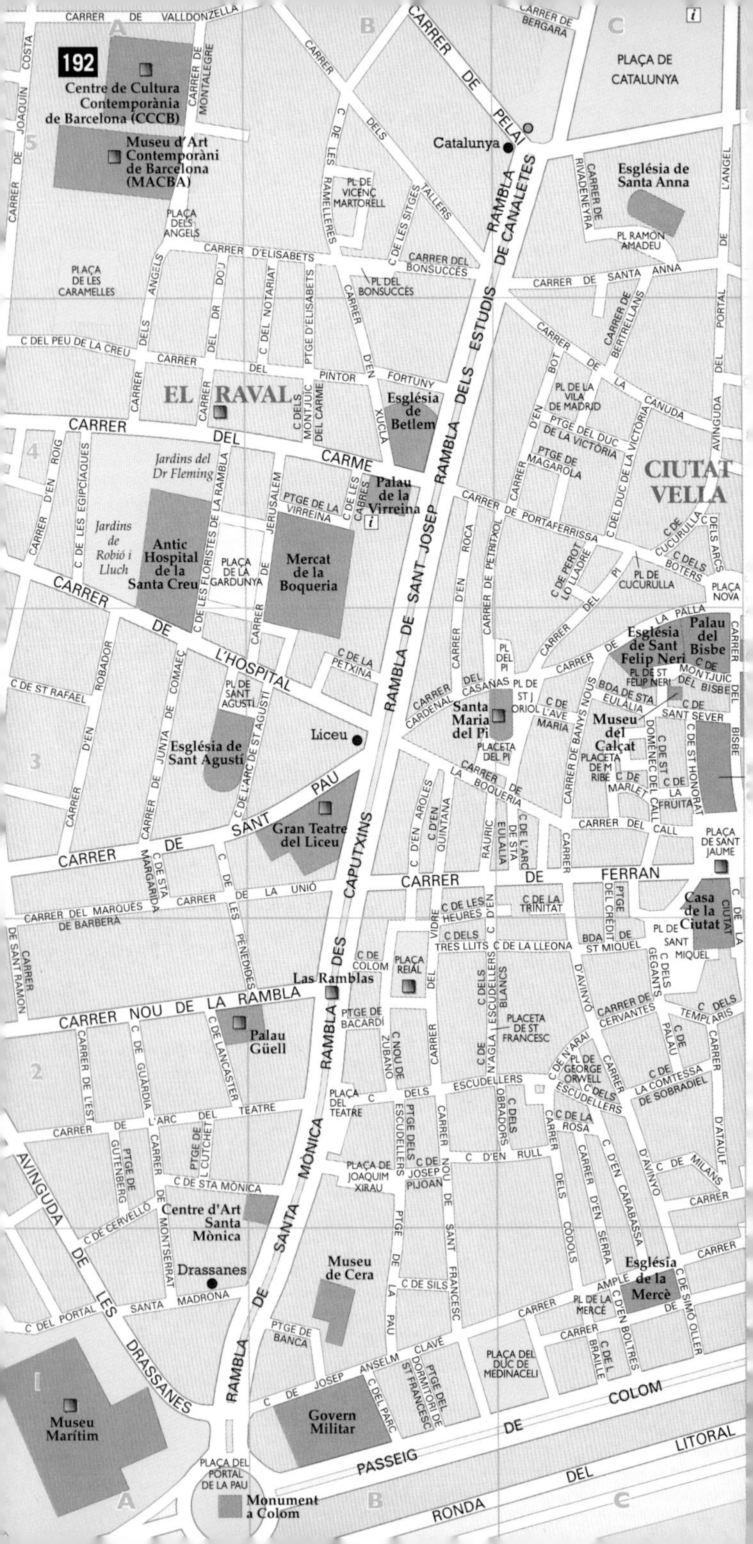
Centre de Cultura Contemporània de Barcelona (CCCB)
Museu d'Art Contemporàni de Barcelona (MACBA)
Plaça de Catalunya
Catalunya
Església de Santa Anna
Plaça dels Angels
Plaça de les Caramelles
PL de Vicenç Martorell
PL del Bonsuccés
PL Ramon Amadeu
EL RAVAL
Església de Betlem
Palau de la Virreina
CIUTAT VELLA
Jardins del Dr Fleming
Jardins de Robió i Lluch
Antic Hospital de la Santa Creu
Plaça de la Gardunya
Mercat de la Boqueria
PL de la Vila de Madrid
PL de Cucurulla
Plaça Nova
Església de Sant Felip Neri
Palau del Bisbe
PL de St Felip Neri
PL de Sant Agustí
Església de Sant Agustí
Liceu
Santa Maria del Pi
PL del Pi
PL de St J Oriol
Placeta del Pi
Museu del Calçat
Placeta de M Ribé
Gran Teatre del Liceu
Plaça de Sant Jaume
Casa de la Ciutat
PL de Sant Miquel
Plaça Reial
Las Ramblas
Palau Güell
Placeta de St Francesc
PL de George Orwell
Plaça del Teatre
Plaça de Joaquim Xirau
Centre d'Art Santa Mònica
Drassanes
Museu de Cera
Església de la Mercè
PL de la Mercè
Plaça del Duc de Medinaceli
Museu Marítim
Govern Militar
Plaça del Portal de la Pau
Monument a Colom
Carrer de Valldonzella
Carrer de Pelai
Carrer de Bergara
Rambla de Canaletes
Rambla dels Estudis
Rambla de Sant Josep
Rambla dels Caputxins
Rambla de Santa Mònica
Carrer del Carme
Carrer de l'Hospital
Carrer de Sant Pau
Carrer Nou de la Rambla
Carrer de Ferran
Carrer de Santa Anna
Carrer de la Canuda
Carrer de Portaferrissa
Carrer d'Elisabets
Carrer del Pintor Fortuny
Carrer dels Escudellers
Passeig de Colom
Ronda del Litoral
Avinguda de les Drassanes
Avinguda del Portal de l'Angel
A
B
C
2
3
4
5

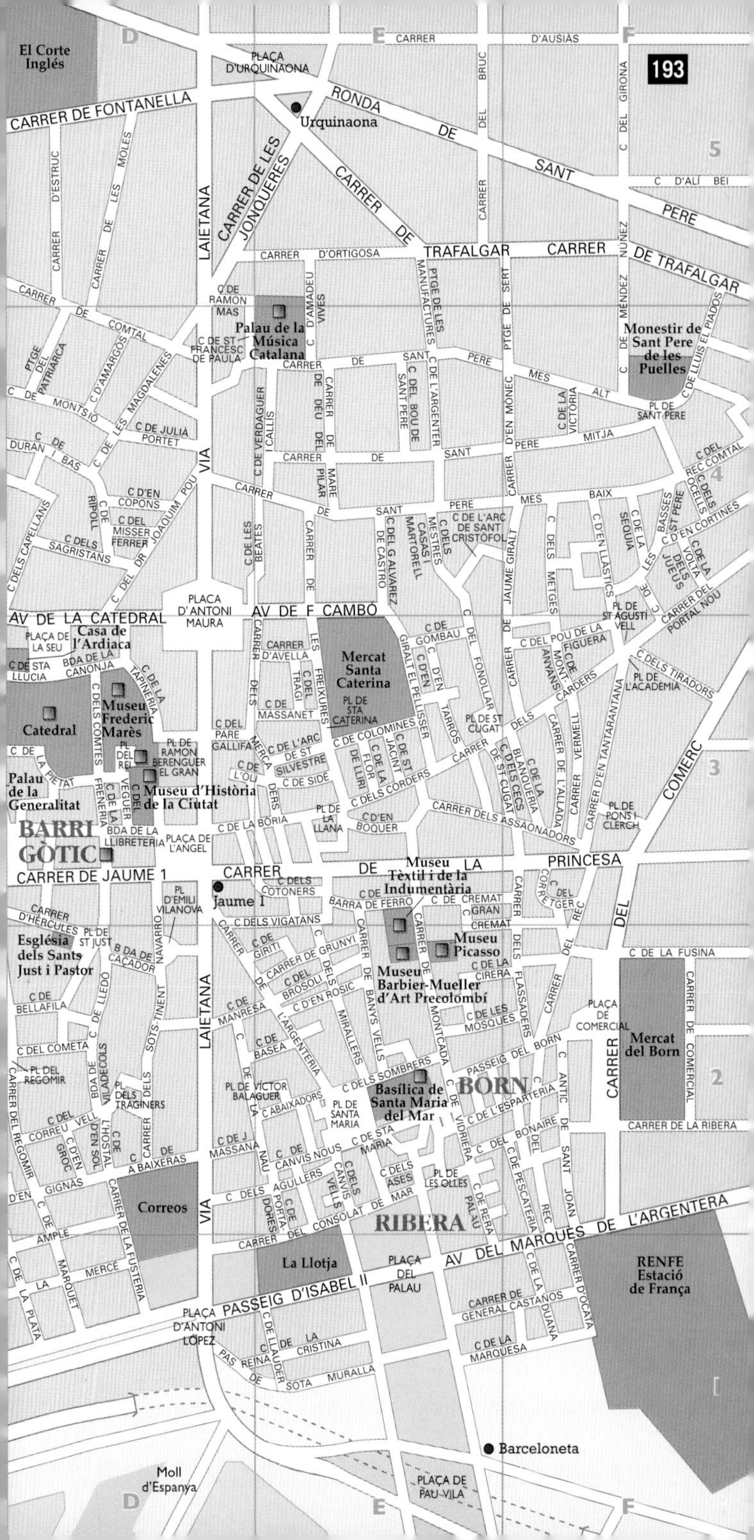

El Corte Inglés
PLAÇA D'URQUINAONA
Urquinaona
CARRER D'AUSIÀS
CARRER DE FONTANELLA
RONDA DE SANT PERE
C DEL BRUC
C DEL GIRONA
C D'ALÍ BEI
CARRER DE LES JONQUERES
CARRER DE TRAFALGAR
LAIETANA
VIA LAIETANA
CARRER D'ORTIGOSA
CARRER D'ESTRUC
CARRER DE LES MOLES
CARRER COMTAL
C DE RAMON MAS
Palau de la Música Catalana
C DE ST FRANCESC DE PAULA
C D'AMADEU VIVES
PTGE DE LES MANUFACTURES
PTGE DE SERT
C DE MÉNDEZ NÚÑEZ
Monestir de Sant Pere de les Puelles
PL DE SANT PERE
C DE LLUÍS EL PIADÓS
CARRER DE SANT PERE MES ALT
CARRER DE SANT PERE MITJÀ
CARRER DE SANT PERE MES BAIX
PTGE DEL PATRIARCA
C D'AMARGÓS
C DE MONTSIÓ
C DE LES MAGDALENES
C DE JULIÀ PORTET
C DE DURAN I BAS
C DE VERDAGUER I CALLÍS
CARRER DE DEU DEL PILAR
CARRER DE MARE DE DÉU DEL PILAR
C DEL BOU DE SANT PERE
C DE L'ARGENTER
CARRER D'EN MONEC
C DE LA VICTÒRIA
C D'EN COPONS
C DE RIPOLL
C DEL MISSER FERRER
C DELS SAGRISTANS
C DELS CAPELLANS
C DEL DR JOAQUIM POU
C DE LES BEATES
C DEL G ALVAREZ DE CASTRO
C DE MESTRES CASAS I MARTORELL
C DE L'ARC DE SANT CRISTÒFOL
C DE JAUME GIRALT
C DELS METGES
C D'EN LLÀSTICS
C DE LA SÈQUIA
C DE LES BASSES DE ST PERE
C D'EN CORTINES
C DE LA VOLTA DELS JUEUS
C DEL REC COMTAL
C DELS OCELLS
PLAÇA D'ANTONI MAURA
AV DE LA CATEDRAL
AV DE F CAMBÓ
PLAÇA DE LA SEU
Casa de l'Ardiaca
BDA DE LA CANONJA
C DE STA LLÚCIA
C DE LA TAPINERIA
Museu Frederic Marès
Catedral
C DELS COMTES
PL DEL REI
PL DE RAMON BERENGUER EL GRAN
Museu d'Història de la Ciutat
C DE LA PIETAT
Palau de la Generalitat
C DE LA FRENERIA
C DEL VEGUER
BARRI GÒTIC
BDA DE LA LLIBRETERIA
PLAÇA DE L'ANGEL
CARRER D'AVELLA
C DEL TRAGÍ
C DE MASSANET
C DEL PARE GALLIFA
Mercat Santa Caterina
PL DE STA CATERINA
C DE GOMBAU
C D'EN GIRALT EL PELLISSER
C D'EN TARRÒS
C DEL FONOLLAR
PL DE ST AGUSTÍ VELL
CARRER DEL PORTAL NOU
C DEL POU DE LA FIGUERA
C DE MONT-ANYANS
C DELS CARDERS
C DELS TIRADORS
PL DE L'ACADÈMIA
PL DE ST CUGAT
C DE COLOMINES
C DE L'ARC DE ST SILVESTRE
C DE L'OLI
C DE SIDÉ
C DE LA FLOR DE LLIRI
C DE ST JACINT
C DELS CORDERS
C DELS CECS DE ST CUGAT
C DE LA BLANQUERIA
CARRER DE L'ALLADA VERMELL
CARRER D'EN TANTARANTANA
CARRER DEL COMERÇ
PL DE PONS I CLERCH
CARRER DELS ASSAONADORS
C DE LA BÒRIA
PL DE LA LLANA
C D'EN BOQUER
CARRER DE LA PRINCESA
CARRER DE JAUME I
Jaume I
Museu Tèxtil i de la Indumentària
C DELS COTONERS
BARRA DE FERRO
C DE CREMAT GRAN
C DEL CORRETGER
C DEL REC
C DELS VIGATANS
CARRER D'HÈRCULES
PL D'EMILI VILANOVA
PL DE ST JUST
Església dels Sants Just i Pastor
BDA DE CAÇADOR
C DE NAVARRO
C DE GIRITI
CARRER DE GRUNYÍ
C DEL BROSOLÍ
Museu Picasso
Museu Barbier-Mueller d'Art Precolombí
C DE LA CIRERA
C DE LA FUSINA
C DE BELLAFILA
C DE LLEDÓ
C DELS SOTS-TINENT NAVARRO
C DE MANRESA
C D'EN ROSIC
C DELS MIRALLERS
C DELS BANYS VELLS
C DE MONTCADA
C DE LES MOSQUES
PLAÇA DE COMERCIAL
Mercat del Born
CARRER DE COMERCIAL
C DEL COMETA
PL DEL REGOMIR
BDA DE VILADECOLS
PL DELS TRAGINERS
C DE BASEA
C DE L'ARGENTERIA
C DELS SOMBRERERS
Basílica de Santa Maria del Mar
BORN
PASSEIG DEL BORN
C DE L'ESPARTERIA
C DE FLASSADERS
C ANTIC DE SANT JOAN
CARRER DE LA RIBERA
PL DE VÍCTOR BALAGUER
C ABAIXADORS
PL DE SANTA MARIA
C DE STA MARIA
C DE VIDRIERA
C DEL BONAIRE
C DEL CORREU VELL
C D'EN GROC
C D'EN SOL
C DE L'HOSTAL
C DE J MASSANA
C DE CANVIS NOUS
C DELS CANVIS VELLS
C DE LES ASES
PL DE LES OLLES
C DE PESCATERIA
C DE GIGNÀS
CARRER DE A BAIXERAS
Correos
C DELS AGULLERS
C DE LA NAU
C DE PORTA DORES
CARRER DEL CONSOLAT DE MAR
C DE RERA PALAU
C DEL REC
RIBERA
AV DEL MARQUÈS DE L'ARGENTERA
C D'EN AMPLE
CARRER DE LA FUSTERIA
CARRER DE LA MERCÈ
C DE LA PLATA
C DEL MARQUET
La Llotja
PLAÇA DEL PALAU
PASSEIG D'ISABEL II
C DE LA DUANA
CARRER D'OCATA
RENFE Estació de França
CARRER DE GENERAL CASTAÑOS
PLAÇA D'ANTONI LÓPEZ
PAS REINA CRISTINA
C DE LLAUDER
PAS DE SOTA MURALLA
C DE LA MARQUESA
Barceloneta
Moll d'Espanya
PLAÇA DE PAU VILA
D
E
F
5
4
3
2

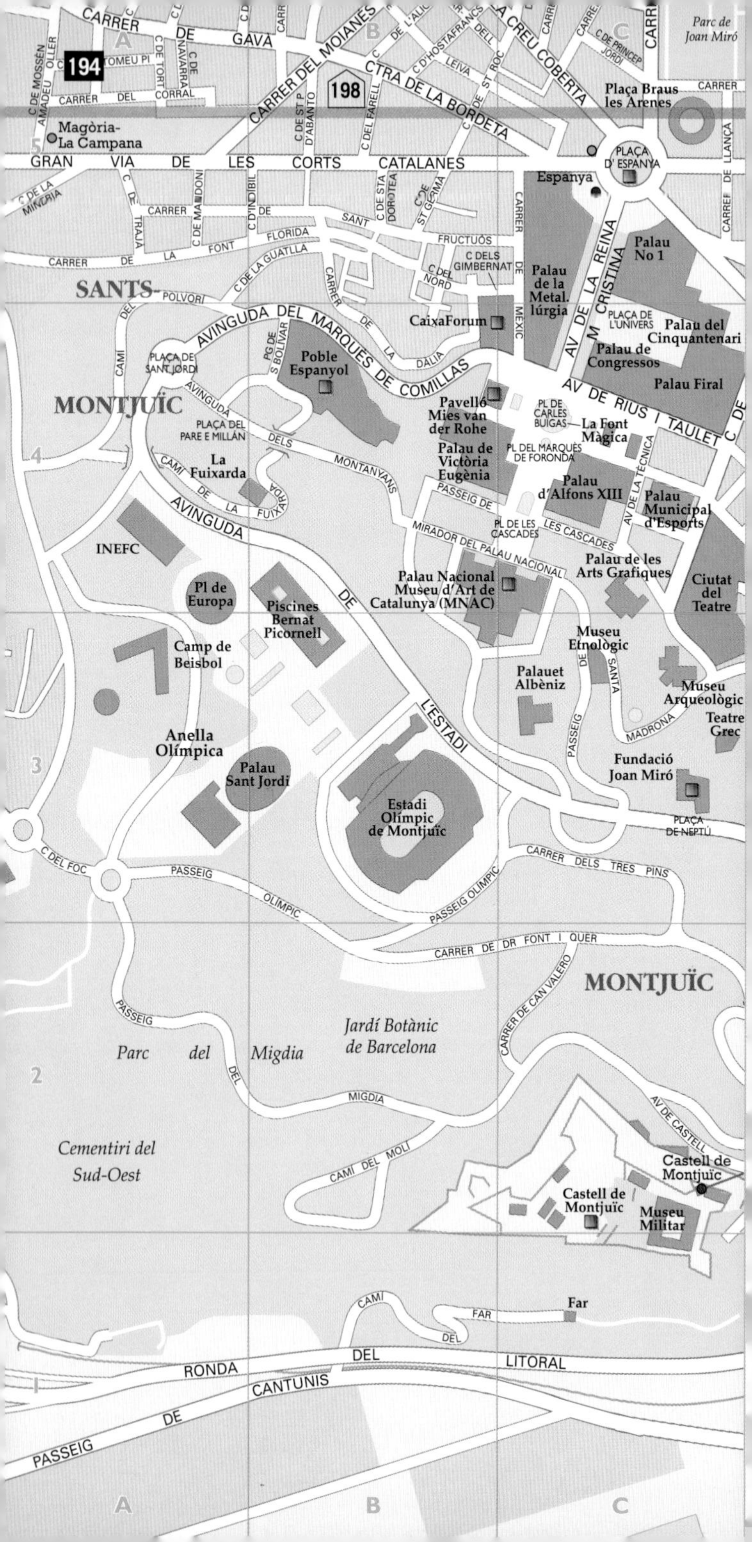
198
Carrer de Gavà
Carrer del Moianès
Ctra de la Bordeta
La Creu Coberta
Parc de Joan Miró
Plaça Braus les Arenes
Magòria-La Campana
Gran Via de les Corts Catalanes
Plaça d'Espanya
Espanya
Carrer Florida
Carrer de la Font
Carrer de Sant Fructuós
Carrer de Mèxic
Sants-Montjuïc
Montjuïc
Av de la Reina M Cristina
Palau No 1
Palau de la Metal. lúrgia
Plaça de l'Univers
Palau del Cinquantenari
Palau de Congressos
Palau Firal
CaixaForum
Avinguda del Marquès de Comillas
Poble Espanyol
Plaça de Sant Jordi
Av de Rius i Taulet
Pavelló Mies van der Rohe
Pl de Carles Buigas
La Font Màgica
Plaça del Pare e Millán
Avinguda dels Montanyans
La Fuixarda
Camí de la Fuixarda
Palau de Victòria Eugènia
Pl del Marquès de Foronda
Palau d'Alfons XIII
Palau Municipal d'Esports
Passeig de les Cascades
Pl de les Cascades
Mirador del Palau Nacional
INEFC
Avinguda de l'Estadi
Palau Nacional Museu d'Art de Catalunya (MNAC)
Palau de les Arts Gràfiques
Ciutat del Teatre
Pl de Europa
Piscines Bernat Picornell
Museu Etnològic
Camp de Beisbol
Palauet Albèniz
Museu Arqueològic
Teatre Grec
Passeig de Santa Madrona
Anella Olímpica
Fundació Joan Miró
Palau Sant Jordi
Estadi Olímpic de Montjuïc
Plaça de Neptú
C del Foc
Passeig Olímpic
Carrer dels Tres Pins
Carrer de Dr Font i Quer
Carrer de Can Valero
Jardí Botànic de Barcelona
Parc del Migdia
Passeig del Migdia
Av de Castell
Cementiri del Sud-Oest
Camí del Molí
Castell de Montjuïc
Museu Militar
Far
Camí del Far
Ronda del Litoral
Passeig de Cantunis

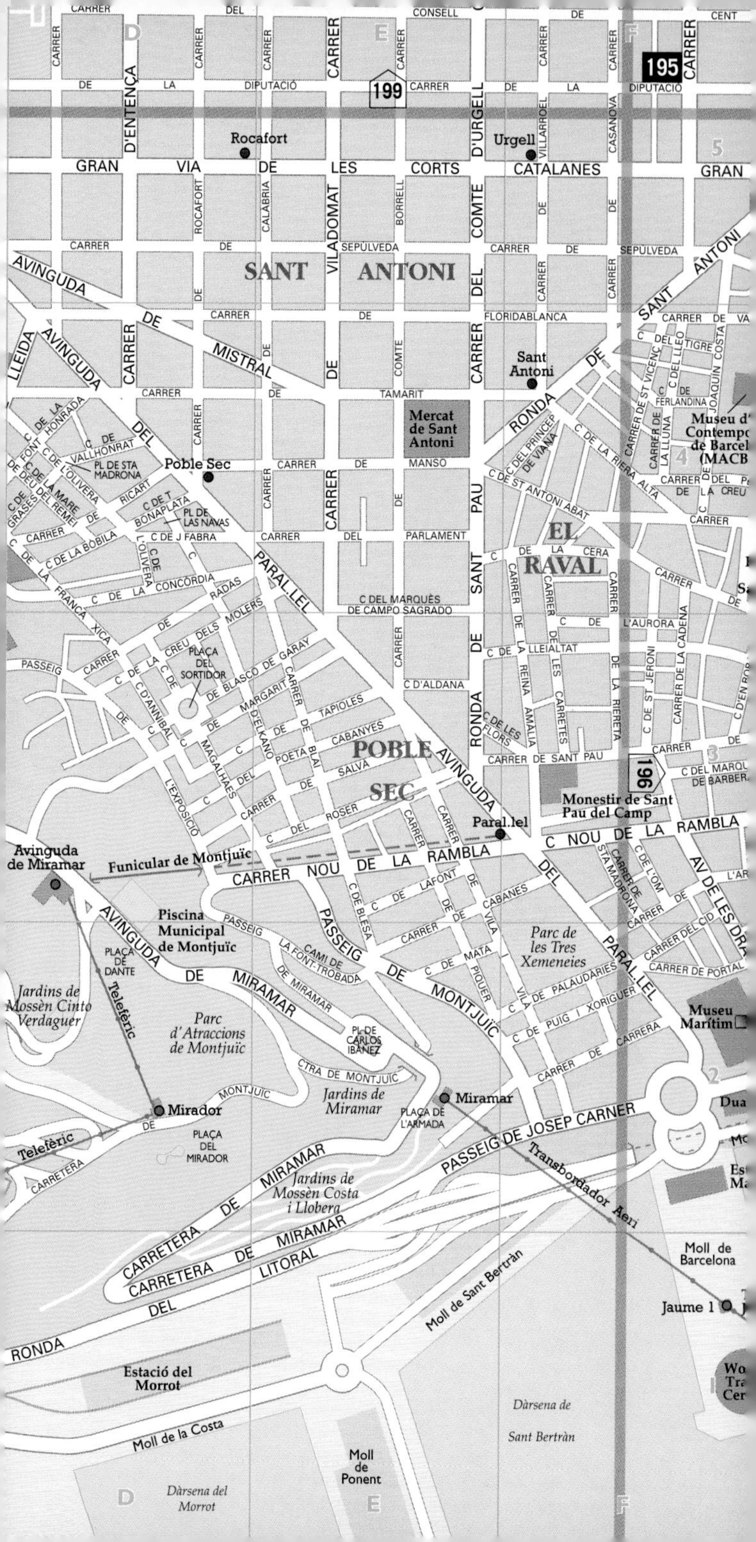

SANT ANTONI
POBLE SEC
EL RAVAL
Rocafort
Urgell
Sant Antoni
Poble Sec
Paral.lel
Mercat de Sant Antoni
Monestir de Sant Pau del Camp
Museu Marítim
Avinguda de Miramar
Funicular de Montjuïc
Piscina Municipal de Montjuïc
Jardins de Mossèn Cinto Verdaguer
Parc d'Atraccions de Montjuïc
Jardins de Miramar
Parc de les Tres Xemeneies
Mirador
Miramar
Telefèric
Transbordador Aeri
Jardins de Mossèn Costa i Llobera
Moll de Barcelona
Jaume 1
Moll de Sant Bertràn
Estació del Morrot
Moll de la Costa
Moll de Ponent
Dàrsena de Sant Bertràn
Dàrsena del Morrot
GRAN VIA DE LES CORTS CATALANES
AVINGUDA DE MISTRAL
AVINGUDA DEL PARAL.LEL
RONDA DE SANT PAU
RONDA DE SANT ANTONI
CARRER NOU DE LA RAMBLA
PASSEIG DE MONTJUÏC
AVINGUDA DE MIRAMAR
PASSEIG DE JOSEP CARNER
CARRETERA DE MIRAMAR
RONDA DEL LITORAL
195
199
196

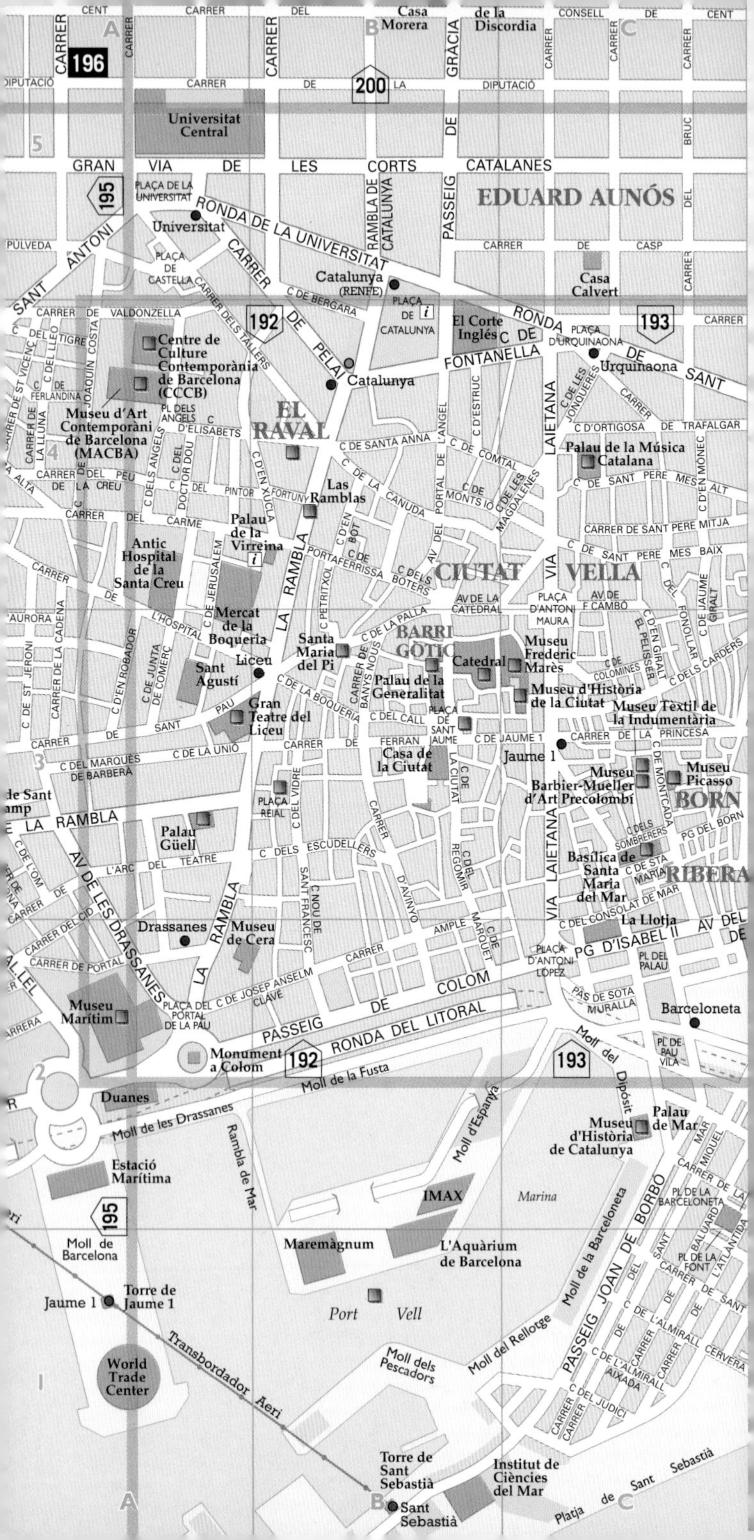

196
200
195
192
193
Casa Morera
Casa de la Discordia
Universitat Central
Gran Via de les Corts Catalanes
Eduard Aunós
Plaça de la Universitat
Universitat
Ronda de la Universitat
Rambla de Catalunya
Passeig de Gràcia
Carrer de Casp
Casa Calvert
Catalunya (RENFE)
Plaça de Catalunya
El Corte Inglés
Ronda de Sant
Plaça d'Urquinaona
Urquinaona
Carrer de Pelai
Catalunya
Centre de Culture Contemporània de Barcelona (CCCB)
Museu d'Art Contemporàni de Barcelona (MACBA)
El Raval
Las Ramblas
Palau de la Virreina
Antic Hospital de la Santa Creu
Mercat de la Boqueria
Sant Agustí
Liceu
Gran Teatre del Liceu
Santa Maria del Pi
Barri Gòtic
Ciutat Vella
Catedral
Museu Frederic Marès
Palau de la Generalitat
Museu d'Història de la Ciutat
Palau de la Música Catalana
Museu Tèxtil de la Indumentària
Casa de la Ciutat
Jaume 1
Museu Barbier-Mueller d'Art Precolombí
Museu Picasso
Born
Basílica de Santa Maria del Mar
Ribera
La Llotja
Plaça Reial
Palau Güell
Drassanes
Museu de Cera
Museu Marítim
Monument a Colom
Passeig de Colom
Ronda del Litoral
Barceloneta
Via Laietana
Pg d'Isabel II
Duanes
Moll de la Fusta
Moll de les Drassanes
Moll d'Espanya
Moll del Dipòsit
Museu d'Història de Catalunya
Palau de Mar
Estació Marítima
IMAX
Marina
Maremàgnum
L'Aquàrium de Barcelona
Moll de Barcelona
Torre de Jaume 1
Port Vell
Rambla de Mar
Moll de la Barceloneta
Passeig Joan de Borbó
Moll del Rellotge
Moll dels Pescadors
World Trade Center
Transbordador Aeri
Torre de Sant Sebastià
Institut de Ciències del Mar
Sant Sebastià
Platja de Sant Sebastià

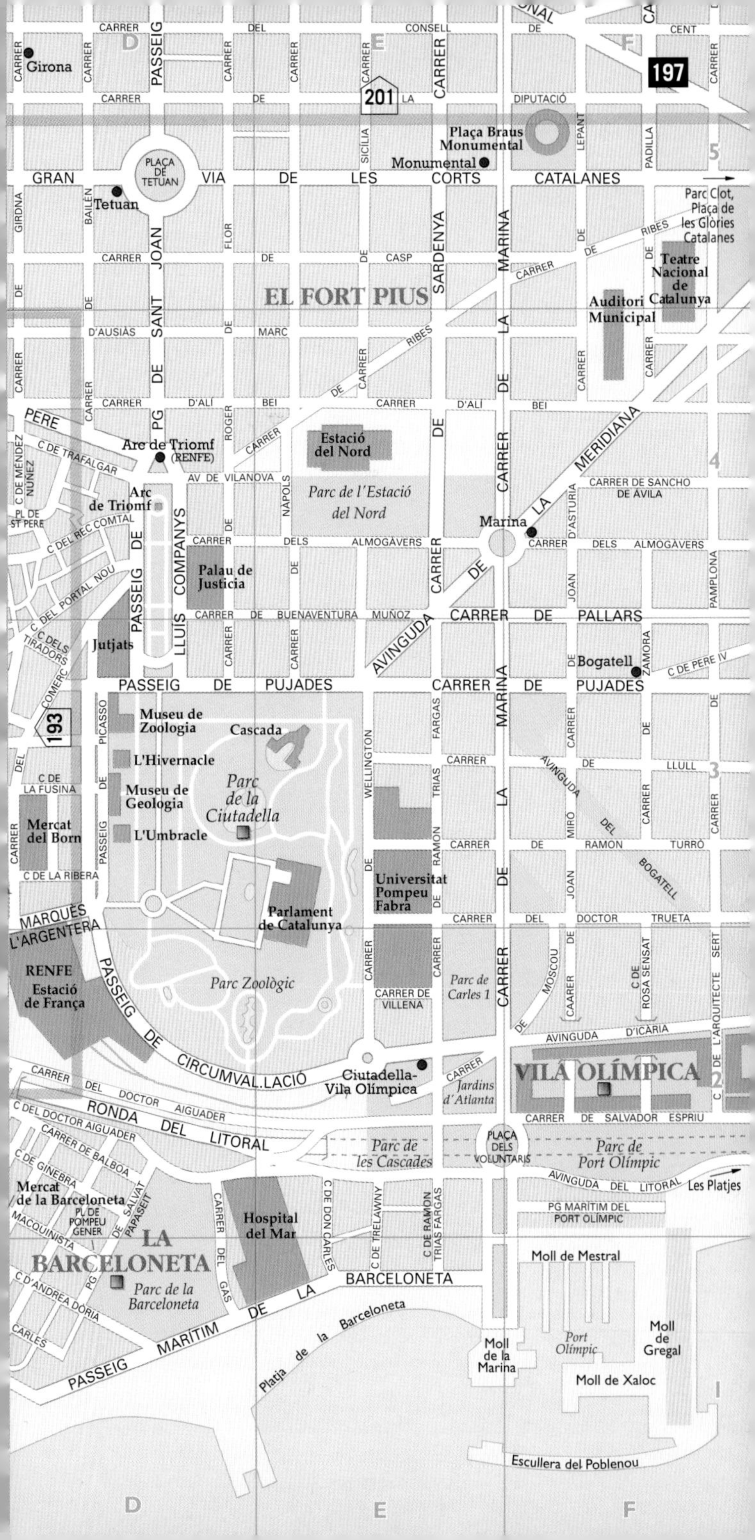

197
201
193
D
E
F
5
4
3
2
1
Girona
Tetuan
Plaça de Tetuan
Gran Via de les Corts Catalanes
Plaça Braus Monumental
Monumental
Parc Clot, Plaça de les Glòries Catalanes
Teatre Nacional de Catalunya
Auditori Municipal
EL FORT PIUS
Carrer del Consell de Cent
Carrer de la Diputació
Carrer de Casp
Carrer d'Ausiàs Marc
Carrer d'Alí Bei
Carrer de Ribes
Passeig de Sant Joan
Carrer de Sardenya
Carrer de la Marina
Carrer de Sicília
Lepant
Padilla
Girona
Bailèn
Flor
Roger
Estació del Nord
Parc de l'Estació del Nord
Arc de Triomf (RENFE)
Arc de Triomf
Av de Vilanova
Nàpols
Pere
C de Trafalgar
C de Méndez Núñez
Pl de St Pere
C del Rec Comtal
C del Portal Nou
C dels Tiradors
Comerç
Carrer dels Almogàvers
Carrer de Sancho de Ávila
Avinguda Meridiana
Marina
D'Astúria
Joan
Pamplona
Palau de Justicia
Passeig de Lluís Companys
Carrer de Buenaventura Muñoz
Avinguda de la Meridiana
Carrer de Pallars
Jutjats
Bogatell
Zamora
C de Pere IV
Passeig de Pujades
Carrer de Pujades
Picasso
Museu de Zoologia
Cascada
L'Hivernacle
Museu de Geologia
L'Umbracle
Parc de la Ciutadella
Parlament de Catalunya
Parc Zoològic
Wellington
Fargas
Trias
Ramon
Carrer de Llull
Avinguda del Bogatell
Miró
Carrer de Ramon Turró
Universitat Pompeu Fabra
Carrer del Doctor Trueta
Carrer de Villena
Parc de Carles 1
Moscou
C de Rosa Sensat
C de l'Arquitecte Sert
Avinguda d'Icària
C de la Fusina
Mercat del Born
C de la Ribera
Marquès de l'Argentera
RENFE Estació de França
Passeig de Circumval.lació
Carrer del Doctor Aiguader
C del Doctor Aiguader
Ronda del Litoral
Ciutadella-Vila Olímpica
Jardins d'Atlanta
VILA OLÍMPICA
Carrer de Salvador Espriu
Plaça dels Voluntaris
Parc de les Cascades
Parc de Port Olímpic
Avinguda del Litoral
Les Platjes
PG Marítim del Port Olímpic
Carrer de Balboa
C de Ginebra
Mercat de la Barceloneta
Pl de Pompeu Gener
Salvat Papaseit
Macquinista
LA BARCELONETA
Parc de la Barceloneta
C d'Andrea Doria
Carles
Carrer del Gas
Hospital del Mar
C de Don Carles
C de Trelawny
C de Ramon Trias Fargas
Passeig Marítim de la Barceloneta
Platja de la Barceloneta
Moll de Mestral
Moll de la Marina
Port Olímpic
Moll de Gregal
Moll de Xaloc
Escullera del Poblenou

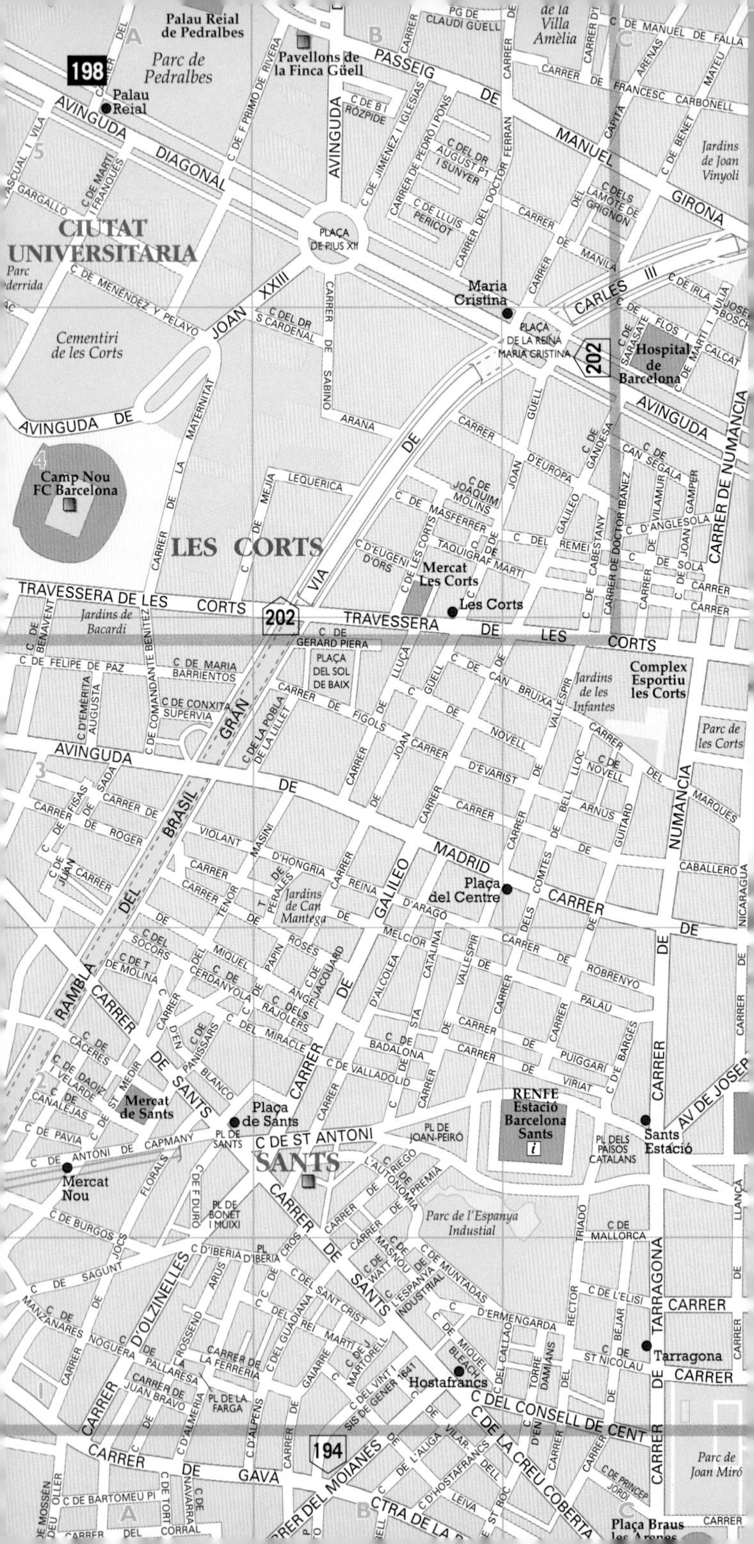
198
Palau Reial de Pedralbes
Parc de Pedralbes
Palau Reial
Pavellons de la Finca Güell
PG DE CLAUDI GÜELL
de la Villa Amèlia
C DE MANUEL DE FALLA
PASSEIG DE MANUEL GIRONA
CARRER DE FRANCESC CARBONELL
AVINGUDA DIAGONAL
AVINGUDA JOAN XXIII
PLAÇA DE PIUS XII
C DE JIMENEZ I IGLESIAS
CARRER DE PEDRO I PONS
C DEL DR AUGUST PI I SUNYER
C DE LLUIS PERICOT
CARRER DEL DOCTOR FERRAN
C DELS LAMOTE DE GRIGNON
CARRER DE MANILA
Jardins de Joan Vinyoli
CIUTAT UNIVERSITARIA
C DE MENENDEZ Y PELAYO
C DEL DR S CARDENAL
CARRER DE SABINO ARANA
Cementiri de les Corts
Maria Cristina
PLAÇA DE LA REINA MARIA CRISTINA
CARLES III
C DE IRLA
Hospital de Barcelona
C DE SARASATE
202
AVINGUDA DE
AVINGUDA CARRER DE NUMANCIA
Camp Nou FC Barcelona
CARRER DE LA MATERNITAT
LEQUERICA
C DE MEJIA
LES CORTS
VIA
C DE JOAQUIM MOLINS
C DE MASFERRER
TAQUIGRAF MARTI
C D'EUGENI D'ORS
C DE LES CORTS
Mercat Les Corts
Les Corts
CARRER D'EUROPA
C DE GANDESA
C DEL REMEI
CARRER DE DOCTOR IBANEZ
C D'ANGLESOLA
C DE SOLA
TRAVESSERA DE LES CORTS
Jardins de Bacardi
C DE BENAVENT
C DE FELIPE DE PAZ
C DE MARIA BARRIENTOS
C DE CONXITA SUPERVIA
C DE COMANDANT BENITEZ
C D'EMERITA AUGUSTA
C DE GERARD PIERA
PLAÇA DEL SOL DE BAIX
CARRER DE FIGOLS
C DE CAN BRUIXA
Jardins de les Infantes
Complex Esportiu les Corts
Parc de les Corts
CARRER DE NOVELL
CARRER D'EVARIST ARNUS
CARRER DEL MARQUES
AVINGUDA DE MADRID
GRAN VIA
RAMBLA DEL BRASIL
CARRER DE ROGER
VIOLANT D'HONGRIA
CARRER REINA
Jardins de Can Mantega
CARRER DE GALILEO
Plaça del Centre
CARRER DELS COMTES DE BELL LLOC
CABALLERO
NICARAGUA
CARRER DE ROBRENYO
CARRER DE PALAU
CARRER DE SANTS
C DE VALLADOLID
Mercat de Sants
Plaça de Sants
RENFE Estació Barcelona Sants
PL DELS PAISOS CATALANS
Sants Estació
AV DE JOSEP
PL DE JOAN-PEIRÓ
C DE ST ANTONI
SANTS
Mercat Nou
Parc de l'Espanya Industial
C DE MALLORCA
CARRER DE TARRAGONA
Tarragona
C D'OLZINELLES
C DE BURGOS
C DE SAGUNT
PL DE BONET I MUIXI
C DE MANZANARES
CARRER DE LA FERRERIA
PL DE LA FARGA
Hostafrancs
C DEL CONSELL DE CENT
C DE LA CREU COBERTA
194
CARRER DE GAVA
CARRER DEL MOIANES
CTRA DE LA
Parc de Joan Miró
Plaça Braus les Arenes

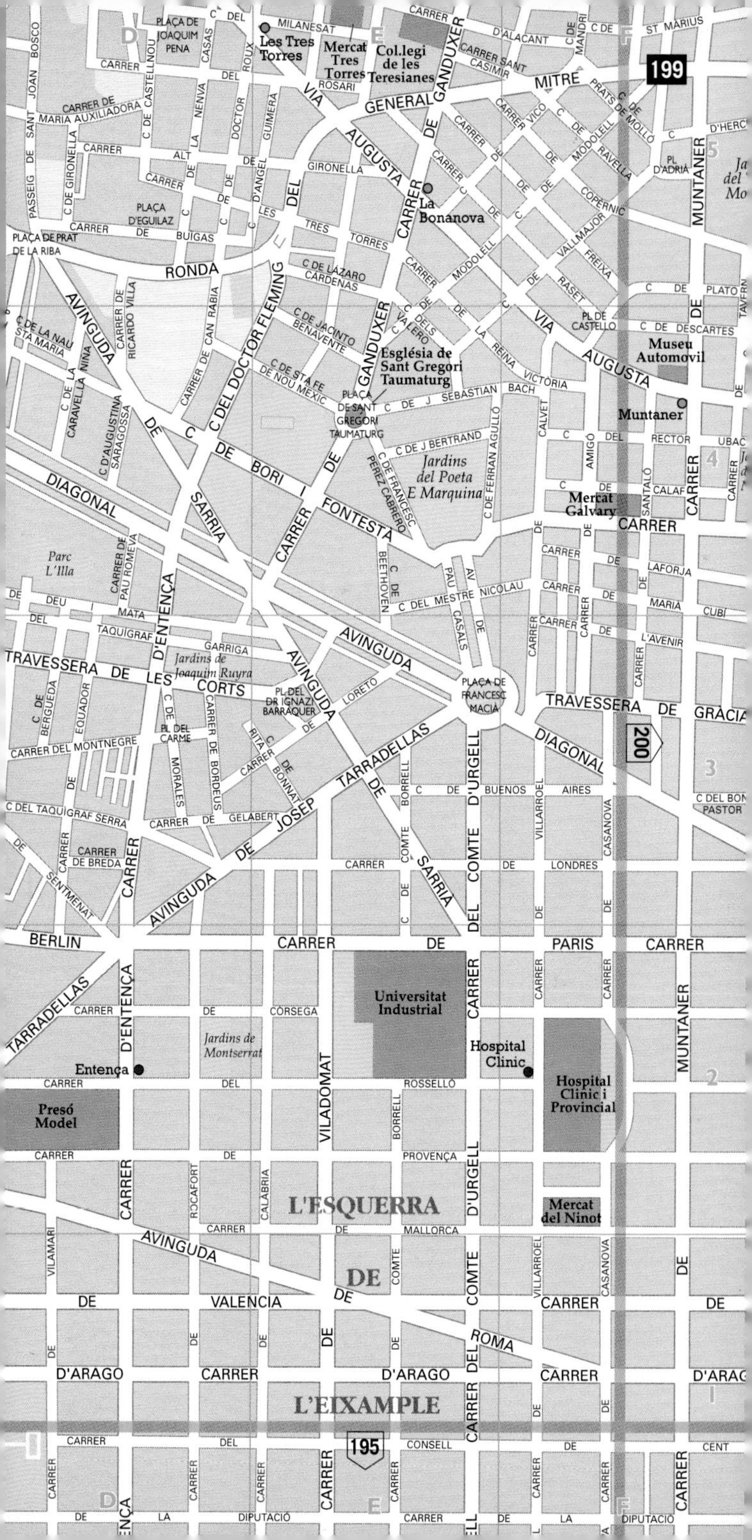

199
Les Tres Torres
Mercat Tres Torres
Col.legi de les Teresianes
PLAÇA DE JOAQUIM PENA
CARRER DE MARIA AUXILIADORA
PASSEIG DE SANT JOAN BOSCO
VIA AUGUSTA
GENERAL MITRE
CARRER DE GANDUXER
La Bonanova
PLAÇA D'EGUILAZ
PLAÇA DE PRAT DE LA RIBA
RONDA DEL GENERAL MITRE
C DE LÁZARO CARDENAS
C DE JACINTO BENAVENTE
C DE STA FE DE NOU MEXIC
Església de Sant Gregori Taumaturg
PLAÇA DE SANT GREGORI TAUMATURG
C DE J SEBASTIAN BACH
C DE J BERTRAND
Jardins del Poeta E Marquina
C DEL DOCTOR FLEMING
C DE BORI I FONTESTÀ
Museu Automovil
Muntaner
Mercat Galvany
PL DE CASTELLÓ
C DE DESCARTES
CARRER DE MUNTANER
AVINGUDA DE SARRIÀ
AVINGUDA DIAGONAL
Parc L'Illa
CARRER DE PAU ROMEVA
Jardins de Joaquim Ruyra
TRAVESSERA DE LES CORTS
PL DEL DR IGNAZI BARRAQUER
PLAÇA DE FRANCESC MACIÀ
TRAVESSERA DE GRÀCIA
200
AVINGUDA DE JOSEP TARRADELLAS
C DE BUENOS AIRES
CARRER DE LONDRES
CARRER DEL COMTE D'URGELL
CARRER DE BERLIN
CARRER DE PARIS
CARRER D'ENTENÇA
Universitat Industrial
CARRER DE CORSEGA
Jardins de Montserrat
Entença
Hospital Clinic
Hospital Clinic i Provincial
CARRER DEL ROSSELLO
Presó Model
CARRER DE PROVENÇA
L'ESQUERRA DE L'EIXAMPLE
Mercat del Ninot
CARRER DE MALLORCA
AVINGUDA DE ROMA
CARRER DE VALENCIA
CARRER D'ARAGO
CARRER DEL CONSELL DE CENT
195
CARRER DE LA DIPUTACIÓ
CARRER DE VILADOMAT
CARRER DE CASANOVA
CARRER DE VILLARROEL
CARRER DE BORRELL

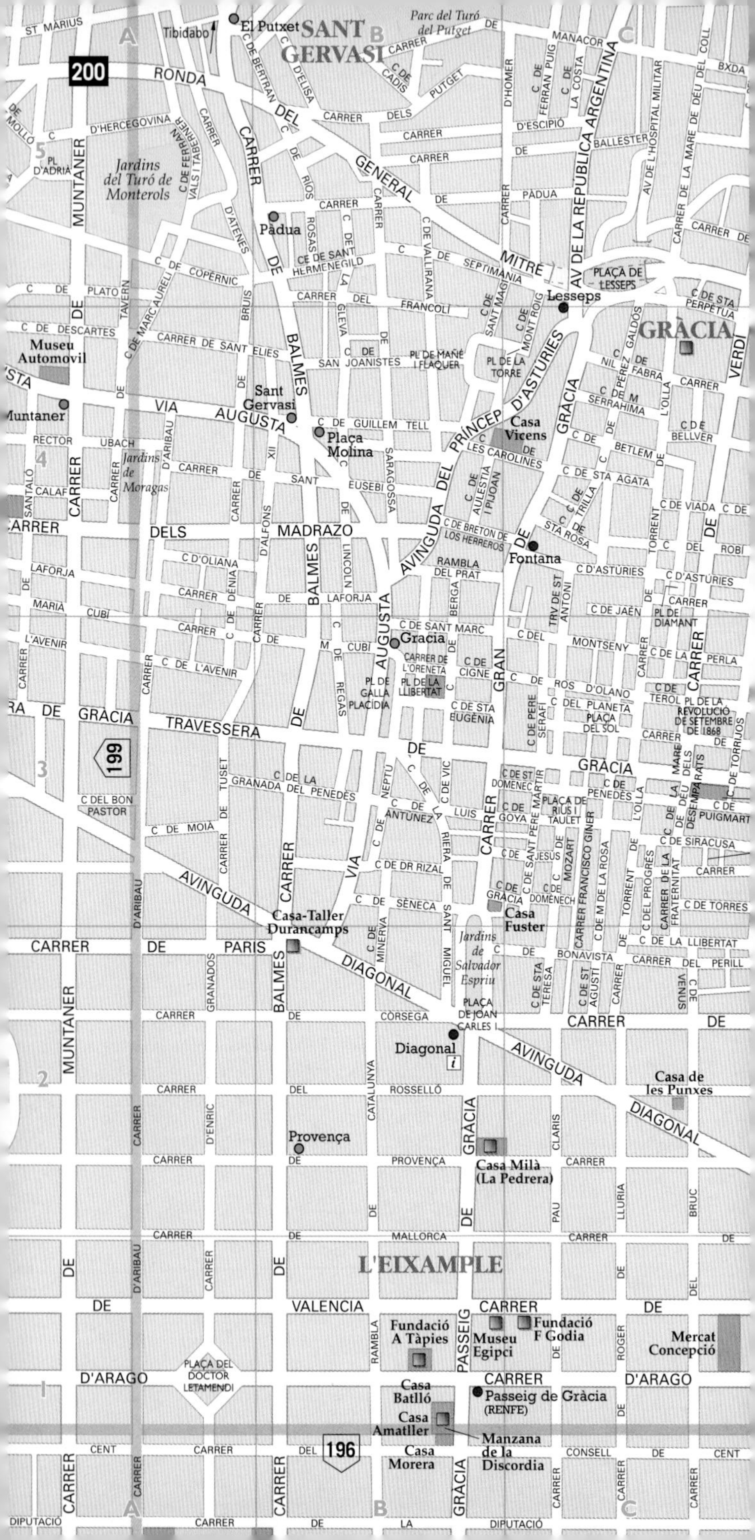
El Putxet
Tibidabo
SANT GERVASI
Parc del Turó del Putget
Jardins del Turó de Monterols
RONDA DEL GENERAL MITRE
MUNTANER
PL D'ADRIÀ
Pàdua
PLAÇA DE LESSEPS
Lesseps
GRÀCIA
Museu Automovil
Muntaner
Sant Gervasi
VIA AUGUSTA
Plaça Molina
Casa Vicens
AVINGUDA DEL PRINCEP D'ASTÚRIES
AV DE LA REPÚBLICA ARGENTINA
Jardins de Moragas
CARRER DELS MADRAZO
BALMES
Fontana
RAMBLA DEL PRAT
Gracia
PL DE GALLA PLACÍDIA
PL DE LA LLIBERTAT
PLAÇA DEL SOL
PL DE LA REVOLUCIÓ DE SETEMBRE DE 1868
TRAVESSERA DE GRÀCIA
199
PLAÇA DE RIUS I TAULET
AVINGUDA DIAGONAL
Casa-Taller Durancamps
CARRER DE PARIS
Casa Fuster
Jardins de Salvador Espriu
PLAÇA DE JOAN CARLES I
Diagonal
Casa de les Punxes
Provença
Casa Milà (La Pedrera)
L'EIXAMPLE
Fundació A Tàpies
Museu Egipci
Fundació F Godia
Mercat Concepció
PLAÇA DEL DOCTOR LETAMENDI
D'ARAGO
Casa Batlló
Casa Amatller
Passeig de Gràcia (RENFE)
Manzana de la Discordia
196
Casa Morera
PASSEIG DE GRÀCIA
CARRER DEL CONSELL DE CENT
DIPUTACIÓ

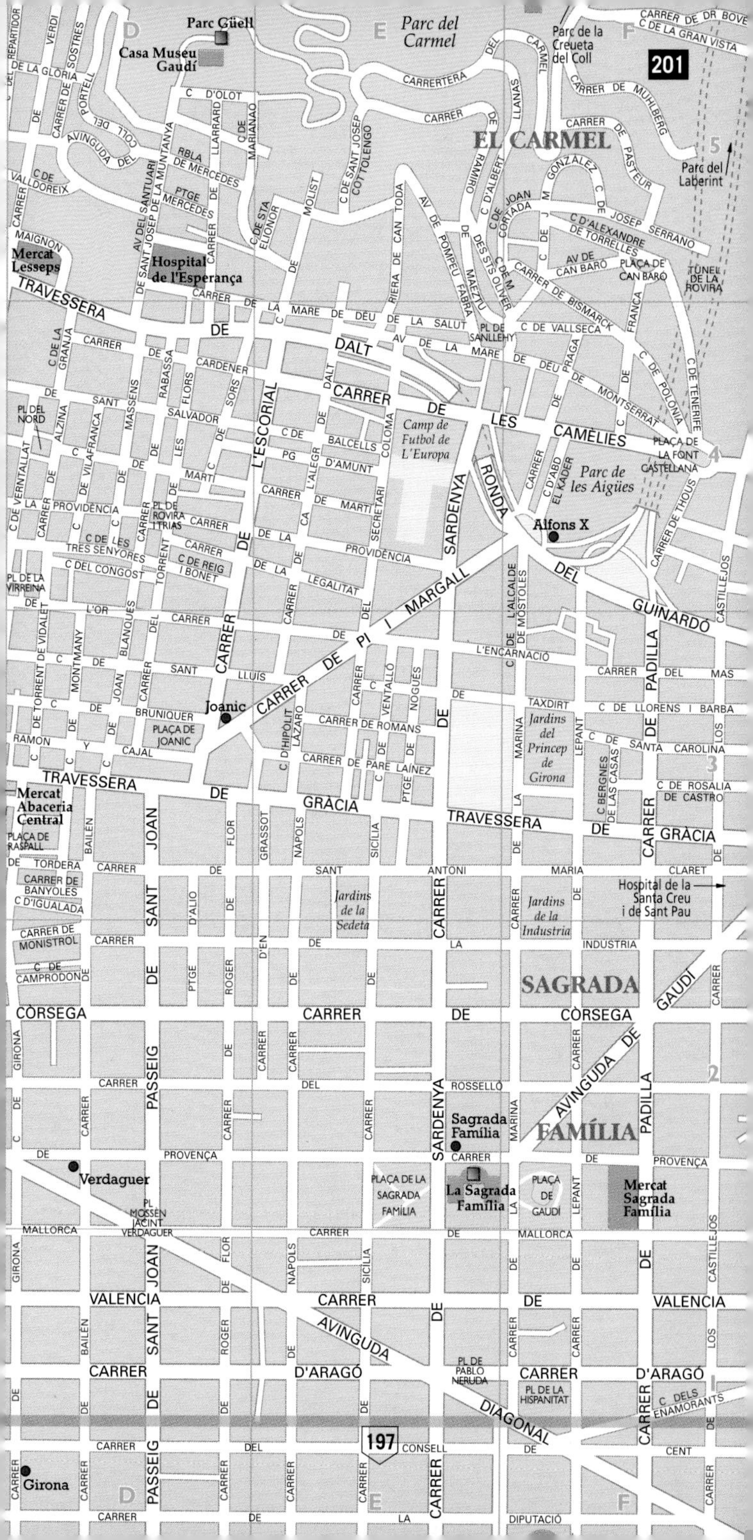
Parc Güell
Casa Museu Gaudí
Parc del Carmel
Parc de la Creueta del Coll
EL CARMEL
Parc del Laberint
Mercat Lesseps
Hospital de l'Esperança
Túnel de la Rovira
Travessera de Dalt
Carrer de les Camèlies
Camp de Futbol de L'Europa
Parc de les Aigües
Alfons X
Ronda del Guinardó
Carrer de Pi i Margall
Joanic
Plaça de Joanic
Jardins del Princep de Girona
Mercat Abaceria Central
Plaça de Raspall
Travessera de Gràcia
Hospital de la Santa Creu i de Sant Pau
Jardins de la Sedeta
Jardins de la Industria
SAGRADA FAMÍLIA
Carrer de Còrsega
Avinguda de Gaudí
Passeig de Sant Joan
Sagrada Família
Verdaguer
Plaça de la Sagrada Família
La Sagrada Família
Plaça de Gaudí
Mercat Sagrada Família
Carrer de Mallorca
Carrer de València
Avinguda Diagonal
Carrer d'Aragó
Pl de Pablo Neruda
Pl de la Hispanitat
Carrer del Consell de Cent
Girona
Carrer de la Diputació
197

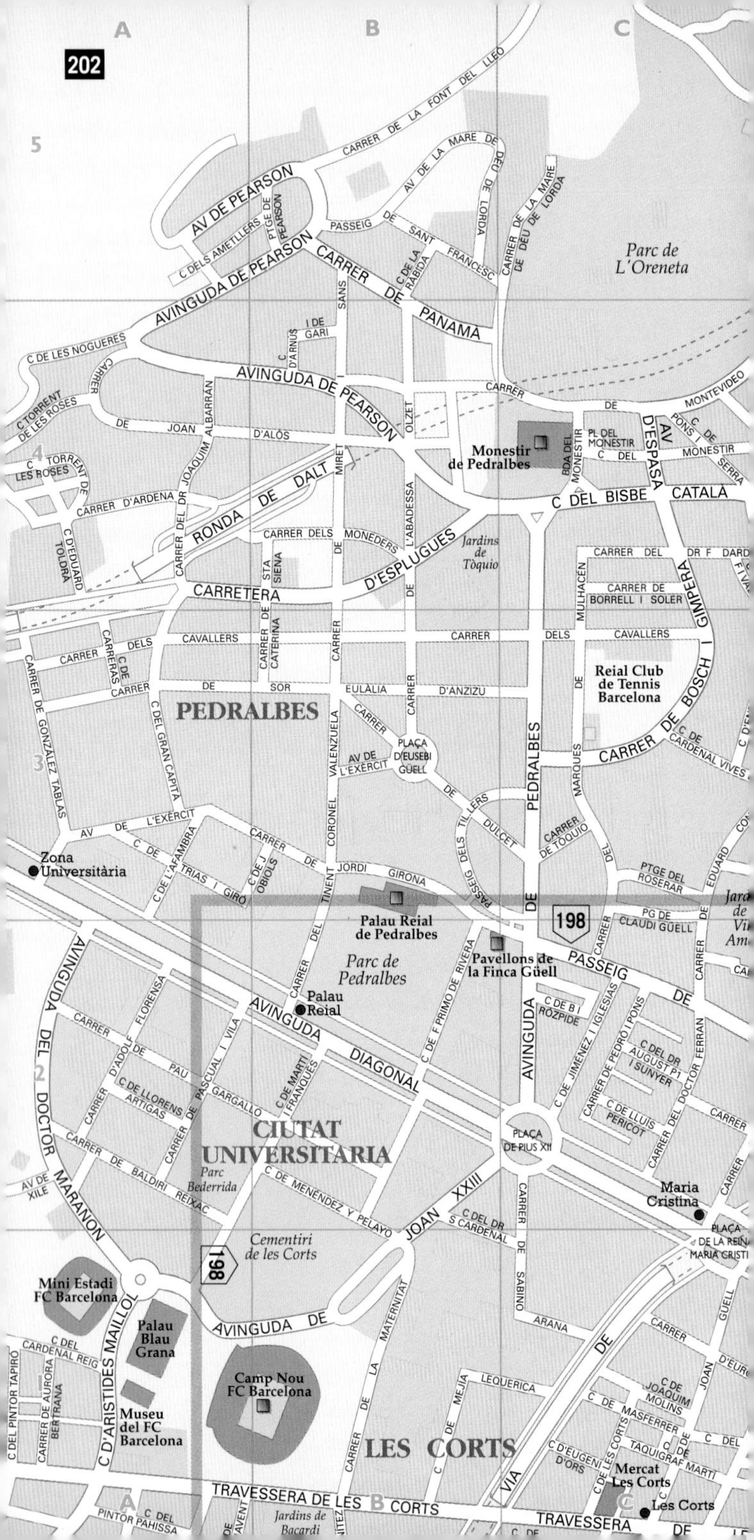
A
B
C
5
4
3
2
1
CARRER DE LA FONT DEL LLEO
AV DE PEARSON
C DELS AMETLLERS
PTGE DE PEARSON
AVINGUDA DE PEARSON
CARRER DE PANAMÁ
PASSEIG DE SANT FRANCESC
AV DE LA MARE DE DÉU DE LORDA
CARRER DE LA MARE DE DÉU DE LORDA
C DE LA RÀBIDA
Parc de L'Oreneta
C DE LES NOGUERES
I DE GARI
SANS
C D'ARNÚS
CARRER DE JOAN D'ALÒS
C TORRENT DE LES ROSES
ALBARRÁN
OLZET
CARRER DE MONTEVIDEO
Monestir de Pedralbes
PL DEL MONESTIR
BDA DEL MONESTIR
C DEL MONESTIR
AV D'ESPASA
C PONS I SERRA
C DEL BISBE CATALÀ
RONDA DE DALT
MIRET
L'ABADESSA
CARRER D'ARDENA
CARRER DEL DR JOAQUIM
C D'EDUARD TOLDRÀ
CARRER DELS MONEDERS
D'ESPLUGUES
Jardins de Tòquio
CARRETERA
STA SIENA
CARRER DEL DR F DARDER
CARRER DE BORRELL I SOLER
MULHACÉN
CARRER DE STA CATERINA
CARRER DELS CAVALLERS
CARRERAS
C DE CARRER DE SOR EULÀLIA D'ANZIZU
CARRER DE GONZÁLEZ TABLAS
C DEL GRAN CAPITÀ
PEDRALBES
Reial Club de Tennis Barcelona
CARRER DE BOSCH I GIMPERA
C DE CARDENAL VIVES
PLAÇA D'EUSEBI GÜELL
AV DE L'EXÈRCIT
CORONEL VALENZUELA
CARRER DE DULCET
PASSEIG DELS TILLERS
AVINGUDA DE PEDRALBES
MARQUÉS DE MULHACÉN
CARRER DE TÒQUIO
Zona Universitària
C DE L'AFAMBRA
TRIAS I GIRÓ
C DE J OBIOLS
CARRER DE JORDI GIRONA
PTGE DEL ROSERAR
C DEL EDUARD
Palau Reial de Pedralbes
198
PG DE CLAUDI GÜELL
Pavellons de la Finca Güell
PASSEIG DE
Parc de Pedralbes
CARRER DEL TINENT
Palau Reial
C DE F PRIMO DE RIVERA
C DE B I ROZPIDE
AVINGUDA DIAGONAL
C DE JIMÉNEZ I IGLESIAS
CARRER DE PEDRO I PONS
C DEL DR AUGUST PI I SUNYER
CARRER DEL DOCTOR FERRAN
AVINGUDA DEL DOCTOR MARAÑÓN
CARRER D'ADOLF FLORENSA
CARRER DE PAU GARGALLO
C DE LLORENÇ ARTIGAS
CARRER DE PASCUAL I VILA
C DE MARTÍ I FRANQUÈS
C DE LLUÍS PERICOT
PLAÇA DE PIUS XII
CIUTAT UNIVERSITARIA
CARRER DE BALDIRI REIXAC
Parc Bederrida
C DE MENÉNDEZ Y PELAYO
JOAN XXIII
C DEL DR S CARDENAL
CARRER DE SABINO ARANA
Maria Cristina
PLAÇA DE LA REINA MARIA CRISTINA
AV DE XILE
Cementiri de les Corts
Mini Estadi FC Barcelona
Palau Blau Grana
AVINGUDA DE
MATERNITAT
C DEL CARDENAL REIG
C D'ARÍSTIDES MAILLOL
C DEL PINTOR TAPIRÓ
CARRER DE AURORA BERTRANA
Camp Nou FC Barcelona
Museu del FC Barcelona
C DE MEJÍA LEQUERICA
VIA DE
CARRER D'EUROPA
C DE JOAQUIM MOLINS
C DE MASFERRER
C DEL TAQUÍGRAF MARTÍ
C D'EUGENI D'ORS
C DE LES CORTS
Mercat Les Corts
LES CORTS
Les Corts
TRAVESSERA DE LES CORTS
PINTOR PAHISSA
Jardins de Bacardi
TRAVESSERA DE

Streetplan Index

Picture credits

The Automobile Association wishes to thank the following photographers, libraries and associations for their assistance in the preparation of this book.

ALLSPORT UK LTD 20/1 (Mark Thompson), 20, 21, 27bl (Clive Brunskill), 158 (Simon Bruly); AXIOM PHOTOGRAPHIC AGENCY 44l (Heidi Grassley), 44r (Heidi Grassley); ANDREW BENSON 11t, 11b, 15, 63, 74, 119t, 177l; THE ANTHONY BLAKE PICTURE LIBRARY 12t (Phototeque Culinaire), 13t (Tony Robins), 13cb (Graham Kirk), 13cr (Tony Robins); BRIDGEMAN ART LIBRARY 47t Menu from "Els Quatre Gats", 1899 by Pablo Picasso (1881-1973), (Museu Picasso, Barcelona, Spain/Index), © Succession Picasso/DACS, London, 2001, 61t The grand hall, designed by Antonio Gaudi (1852-1926), 1885-89 (photo), (Palacio Guell, Barcelona, Spain), 65t Road to Calvary, Blanquers Altarpiece by Jaume Huget (1415-92), (Museo Mares, Barcelona, Spain), 82r Maria Picasso Lopez, The Artist's Mother, 1896 by Pablo Picasso (1881-1973), (Museo Picasso, Barcelona, Spain), © Succession Picasso/DACS, London, 2001, 84/5 Las Meninas, 1957 by Pablo Picasso (1881-1973), Museo Picasso, Barcelona, Spain/Index), © Succession Picasso/DACS, London, 2001, 117b Guell Crypt with its "tilted column" built by Antonio Gaudi (1852-1926) in 1884-91 (photo), (Sagrada Familia, Barcelona, Spain), 139 Self Portrait of Casas with Pere Romeu on a Tandem, 1897 by Ramon Casas (1866-1932), (Museu Nacional d'Art de Catalunya, Spain/Index), 149 Drummer, Tile from the "Palmita" Series, Catalan, 19th century, (Museo de Ceramica, Barcelona, Spain/Index); CEPHAS PICTURE LIBRARY 166b (Mick Rock); COSMOCAIXA 152, 153; DACS, London, 2001 130, 135; DORLING KINDERSLEY 9, FUNDACIO GODIA 119b, GETTYONE/STONE 2(i), 5, 29l, 57, 102/3, 113, 167; GODO-FOTO 6b, 10t, 24bl, 25t, 27bl, 58b, 77t, 177r, 179; HULTON GETTY PICTURE COLLECTION 24t, 25b, 26t; INDEX-FOTOTECA 10b, 16, 26b, 54b, 82l, 83t, 121b; MUSEU NACIONAL D'ART DE CATALUNYA/Servei Fotogràfic (Calveras, Mèrida, Sagristà) 136, 137; MUSEO THYSSEN-BORNEMISZA, MADRID/Monastery of Pedralbes, Barcelona) 138; PALAU DE LA MUSICA, CATALANA 79; PICTOR INTERNATIONAL 154; PICTURES COLOUR LIBRARY 22, 29r, 76t, 116t, 163; POWERSTOCK ZEFA 11br, 48; REX FEATURES 24br, 27t, 27c; SUPERSTOCK LTD 19; ROGER-VIOLLET 83b; WORLD PICTURES 28r, 46t, 164t, 164b, 165.

All remaining pictures are held in the Association's own library (AA PHOTO LIBRARY) and were taken by MAX JOURDAN with the exception of the following:

MICHELLE CHAPLOW 3(ii), 6/7, 12b, 13ct, 14t, 14b, 90, 161, 166tr, 168, 187br; STEVE DAY Front & back covers and spine, 2(ii), 3(i), 8, 17c, 17b, 18, 22/3, 28c, 31, 45, 50l, 50r, 53t, 54cr, 58t, 59t, 59b, 77b, 87, 88, 98b, 99, 100t, 100b, 101t, 101c, 101b, 103, 104, 106, 108r, 109t, 116b, 117t, 134, 141, 145, 147, 155, 156, 157, 170, 171l, 171r, 172, 173, 174l, 174r, 176, 178, 180, 181, 182; PETER WILSON 65b, 78, 135, 166tl.

Author's acknowledgement

Andrew Benson wishes to thank Olga Pena, Carles Orriols, Maria Lluïsa Albacar and Marcel Forns Bernhardt for their assistance during the research of this book.

SPIRAL GUIDES

Questionnaire

Dear Traveler

Your comments, opinions and recommendations are very important to us. So please help us to improve our travel guides by taking a few minutes to complete this simple questionnaire.

Send to: Spiral Guides, MailStop 66, 1000 AAA Drive, Heathrow, FL 32746–5063

Your recommendations...

We always encourage readers' recommendations for restaurants, nightlife or shopping – if your recommendation is added to the next edition of the guide, we will send you a FREE AAA Spiral Guide of your choice. Please state below the establishment name, location and your reasons for recommending it.

____

____

____

____

____

Please send me AAA Spiral ______________________________

(see list of titles inside the back cover)

About this guide...

Which title did you buy?

______________________________ AAA Spiral

Where did you buy it? ______________________________

When? mm/ y y

Why did you choose a AAA Spiral Guide? ______________________________

____

____

____

Did this guide meet your expectations?

Exceeded ☐ Met all ☐ Met most ☐ Fell below ☐

Please give your reasons ______________________________

____

____

____

continued on next page...

Were there any aspects of this guide that you particularly liked?

Is there anything we could have done better?

About you...

Name (Mr/Mrs/Ms)

Address

Zip

Daytime tel nos.

Which age group are you in?

Under 25 ☐ 25–34 ☐ 35–44 ☐ 45–54 ☐ 55–64 ☐ 65+ ☐

How many trips do you make a year?

Less than one ☐ One ☐ Two ☐ Three or more ☐

Are you a AAA member? Yes ☐ No ☐

Name of AAA club

About your trip...

When did you book? m m/ y y When did you travel? m m/ y y

How long did you stay?

Was it for business or leisure?

Did you buy any other travel guides for your trip? ☐ Yes ☐ No

If yes, which ones?

Thank you for taking the time to complete this questionnaire.